DATE DUE

SEP 1 5 1994		APR 2 8 1994	

Demco, Inc. 38-293

POPULATION AND SOCIETY
IN THE ARAB EAST

POPULATION AND SOCIETY IN THE ARAB EAST

by

GABRIEL BAER

translated from the Hebrew by

HANNA SZŐKE

FREDERICK A. PRAEGER, *Publisher*

NEW YORK

Published in the United States
of America in 1964
by Frederick A. Praeger, Inc., *Publisher*
64 University Place, New York 3, N.Y., U.S.A.

First published in Hebrew as
ערבי המזרח התיכון
© Hakibbutz Hameuchad Publishing House Ltd 1960
© Routledge & Kegan Paul Ltd 1964

Library of Congress Catalog Card Number: 63-18535

Printed in Great Britain

CONTENTS

v

Contents

MAPS

PREFACE

THIS book originated in lectures given during the last few years at the Hebrew University of Jerusalem and other institutions in Israel. The lectures were conceived as an introduction to the study of modern Middle Eastern history, economy, or politics; their aim was to present the main facts of population structure and the problems and trends of development of Middle Eastern Arab society. The book was written in 1958 and published in Hebrew early in 1960. For the English translation figures have been brought up to date where possible, research conducted during the last three years has been included, and books, articles, or other material published during this period have been taken into account. This edition is, therefore, a somewhat enlarged version of the original book.

Arabic names and terms have been transliterated as accurately as possible, but diacritical marks had to be omitted for the sake of simplicity. In some cases a conventional English spelling has been adopted. As one of the aims of this book is to make the student familiar with the literature on its subject, sources have been mentioned in detail in footnotes.

I wish to express my gratitude to my colleagues, my students, and the reviewers of the Hebrew edition for their critical remarks, for drawing my attention to additional material, and for encouragement. In particular, I wish to thank Professor S. D. Goitein, Dr Hayim Blanc, Dr Yonina Talmon, Mr Daniel Dishon, Mr Eliezer Be'eri, and Mr Hayim Shaked. I am greatly indebted to my parents Dr Albert and Mrs Kaete Baer for help in several ways with the preparation of this edition; and I am grateful to the translator Mrs Hanna Szőke for her patient and efficient work.

A few sections of the book have appeared in English in *New Outlook* (Tel-Aviv) and *Middle Eastern Affairs* (New York); the permission of these journals to reproduce the articles (with small changes and additions) is hereby acknowledged.

G. B.

October 1962

INTRODUCTION

'POPULATION and Society in the Arab East' is a subject whose scope must be defined both in terms of the geographical territory covered and in terms of the matters under discussion in this book.

If we survey the literature of recent years, we scarcely find any two books on the 'Middle East' which in fact deal with exactly the same countries. Usually the Maghrib, the countries of North Africa, are not included, but where exactly is the boundary between the Maghrib and the Middle East? From a geographical or historical viewpoint, the line should be drawn between Cyrenaica, which has always been associated with Egypt, and Tripolitania (Tarablus al-Gharb). As the two regions, however, are now united in one state, they have both been included in the present discussion.

Other boundaries have been set using the criterion that the Arabic language is spoken by the majority of the population under review. Israel, Turkey, and Persia have thus been excluded. On the other hand, non-Arabic-speaking minorities in the Arab countries are briefly described. The 'Arab East' is thus the best name for this area, since the 'Arab countries' would include the Maghrib, and the 'Middle East' includes Israel, Turkey, and Persia. In short, then, this book is concerned with the population of Egypt, with roughly 26 million inhabitants, Sudan (10 million), the Arabian Peninsula (13–14 million), Iraq (6½ million), Syria and Lebanon (6 million), Jordan (1½ million), and Libya (1 million); in all, some 65 million people.

Most works on the Arabs written during the last generation are concerned with problems of a political and economic nature. In the author's view a fundamental knowledge of the population, demographic problems, and social development of the Arabs is essential for the understanding of events in other spheres.

The contents of *Population and Society in the Arab East* are arranged according to the following scheme. In Chapter I the demographic structure and demographic trends are surveyed. In each of the following sections the discussion centres around one of the criteria by which population may be classified: sex, kinship, religion and language, way of life (ecology), and socio-economic stratification. Hence the chapters are concerned with woman and the family; religious and linguistic communities; beduins, fellahs, and townsmen; and finally, the various social and economic classes and strata. It was hoped by these means to underline the particular character of each of these groups and the differences between them and their counterparts in other societies (in so far as comparison is possible). Stress is laid on the problems specific to each group and the changes which have occurred within the last generation, up to the very latest developments.

Thus there are no special sections devoted to geography, economics, culture, trends of thought, and the historical and political developments of the Arab Eastern countries. However, these spheres of interest have not been disregarded; on the contrary, there is scarcely a page which does not touch on one or another of them, not indeed as the central theme, but as a factor influencing the character or development of this or that population group or of some demographic problem.

The difficulty in preparing this book has been not only scarcity of source material but also its unevenness: some countries and some subjects are much better covered than others. Statistical data of basic importance are lacking for most of the countries; there are few monographs, and on some subjects no data whatsoever are to be found. Hence it was impossible to maintain the desirable balance between the chapters, and a few subjects have been treated somewhat summarily because of lack of sources. Theories that are not well established have been avoided completely, in the hope that, in the not far distant future, new investigations will complement this incomplete picture of the population and society of the Arabs of the Middle East.

I

DEMOGRAPHY

A. SIZE AND DISTRIBUTION OF POPULATION

1. *SIZE*

Population is counted by the *census*. It is also advisable to rely on a census for certain aspects of population classification, e.g., distribution of nomads, division between village and town, distribution by occupation, etc. The main difficulty encountered in any research on the population of the Middle East is the total absence of any such census in some countries, and its confused results in others. There are three reasons why some countries of the Middle East have never carried out a census:

- (*a*) the structure of the population;
- (*b*) lack of modern administrative method;
- (*c*) political factors.

The lack of modern administrative methods is nowadays being tackled by means of foreign technical assistance. For example, the Sudanese and Jordanian governments have been aided by United Nations experts in carrying out their censuses. It was found that the administrative problem is, in fact, not of primary importance. The structure of the population, however, is and will continue to be a serious problem wherever nomadism is prevalent (as, for example, in some parts of the Arabian Peninsula). The political factor actually exists only in the Lebanon, where communal distribution has assumed political significance.

The following factors are responsible for inexact results of population counts:

I

(*a*) The unsettled nature of part of the population; the number of beduins has thus been estimated only roughly.

(*b*) Illiteracy: much of the population does not understand the questions posed by the census-takers, and this may, of course, falsify the results. In particular, among large sectors of the population of these countries there is no conception of accurate numbers. Age is often stated in 'round' figures. There is no sense of objective truth, and replies are designed to satisfy the census-takers.

(*c*) Traditional mistrust on the part of the population, particularly the fellahs, when confronted by representatives of the Government; they always suspect that any correct information elicited will be used to their disadvantage.

(*d*) Hence also transitory factors, such as reduction of numbers to avoid conscription or taxes. This is what happened in Syria and Lebanon in the 1920s, and apparently also in Iraq in 1947. On the other hand, numbers are augmented in times of rationing. This seems to have occurred in Egypt in 1947, and in refugee population counts.

(*e*) Social causes: opposition on the part of beduins, who resent interference in their affairs; inflation of numbers for the sake of family prestige; silence on the subject of new-born sons as a precautionary measure against the evil eye, on the subject of girls because no importance is attached to them, or on the subject of wives which is considered to be a private matter (the census-takers are unable to check the veracity of such statements, as they cannot enter the women's apartments). Sometimes sons are declared as daughters, again for fear of the evil eye. The existence of an unmarried daughter over the age of 15 is considered shameful.

Taking these factors into account, we may now set about determining what was, in fact, the population of the Arab Middle East, on the basis of data relating to the years between 1950 and 1960.

The country with the longest tradition of census-taking and the best-developed administrative machinery to deal with it is Egypt. Here, censuses have been taken at ten-year intervals from 1897 onwards. In 1957 the census was omitted for political reasons. The preliminary results of a census of September 1960 show that the number of inhabitants of Egypt reached 26,080,000.

The first census ever to be undertaken in the Sudan was taken in 1955–6. Results of this count give 10,262,536 for the Sudanese population. The Sudan is, then, the country having the second largest population of all those under discussion.

Population counts of the Arabian Peninsula exist only for Aden (colony) as of 1955 (but not for the Aden Protectorate), Bahrain (1959), and Kuwait (1961). For the other countries of the Peninsula there are only estimates. It is generally agreed that Saudi Arabia has the largest population, but the actual figure is a subject of controversy. The Government of that country claimed 6 million inhabitants in 1947, but other estimates increase or reduce this figure by as much as a million. No data whatsoever have been published on the basis of which the situation could be reviewed and a reliable estimate chosen.

Second place in the Arabian Peninsula is undoubtedly taken by Yemen. An article purporting to give numbers representing the population in the early 1940s was published in 1947.[1] According to its author, these numbers were based on official Yemenite statistics (no census exists), and the figure quoted was 4,069,087. More recent evaluations have generally used this number as a standard, and the present estimate is in the region of 5 millions.

The population of the other countries of the Arabian Peninsula between 1955 and 1960 is generally assessed as follows:

Aden (colony)	138,230	(1955 census)
Aden (protectorate)	750,000	
Muscat and Oman	500,000	
Trucial Oman	80,000	
Qatar	25,000	
Kuwait	321,621	(1961 census)
Bahrain	142,213	(1959 census)
In all, about	2,000,000	

The total population of the Arabian Peninsula is, then, of the order of 13–14 millions.

In Iraq the first population census was taken in 1947. Its

[1] N. Lambardi, 'Divisione amministrative del Yemen con notizie economiche e demografiche', *Oriente Moderno* (*OM* in later references), 1947, No. 7–9.

results were too low; the small percentage of males enumerated suggests that many men evaded the count for fear of conscription. Apparently more dependable are the results of the 1957 census, according to which there were 6,538,109 Iraqis.

In Syria no population count took place between 1922 and 1960, when, according to a combined census of the U.A.R., the inhabitants of Syria numbered 4,561,000 persons.[1]

The most recent census in Lebanon was that of 1932. An estimate published by the Lebanese Government in 1959 gave the figure for its population at that date as 1,550,000.

The first Jordanian census was taken in October 1961; the number of inhabitants of the kingdom counted was 1,752,095 (distributed as follows: Transjordan, 826,618; Arab Palestine, 805,940; Jordanians residing abroad, 62,000; unsettled beduins, 56,000; and foreigners, 2,000. The last three figures are estimates.)[2]

The population of the Gaza Strip is about 300,000, at least two-thirds of which is made up of refugees.

A Libyan count of 1954 yielded a figure of 1,091,830 as the country's population. Tripolitania contributed 746,064 inhabitants, Cyrenaica 291,328, and Fezzan 54,438.

The addition of these numbers gives 65 millions as a very rough estimate of the number of inhabitants of the Arab Middle East in the middle of the twentieth century.

2. *GEOGRAPHICAL DISTRIBUTION*

One important point emerges from this survey of the range of population of the Middle East: more than half the Arabs are found in Africa. If the Arab population of North Africa is added the weight of this sector of the Arab world becomes even greater. (The non-Arab population of both subcontinents is here ignored; it includes the Kurds of Iraq, the Negro tribes of Southern Sudan, the Berbers of North Africa, the Europeans of Egypt and North Africa, etc., the inclusion of all of whom would not change the general picture.)

[1] *al-Ahram*, 24 October 1960. According to the Syrian newspaper *al-Wahda* of 20 May 1961, the population of Syria amounted to 4,780,322 at the end of 1960.

[2] Figures according to the Director of the Jordanian Statistical Office, as published in *al-Manar* (Jordan) of 27 February 1962. See also *OM*, March 1962, pp. 202–3.

A second point of note is that the North is more densely populated than the South—Egypt more than the Sudan, the Fertile Crescent countries more than the Arabian Peninsula, although the Peninsula is much larger than the Fertile Crescent. The reasons for this are clear: (*a*) rivers; and (*b*) proximity to the Mediterranean, well-developed trade with Europe, a passage for trade between Europe and the East, etc. As against this, the South has desert stretches and the Sudan, in particular, swamps and forests. Among the Northern countries themselves there are further significant variations of population density.

What is the correct measure of density? Certainly it is not the number of persons per square kilometre of total land, since a considerable proportion of the total area of these countries is arid desert. A calculation on this basis is, then, misleading; it would suggest that Egypt is one of the most sparsely populated nations, with 19 inhabitants per square kilometre. It would also be a mistake to count the number of inhabitants per square kilometre of populated or currently cultivated land, since the countries of the Middle East are among those termed under-developed, and much of the land suitable for cultivation and settlement has not yet been exploited. The method here used will be to count heads per square kilometre of land currently or potentially under cultivation, or in short, per sq. km. of arable land. On this basis, the Northern Arab countries may be divided into three groups:[1]

(*a*) Egypt, whose population density was 593 persons per sq. km. of arable land in 1947—a density easily exceeding that of highly populated industrial countries. The reasons for this are geographical (the Nile Valley and Delta, bordered by desert) and demographical (rapid natural population increase, of which more will be said later).

(*b*) Lebanon, whose population is far less dense than that of Egypt, and approaches that of the industrial nations of Europe (260 per sq. km. of arable land, in 1951). Here the reasons for a high density are twofold: (1) historical—the concentration of non-Muslim communities, which found a shelter in the

---

[1] Figures of arable land according to A. Bonne, 'Land and Population in the Middle East', *Middle East Journal* (*MEJ* in later references), Winter 1951, pp. 54–5. No estimates of cultivable land in the southern countries (the Sudan and the Arabian Peninsula) are available.

Lebanese mountains and enjoyed a certain degree of autonomy and protection from various depopulating factors; development of Lebanon as a centre of trade with Europe, and so on; (2) geographical—the area of arable land is limited because of the mountainous nature of the country.

(*c*) Syria, Iraq, and Libya (not all on a par).

Syria (1951)	82·5 per sq. km. of arable land
Iraq (1947)	53 per sq. km. of arable land
Libya (1950)[1]	50 per sq. km. of arable land

These three may be considered as sparsely populated countries with potentialities of further development. This is due to a number of causes, among them lack of development during the period of the Ottoman Empire; weakness on the part of the central government which left them open to attack by desert beduins and to wars which thinned out the population. Transjordan also belonged to this group of countries, but since the annexation of part of Palestine and the influx of most of the Palestinian refugees new Jordan is closer to the second group (Lebanon). In 1952 there were in Transjordan alone 100 persons per sq. km. of arable land.

Within each of the Middle Eastern countries there are considerable variations of population density. From population maps of Syria and Iraq the following general trends may be observed:

(*a*) Large territorial concentrations of population along the river banks, forming fertile strips in desert surroundings. This description is true of the Euphrates in Syria and Iraq, the Tigris north of Baghdad, Shatt al-'Arab, and to a certain extent the Orontes (al-'Asi) in Syria.

(*b*) High concentrations in the environs of the cities of Damascus, Aleppo, and Baghdad. These cities, which grew up as trade centres for the fertile rural regions, attracted more people, who saw in them a haven of protection from beduin attack and a convenient market for their produce. Similarly, dense settlements have grown up around the coastal cities of Beirut and Latakia.

---

[1] On cultivable land in Libya see J. Lindberg, *A General Economic Appraisal of Libya*, United Nations, New York, 1952, p. 9.

Different causes are responsible for the distribution of population among the provinces of Egypt, although here, too, the provinces around Cairo are the most densely populated (Giza 809 persons per sq. km., Minufiya and Qalyubiya 733). The first point to be noted is the denser population of Upper Egypt (an average of 600 per sq. km.) than of the Delta (337 per sq. km.). There are some crowded provinces in which the area under cultivation has not been extended appreciably over the past 150 years, and the scope for further development is also restricted, such as Girga (837), Asyut (678), and Qena (617). There are also the relatively less well-populated provinces, which are the main development regions, such as Fayyum (383) and Aswan (342) in Upper Egypt, and Buhaira (276), Gharbiya (333), and Sharqiya (269) in the Delta. The Northern Delta, the coastal region of Egypt, is not settled densely (as are the coastal areas of other Arab countries) because of the number of lakes and the nature of the soil.

In the Sudan most of the populace north of Khartoum is to be found on the shores of the Nile, and a little between the Nile and the Red Sea; south of the capital, the inhabited region is more diffuse. The most highly populated zone is Khartoum and its south-easterly environs (province of the Blue Nile).

With the exception of such populated areas as Aden and Bahrain, the Arabian Peninsula is very sparsely settled. The most densely populated area is the south-westernmost corner. Yemen, for example, constitutes only 6% of the area of the Peninsula, while its population is over a third of the whole. 'Asir, again, is considered to be the most highly populated region of Saudi Arabia (with the exception of certain oil regions of the Persian Gulf). The extensive south-easterly region of Najd is, with some justice, known as 'ar-Rub' al-Khali' (the empty quarter).

Most of the inhabitants of Libya are concentrated in a strip along the coast, and the density is greater in Tripolitania than in Cyrenaica. In the southern desertland (of which Fezzan is a part) the population is especially low.

A notable feature of Jordan is that Arab Palestine, constituting less than 6% of the total area of the country, contains almost one-half of its inhabitants. Much of Transjordan, however, is desertland.

7

3. *AGE GROUPINGS*

Apart from the general factors which tend to falsify the results of a census, there are a number of others which cause trouble when attempting to present an exact statistical analysis of population age groupings in the Arab Middle East. These include unwillingness to admit the correct age because of conscription, the tendency of adults to exaggerate their age, the practice of 'rounding off' numbers in all questions of age, and the common lack of an appreciation of exact numbers.

A complete statistical analysis of age groupings exists only for Egypt; it is summarised in the following chart. For comparison, age-distribution pyramids for France and Japan are also given; these exhibit the most distinctive trait of the Egyptian age distribution (and one that is typical of the other Arab countries too, as well as of many Asian countries, to a greater or lesser degree): the broad base of the pyramid—i.e., the unusually large proportion of young people. This is due to the high birth and mortality rates, discussed more fully in Section B.

However, examination of the age distribution of the population of Egypt over the past few decades shows a well-defined tendency towards a drop in the percentage of young people.

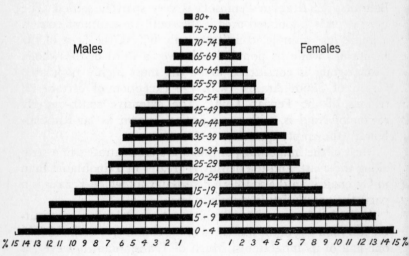

Age Groupings of Egypt, 1947

8

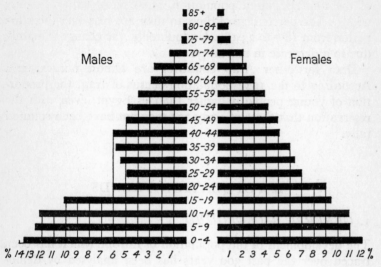

Age Groupings of Japan, 1945

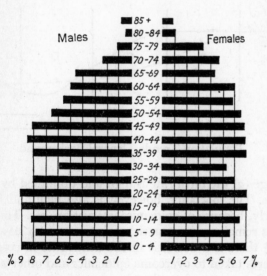

Age Groupings of France, 1948

9

Thus, for example, in 1907 the 0–9 age group made up 30·1% of the total Egyptian population, while in 1947 it was only 26·4%. The percentage of those in their 40s rose over the same period from 18·7 to 23·1%. Undoubtedly, the change is mainly due to a decrease in mortality.

Data for other Arab countries are almost non-existent. According to the 1947 population census of Iraq, the proportion of young people is higher than in Egypt, even with the reservation that those of army age may not have been counted fully.

B. POPULATION TRENDS

1. *GENERAL BACKGROUND*

The development of the population of Europe which has been traced over the past 300 years has been analysed by demographers into five main stages (see following diagram):

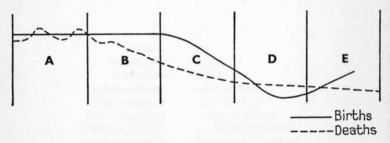

Population Trends, General Background

In stage (*a*) the birth rate is high and unlimited by artificial measures. The mortality, however, is also high and fluctuates irregularly, because of epidemics, starvation, etc. The population thus remains almost static, or increases at a slow rate. In stage (*b*) there is a decrease in the death rate in consequence of measures taken to overcome epidemics and other afflictions. The birth rate, on the other hand, remains high, and consequently a rise in the natural population increase is observed (nineteenth century in Europe). In stage (*c*) the mortality continues to fall, but the birth rate now also starts to go down because of control, and some degree of equilibrium is achieved. In stage (*d*) there is a further fall in both rates, but the birth-rate curve meets, or in some countries even crosses, the death-rate curve. In stage (*e*) a renewed rise in the birth rate, and thus in the natural increase, makes its appearance, the mortality remaining fixed or falling still further.

What are the reasons for this series of occurrences? The continuous fall in mortality, beginning at stage (*b*), is due to: (1) development of the medical sciences and hygiene; (2) development of preventive and curative health services; (3) improvements in personal hygiene; (4) cultural development— in some countries the death rate fell when compulsory schooling was introduced; and (5) general development—directly, by the transport system (helping to prevent starvation and disease), and indirectly, by a rise in the standard of living of the population. Furthermore, countries in good economic state are in a position to establish progressive and expensive health services.

The changes in the birth rate began to appear in Europe towards the end of the nineteenth and the beginning of the twentieth centuries, as a result of the use of contraceptives and artificial abortion. The reasons for limitation of the birth rate are four:

(1) As mortality fell, the number of living persons grew and economic pressure was felt.

(2) The expenses incurred per child rose with the rise in the cultural level and standard of living. Expenses included education, health, etc.

(3) With the change from agriculture to industry and the establishment of laws limiting child labour, children ceased to be a source of income when young, and instead became unproductive up to an advanced age.

(4) A weakening of religious fervour; a change-over from a fatalistic approach to life to a rational attitude; the change in the status of women in society and in the family—all these factors contribute to the reduction of childbirth. Obviously, it was the upper classes which started limiting the birth rate, the lower classes learning from them.

According to these stages, the countries of the world may be divided as follows:

(*a*) the countries of Central Africa, still in stage (*a*);
(*b*) the countries of Southern and Eastern Asia, the Middle East, and North Africa, in stage (*b*);
(*c*) the Soviet Union and Latin America, in stage (*c*);
(*d*) Europe and the United States of America, in stages (*d*) and (*e*), i.e., on the way to a deficit (a death rate greater than the birth rate) or to a renewed fertility at a low rate of natural increase.[1]

Since more than 50% of the world's population is in Africa and Asia, the rapid natural increase has become a serious demographic problem. How does the situation present itself in the Middle East?

2. *BIRTH RATE*

A full answer cannot be given to the question, as some essential data are missing. It has been noted that more or less exact population censuses have, in the past, been taken in Egypt alone. In other countries there are no early figures to compare with the results of recent censuses, or no figures whatsoever exist. Moreover, registration of the newborn and the dead is neither complete nor exact. The problem is undoubtedly more serious in Egypt than in any other Middle Eastern country; all the following data are, then, concerned chiefly with Egypt, although some of the points may be equally valid for other Middle Eastern countries.

The most striking phenomenon in Egypt is the high birth rate, which as yet shows no signs of lessening (stage (*b*)). Before the Second World War the incidence of births reached an average of 42 per thousand; in the early 'forties it fell, possibly because of epidemics, while in the late 40s it returned to the figure of 42 per thousand. In 1950 it rose to 44 per thousand, in 1951 to 45 per thousand. This birth rate is actually one of

---

[1] This is a division on general and rough lines, and obviously there are exceptions. It is also not to be concluded from this division that all countries of the world will of necessity pass through the same stages of development as did Europe.

the highest in all Africa. Only in some countries of Central America is the incidence higher, while few Asiatic countries have a comparable rate.

The reasons for such a high Egyptian birth rate, or more precisely, the reasons why a fall has not set in, are fourfold:[1]

(1) The poverty and ignorance of Egyptian fellahs (who make up the majority of the population) and their fatalism; they are indifferent to limiting the birth rate and lack the knowledge to do so. Even when no more children are desired, witchcraft is evoked.[2]

(2) The child is an essential part of the family working force of the Egyptian fellah, even from his fourth or fifth year. This is particularly true in the cotton-growing areas. An expert on cotton-growing has said: 'Cotton requires not only a dense population but one with a birth rate above the average.'[3]

Many of the tasks connected with the cultivation of cotton, such as insect warfare and cotton-picking, are particularly well suited to child labour. Moreover, this is a cheap form of labour. But not only in the cotton-growing regions do children have essential roles in the family livelihood, as H. Ammar demonstrated in his research on the village of Silwa in Aswan province, published in 1954. He has calculated that a 13-year-old boy is capable of performing two-thirds of the tasks involved in the cultivation of crops in this region. The author shows that at a very young age the child produces more than he consumes. Compulsory education is still not enforced sufficiently to change the picture.[4] In this connection it is interesting to note that Professor Fawzi, on the Sudan, concluded that '52·3% of boys of 5 to under puberty are economically active'.[5]

(3) The larger the family, the more respected its place in society; in some regions, particularly those distant from the central authorities and bordering on the desert, a large family

---

[1] See also R. Patai (ed.), *Jordan*, New Haven, 1957, p. 287. It is doubtful whether all the factors mentioned there do in fact influence the formation of large families.

[2] For details see W. S. Blackman, *The Fellahin of Upper Egypt*, London, 1927, pp. 106–8.

[3] Quoted by Charles Issawi, *Egypt at Mid-Century*, London, 1954, p. 56.

[4] Hamed Ammar, *Growing Up in an Egyptian Village*, London, 1954, pp. 26–33.

[5] Saad ed-Din Fawzi, 'Manpower Distribution in the Sudan', *Middle East Economic Papers* (*MEEP* in later references), Beirut, 1958, p. 27.

even has certain defensive advantages.[1] Women are anxious to have many children as a protection from divorce.

(4) Marriage at an early age, and the high percentage of married as compared with single persons. Marriage at an early age is a tradition founded on early sexual maturity, lack of contraceptive measures, requirements of chastity, and the fact that the position of an unmarried woman is very debased.

It is of interest to compare the percentage of married women over the age of 15 in Egypt with the corresponding percentage for other countries. In Egypt the figure was 65·1% in 1937 and 62·9% in 1947, as in other Asiatic countries. The percentage of married women in European countries in the 'thirties and 'forties was less than 60%, and in many cases less even than 55%. (Only in Bulgaria did the figure reach 70·6% in 1934.) In South America less than 55% is found. It is perhaps more instructive to compare figures for young married women between the ages of 15 and 19. In Egypt the percentage was 23·6% in 1937 (32·8% for the 16–19 age-group) and 24·2% in 1947. Such a high rate is found in some Asiatic countries (Turkey—25·8% in 1945) and an exceedingly high number in India (83·9% in 1951). In Europe the highest figure is that for Bulgaria (16·6% in 1954), while in Western Europe it is below 6%; in South America the country having the highest percentage of young married women is Brazil, with 14·8% in 1950 (except for British Guiana, where special conditions prevail). The corresponding figure for the United States was 16·7% in 1950.

An Egyptian law of 1923 (No. 56) stipulating that the registration of marriage is permissible only for women of 16 and over, and also changes of custom and urbanisation, are responsible for a fall in this percentage (over the years 1907, 1917, and 1927, it fell from 48·4% to 39·3% and to 34·8%). However, the fellahs take various steps to elude the law, as Winkler points out in his book on the village of Kiman in the province of

[1] In conversations with scores of fellahs, which the author held at the end of 1956, the majority expressed a desire for many children. Their main reasons were: (*a*) the need for a working-force to ensure their livelihood; (*b*) the need for protection of the family, in the event of a quarrel with other families. Cf. also A. H. Fuller, *Buarij, Portrait of a Lebanese Village*, Cambridge, Mass., 1961, p. 35.

Qena.[1] The fertility span of the Egyptian woman is longer than that of women of many countries.

There is little information on the age of marriage in other countries of the Arab Middle East. Apparently they do not differ appreciably from Egypt. Dr Salim notes that the accepted age of marriage in Chibayish in Southern Iraq is 14–16 for girls. In a study of five Lebanese villages in the al-Biqaʿ region, Churchill found that the common age of marriage is 15 among young men and 13 among girls, while the legal minimum is 16 for men and 14 for women. In a survey of Palestinian Arab villages carried out in 1944 the high number of marriages at an early age was emphasised. According to Chatila, young women of the Syrian village are married off at an age of 14–18 (beduin girls even earlier), whereas in the city and among higher-class elements there is a clear tendency to raise the age of marriage.[2]

In this connection a common misconception should be mentioned: that polygamy and the high divorce rate are among the principal causes of the high birth rate in the Muslim countries of the Middle East. This opinion is erroneous for two reasons: first, because the decisive factor is the number of married women and the length of the period during which they are married, rather than the structure of the family—polygamic or monogamic. If, out of 100 married women, 50 are married to 25 men—i.e. are members of polygamic families—they will not give birth more often than the other 50, each of whom is married to a separate man. This is conditional, of course, on the absence of a large excess of women, and indeed no such excess exists in the Arab countries. Considering the original proposition, one might almost claim that the opposite is truer: in so far as polygamy has any effect on the general birth rate, its influence is likely to be adverse.[3] Second, it is to be re-

[1] H. A. Winkler, *Bauern zwischen Wasser und Wüste*, Stuttgart, 1934, p. 117. See also A. Boktor, *School and Society in the Valley of the Nile*, Cairo, 1936, p. 67; Blackman, pp. 43–4; etc.

[2] Mustafa S. Salim, *ach-Chibayish*, Vol. I, Baghdad, 1956, p. 104; C. W. Churchill, 'Village Life in the Central Beqaʿ Valley of Lebanon', *MEEP*, Beirut, 1959, p. 4; Govt. of Palestine, 'Survey of Economic Conditions in Arab Villages', *General Monthly Bulletin of Statistics*, 1945, p. 441; Kh. Chatila, *Le Mariage chez les musulmans en Syrie*, Paris, 1934, pp. 25–9. For the Yemen see also C. Fayein, *Hakima—Eineinhalb Jahre Ärztin im Jemen*, Wiesbaden, 1956, pp. 194–9.

[3] H. V. Muhsam, 'Fertility of Polygamous Marriages', *Population Studies*, Cambridge, July 1956, p. 16.

membered that polygamy is no longer a common feature of Middle Eastern life. It has almost disappeared among the middle and upper classes, although not among the lower classes, especially fellahs and beduin shaikhs. Generally speaking, polygamy has become a factor of negligible importance in the Arab countries.

As to divorce, the rate in Egypt is indeed one of the world's highest, but there are no statistical proofs that marriage after divorce has a positive influence on the birth rate.

3. *MORTALITY AND HEALTH*

The Egyptian death rate, like the birth rate, is among the highest in the world. In 1950 it reached 19·1 per thousand, a number exceeding that of any country of Latin America or Asia for which figures are available. (In Africa there are large yearly variations, as is to be expected in stage (*a*).) Particularly high is the Egyptian infant mortality rate.

What are the causes of this prodigious death rate, and especially that among infants? The principal causes are bad sanitary conditions, faulty nutrition, and, as a result of both of these, disease.

Sanitary conditions. The leading aspect of this problem is *housing*. Obviously, there are enormous variations in housing conditions in the Middle East, depending on the region under considera- tion, the ecological conditions, social class, etc. For most of the Middle East there are no relevant statistics. The following comments, however, are of fairly general application.

The houses of fellahs are built of various materials (reed in Southern Iraq and the Persian Gulf; clay and brick in Egypt, the valleys, and riversides; stone in the mountainous regions). Structurally, there are similarities; most of the houses are low, the entrance is low and narrow, and they lack windows except for a single aperture (in many regions, and particularly in Egypt, because of the shortage of wood). The authoress Ibnat ash-Shati' wrote in this connection:

The fellah lives in dark and broken-down hovels which shelter his livestock and his children too, in mean huts of clay covered with a thatch of straw and sugar-cane, most of which are hardly elevated

16

above ground level. Sun and air do not penetrate, apart from a thin ray of light stealing through a tiny window in the wall.[1]

The same picture is drawn by Mirrit Ghali:

> The thousands of villages and farms in which most of the people live are made up of small and low houses, built of clay or unmortared and unpainted brick. The houses have no furniture and the illuminating and purifying light of the sun does not penetrate them. Despite the lack of space, part of each house is set apart for animals, and the fellah with his family sleep in the proximity of the animals and their dung. The houses are set one next to another with no sense of order or planning.[2]

In provinces of Southern Iraq some 50–85% of the population live in tents or huts.

A special problem is covering for the roof, be it straw, sugarcane, reed, or wood; it functions as a store for fuel (wood, animal dung, etc.). Under the climatic conditions of Egypt, fires often occur. Over the years 1926–30, 66 Egyptian villages burnt down. On 15 June 1953, the newspaper *al-Ahram* reported that on the previous day fires had broken out in seven villages and 668 houses were destroyed. About the same number of houses were burnt down in several fires which broke out at the end of January and the beginning of February 1954.

A prominent feature of village housing is the highly crowded conditions. Most village families live in a single room, together with their livestock. Even in so advanced a village as al-Munsif in Lebanon, more than two-thirds of all dwellings had one room, though most of them were two-floor, the lower section serving as a storeroom and animal enclosure.[3] In the five Palestinian villages studied at the end of 1944 (which were by no means poor), 40% of the inhabitants lived in crowded conditions with four or more persons per room, and a quarter of them lived three to four per room.

Reliable data on most of the Middle Eastern cities are again not to be found. Overcrowding and very poor conditions are characteristic of two types of surroundings—the old quarters, having narrow, twisting alleyways and rickety houses, and the

[1] Ibnat ash-Shati', *Qadiyat al-fallah*, Cairo, n.d., p. 52.

[2] Mirrit B. Ghali, *Siyasat al-ghad*, Cairo, 1944, p. 103.

[3] J. Gulick, *Social Structure and Culture Change in a Lebanese Village*, New York 1955, pp. 30, 34–7.

'tin settlements' which have sprung up in the suburbs of expanding cities. The latter category includes the *sarifas* of seasonal
workers in Iraq. In 'al-'Asima' near Baghdad, the scene of a
sample research project in 1957, 94% of those questioned lived
in huts of reed and mud, and 89% of the families had only one
room. On an average, 4·7 persons per room lived in this area.[1]

Fawzi, who made a study of the 'Deims' and 'Fellata
village' in Southern Khartoum, describes them as a 'shanty
town of tin, straw, reed, and wooden hovels'.[2] Another description, now of dwelling conditions in a Cairo district, is due to
Hafiz 'Afifi:

As a doctor who has worked in Cairo for twenty years, I do not
believe there is a single corner of the capital that I have not set foot
in. I have seen the narrow alleyways through which only one person
can pass, whose inhabitants can jump from a house on one side to
the house on the opposite side. I have been in houses from which
evil and contaminating smells issue, the walls of which are damp in
summer and winter; the sun does not penetrate them and there is
neither air nor light within. I have been in houses whose walls and
roofs are made of old petrol tins, one-room huts which house father,
mother, and children, sometimes together with animals or fowls.
This is no exaggeration, and anyone who wants to verify my words
should go to the 'Arab al-Yasar or 'Ishash at-Turgeman quarters
where he will see for himself the very conditions I have described
here. This is not the only such district in Cairo; there is also the
Bulaq quarter, ad-Darb al-Ahmar, as-Sayyida Zainab, al-Gammal-
iya, 'Abdin, Old Cairo, and in fact all quarters of the city are full of
such conditions.[3]

A detailed description of the Bulaq quarter has been published by 'Umar Shawqi in the *Journal of the Association of
University Graduates, at-Tali'a*,[4] under the heading 'Bulaq—the
Quarter of Sweat, Blood, and Tears'. This is how Dr Shawqi
wrote of housing conditions in Bulaq:

[1] D. G. Phillips, 'Rural-to-Urban Migration in Iraq', *Economic Development and Cultural Change* (*EDCC* in later references), Chicago, Vol. VII, July 1959, p. 416.
[2] Saad ed-Din Fawzi, *Social Aspects of Low-Cost Housing in the Northern Sudan*, Khartoum, 1954, pp. 41 ff. Also G. Hamdan, 'The Growth and Functional Structure of Khartoum', *Geographical Review* (*GR*), New York, January 1960, pp. 35–6.
[3] Hafiz 'Afifi, *'Ala hamish as-siyasa*, Cairo, 1938, p. 22.
[4] Vol. I, No. 5, 15 January 1946.

The by-passer in one of the lanes of this quarter may have to twist his shoulder because of the extreme narrowness. The dwellings on the two sides are so close to one another that a person on one side can shake his neighbour's hand through the window. The sun scarcely penetrates the alley and its houses, and the dampness from the earth reaches half way up the walls. In every alley there are scores of naked and filthy infants to be seen, and you are at a loss to understand how such children remain alive and even grow up.

In the textile manufacturing town of al-Mahalla al-Kubra the housing conditions of workers (for some of whom housing projects have recently been undertaken) are described by an Egyptian author in the following terms:

Working men and women live in hovels, known as *'izba*, which surround al-Mahalla al-Kubra on all sides ... the houses are all made of unbaked brick and are rarely more than one floor high. The throughways are narrow and dirty, covered with rubbish and filth. I have seen ruins of houses and shops in any of which twenty workers sleep together at a time, group succeeding group. When a group of workers on the first shift finishes sleeping, they go off to the factory and their places are taken by workers on the second and third shifts, and so it continues. The same room or shop which serves for their accommodation is also the place where they eat and deal with all other necessities.[1]

Nevertheless, it should be noted that in this particular respect the Egyptian Government of the revolution has done much in the way of undertaking housing projects. The published figures do not give a very clear idea of what is still in the planning stage and what is already completed, but the rate of building is certainly greater now than it was under the old régime. It is unlikely, however, that the construction rate can keep in step with demands.

Quite apart from the specific influence of housing, the general sanitary conditions contribute to the prevalence of disease and high mortality. In this respect, too, the situation in Egypt is highly unsatisfactory. The fellahs of Egypt use irrigation canals as a source of drinking water, for laundry, and for washing down farm animals, as well as for other (and their original)

---

[1] M. K. Munib, 'Lamha 'an hayat al-'ummal fi'l-Mahalla al-Kubra', *al-Ba'th* (Cairo), 22 March 1946. For similar conditions of seasonal workers in Iraq see J. S. Simmons and others, *Global Epidemiology*, Vol. III, The Near and Middle East, 1954, p. 26.

purposes. Clay for the construction of their hovels is dug up by the village, and in time that area turns into a pool of stagnant water (*birka*), a breeding ground for germs and insects. Provision of clean drinking water and blocking of the *birkas* have become most pressing problems of the Egyptian administration.

The situation in other countries is in this respect better, although similar problems do exist in some areas. It is to be noted that in most Middle Eastern cities there is no central sewerage system. Pits serve as privies, new ones being dug whenever required. Waste water is led through open ditches into the wadis (seasonal river-beds) or simply into the open country beyond the built-up area of the city. In only a few places is there a real sewerage system. In some cities drinking water reaches houses through open canals. Under such conditions it is hardly surprising that hordes of insects infest Middle Eastern cities and villages, spreading disease at large.

A significant portion of all Middle Easterns, particularly villagers, have a low resistance to disease because of *poor nutrition*. Beduins and landless fellahs at times experience genuine hunger.[1] Most fellahs subsist on cereals, legumes, and sometimes vegetables. To all intents and purposes, the fellah eats no meat, fish, milk, or eggs. These foods appear on his table only on special occasions, such as marriage ceremonies or circumcisions, and are likely to add to his burden of debts. There is a lack of agreement on whether the diet of the Middle Eastern fellah is enough to satisfy minimal health requirements; at least in relation to the Iraqi and Egyptian fellah, we may quote the oft-repeated opinion expressed in reports of United Nations institutions: 'The average diet was inadequate from a nutritional point of view.' 'In most Near Eastern countries . . . food supplies were still generally unsatisfactory'.[2] The authors of the book *Global Epidemiology* note that considerable sectors of

[1] This was the case, for example, during the malaria epidemic which struck Upper Egypt in 1943 (see Asma Halim, *Thamaniya ayyam fi's-Sa'id*, Cairo, 1944, p. 20). The same year saw an outbreak of famine in extensive regions of South-West Arabia (*Global Epidemiology*, pp. 238–9).

[2] United Nations, *Review of Economic Conditions in the Middle East 1951–52*, New York, 1953, p. 13; Food and Agriculture Organization of the United Nations, *Agriculture in the Near East, Development and Outlook*, Rome, 1953, p. 9. For Iraq (and other Middle Eastern countries) see D. G. Adams, *Iraq's People and Resources*, University of California Press, 1958, pp. 76–81.

the population of Iraq, Jordan, the villages of Syria, Aden, and Kuwait suffer from malnutrition.

In most of the Middle East no fundamental studies of nutrition have been carried out, but much has been written on the subject in Egypt. An Egyptian economist, Ghali, writes:

> It is well known that inhabitants of Egypt suffer from serious deficiencies in diet, both quantitative and qualitative. The food of most people consists of bread and millet with the addition of a little onion and cheese and minute quantities of sugar and fruit. Meat is eaten only rarely, milk is drunk only during illness . . . millet, the main article of food among villagers, does not supply the body with its essential constituents, particularly in view of the low consumption of wheat, milk and meat.

Ghali reaches two conclusions: (*a*) food rations are lower in Egypt than in most countries and are below minimum requirements; and (*b*) the average rations in Egypt fell over the period from the beginning of the century until the 1930s.[1] Issawi, who tabulated the main food materials consumed per head, shows that food consumption rose slightly from the 'thirties to the 'fifties, but not for all foods and not to a significant extent. It must be remembered that for cotton prices this was a boom period which ended with the Korean war.[2]

The fellah's level of nutrition is in general somewhat better in the Fertile Crescent countries than in Egypt.

Summarising, the poor sanitary conditions and deficient diet have had a direct influence on the spread of disease or weakening of body resistance to virulent and infectious diseases.

Disease. It has been seen that Egypt is in stage '(*b*)' of demographic development, that is, a stage in which epidemics no longer give rise to large fluctuations in the death rate. This is true of most other Middle Eastern countries, excluding Aden, which was subject to six outbreaks of bubonic plague during the twentieth century, and Saudi Arabia, periodically the scene of very severe epidemics because of the assemblage of pilgrims during the season of the *hajj* (pilgrimage to Mecca). The most recent widespread epidemic of smallpox broke out in 1928, since when precautionary measures have been considerably

---

[1] Ghali, *Siyasat al-ghad*, pp. 58–62.
[2] Issawi, *Egypt at Mid-Century*, p. 86.

increased. During such special periods as wartime very extensive epidemics have broken out in Egypt. During the period
1942–7 there were five catastrophic epidemics; typhoid fever
in 1942 with 80,619 victims, 16,706 of whom died; malaria in
1942–4, affecting a quarter of a million inhabitants of Upper
Egypt (the number of dead is not known with any accuracy;
Mustafa an-Nahhas, then Prime Minister, stated that the
death rate in the Aswan province rose from 24·3 per thousand
in 1941 to 43·3 per thousand in 1943);[1] in 1944 relapsing fever,
afflicting 127,426 and killing several thousands; cholera in
1947, suffered by 20,804 persons, of whom 10,277 died, according to the Egyptian Ministry of Health.[2] During the war there
was also an outbreak of bubonic plague in Egyptian ports.
Special note should be taken of the large number of victims of
the malaria epidemic, since this disease is not normally fatal;
defective nutrition and the sanitary conditions of the fellahs in
Upper Egypt were responsible for the numerous deaths which
resulted. This is also the case for the cholera epidemic: 'most if
not all the deaths from this epidemic occurred among classes of
the populace which have no means of medical protection and
subsist at a low standard of living. Such classes are "epidemic-
prone".'[3] Actually, Egyptian epidemics are now nowhere near
as severe as they formerly were. In an epidemic which swept
the country in 1835 more than 80,000 died in Cairo alone—i.e.,
one-third of its population, while the number of deaths for all
Egypt was at least 200,000. In the cholera epidemic of 1863–5
more than 60,000 people died, and in one of 1883 some 48,470.
In epidemics of 1895–6 and 1902 (the last cholera epidemic
previous to that of 1947) the number of fatalities fell to 17,270
and 34,595, but the percentage of deaths from among all those
afflicted was still much higher than in 1947.[4]

Percentage of Deaths out of all Cholera Epidemic Cases

1895–6	85%
1902	85%
1947	49·5%

[1] *al-Ahram*, 29 February 1944.
[2] *Bulletin of the World Health Organization (WHO)*, Geneva, 1948, Vol. I, No. 2;
'Ali al-Badri, 'Khamsat awbi'a fi khamsat a'wam', *al-Ahram*, 30 October 1947.
[3] M. Z. 'Abd al-Qadir, ''Ibrat al-kolira', *al-Ahram*, ibid.
[4] *Bulletin of the WHO*, ibid.

The Middle East has, then, largely succeeded in overcoming epidemics, although the situation remains serious for certain diseases that are endemic to the region. The commonest of these is trachoma. According to various sources, more than 90% of all Egyptians suffer from eye diseases of one form or another; Iraqi statistics register yearly a half-million cases of trachoma and a further half-million cases of other eye diseases (with the reservation that registration is incomplete in Iraq and statistics most unclear). According to a report of the Mandate Government to an Anglo-American committee of enquiry, 40% of all children of Palestinian Arab villages were afflicted with trachoma in 1944, and this was a considerable improvement over the figure for 1925 (78%). Trachoma is also a general problem of central importance in Syria, Southern Lebanon, Saudi Arabia, and Kuwait. Malaria is particularly common in Iraq (about 600,000 cases per annum in the 1940s), in all regions of Syria, in Bahrain (where a decrease has been noted in recent years), in Saudi Arabia, and in Yemen. Tuberculosis is widespread in Saudi Arabia, in Southern Arabia, and in some of the principalities of the Persian Gulf. The disease is probably prevalent in Egypt and some of the Fertile Crescent countries too, but clear information on the situation there is lacking.[1]

Development of irrigation (a change-over from basin to perennial irrigation by canals) brought Egypt its most common disease—bilharziasis, caused by worms which inhabit the canals; the disease destroys some organs and causes weakness and loss of resistance. According to an estimate of Dr Hafiz 'Afifi for the 1930s, 75% of the Egyptian population was afflicted, and it is believed that more than half the Egyptian population now has this disease; in certain rural regions of the Delta all inhabitants suffer from it. Other common endemic diseases of Egypt are ancylostomiasis and pellagra. These and other diseases transmitted by water are also common in Iraq. The prevalence of these diseases, and the addiction to hashish (and qat, frequently taken in south-western parts of the Arabian Peninsula), are all responsible for ravage of the body, enfeeblement, and a consequently high death rate.

[1] See *Global Epidemiology*, passim. For Saudia see G. A. Lipsky and others, *Saudi Arabia, its People, its Society, its Culture*, New Haven, 1959, p. 271.

Measures taken to fight disease in the Middle East are as yet
limited, and physicians especially are in short supply. The
following instructive table is based on yearbooks of the United
Nations and *Global Epidemiology*:[1]

Number of Inhabitants per Physician in the Early 1950s
(Round Figures)

Yemen	583,000	Lebanon	1,300
Sudan	86,000	Bulgaria	1,300
Saudi Arabia	63,000	France	1,100
Libya	13,200	Great Britain	880
Jordan	7,400	United States	770
Iraq	6,400	Soviet Union	666
Syria	5,000	Israel	487
Egypt	4,300		

Furthermore, in these largely rural Middle Eastern countries
most of the physicians are concentrated in the cities, and thus
the scale is effectively greater still.

A similar picture is portrayed in a second table, taken from
the same source:[2]

Number of Hospital Beds per Thousand Persons in the Early 1950s

Syria	0·65	Libya	2·59
Sudan	0·95	Lebanon	6·13
Iraq	1·25	Israel	6·83
Jordan	1·44	Norway	9·00
Egypt	1·63	Britain	10·50

In recent years a steady improvement in health has set in.
Medicine in the Middle East does not have to pass through all
the stages which characterised its growth in Europe. Middle
Eastern countries can take over the latest developments ready-
made, at times with foreign technical aid as well. More difficult
is the problem of organisation of public hygiene. This is not a
question of money and organisation alone. Its solution depends
on whether the population can overcome the superstitions and
habits of generations. Among the fellahs, for example, it is
commonly believed that dirt protects infants from the evil eye.
In his book on Silwa in Upper Egypt, 'Ammar describes the
difficulties encountered in establishing a 'health unit' in the
village; one of them was the villagers' opinion that nothing is
worse than death outside the family circle.[3]

[1] Quoted from A. Cohen, *Ha'olam ha'aravi shel yameinu*, Tel-Aviv, 1958, p. 154.
[2] Ibid., p. 156. [3] Ammar, p. 79.

Much progress has been made, however, particularly in the building of hospitals, inoculations and injections, spraying with D.D.T., and even in the construction of housing which is more hygienic than that in existence. In consequence, there is a growing likelihood that the death rate in the Middle East will decrease more and more. In Egypt indeed this rate has steadily fallen from 27·1 per thousand in 1930–4 to 19·1 per thousand in 1950. According to official figures, deaths of infants of under a year per thousand live births have also fallen from 162 in 1930–2 to 130 in 1950. The same is true of Palestine, where, from the middle of the 1930s to the middle of the 1940s, infant mortality among Muslims fell by at least a quarter. A definite fall in the general death rate and in infant mortality has also been reported from Aden, where the statistics are quite reliable.

4. NATURAL INCREASE, EMIGRATION, AND BIRTH CONTROL

If the trends described above persist, it may be assumed that the natural increase, already great, will rise still further. According to the figures quoted here, the natural population increase in Egypt has gone up over the twenty-year period from 1930 to 1950 from 15 to 25 per thousand approximately— mainly as a result of a drop in the death rate. The *Jordanian Statistical Yearbook* places natural increase in the middle 1950s at about 30 per thousand. Accepting the French estimate of Syria's population in the 1930s, and comparing it with official estimates published in the 1950s, that country should have an average rate of natural increase of 25 per thousand. If it is true that the population of the Sudan at the beginning of the century did not exceed 2 million[1] it turns out that the average natural increase must have gone up by a third every ten years during the first half of the twentieth century for its population to reach its present size, according to official figures. The corresponding figure for Western European countries was no more than 5–7 per thousand per year.

Of all Middle Eastern countries Egypt has the most urgent problem of natural increase. In the first fifty years of this century the population of Egypt has almost doubled, and a

[1] Sir Harold Macmichael, *The Sudan*, London, 1954, p. 73.

further doubling is expected in the next thirty to thirty-five years if there is not a drastic change in the current demographic trend in that country.

For many years there had been a dispute between the economists and demographers concerned with Egypt: does there or does there not exist a state of 'overpopulation' in Egypt? Much of the dispute is over the definition of the term 'overpopulation'. Undoubtedly, the extent of the Egyptian population and the rate of natural increase are very great when set against economic resources and potentialities. Hence Egypt must set about solving the problem of the standard of living of its inhabitants and future employment, not only by increasing production (and in this connection, by working towards a more equitable distribution of wealth) but also by reducing the natural increase. This conclusion is based on the following fundamental facts:

(*a*) The population density of agricultural areas of Egypt is much greater than that of industrial countries of Europe.

(*b*) There is much 'hidden unemployment' in Egyptian agriculture. In other words, a considerable portion of the manpower in Egyptian villages could be taken out without any effect on production. Some have assessed that with half the agricultural population, or even less, the present output could be maintained, and this without any technological changes. According to one study, the average number of working days of fellahs in various provinces of Lower Egypt is 180–220 per year, while in Upper Egypt it is only 150–175. The occurrence of underemployment is also witnessed in the cities, with their tens of thousands of pedlars, beggars, etc.[1]

(*c*) The population's standard of living and consumption is very poor. Egypt is among the countries with the lowest *per capita* rates for consumption of food, textiles, power, etc. The same is true of literacy, newspaper circulation, numbers of radios, average life-span, and so on. Available statistics indicate that the average consumption and standard of living fell still further in the last generation, and on this basis the upper and lower classes have become even more widely separated. Egypt, then, must make urgent efforts to raise the standard of living

[1] E. Gharzuzi, *Thawrat al-islah bi'l-arqam*, Cairo, 1959, p. 37. For underemployment in the cities, see for instance, Dr 'Abbas 'Ammar in *al-Ahram*, 30 August 1954.

and consumption, and the condition for this is higher production which is not reabsorbed by the natural increase.

(*d*) The area of Egyptian land under cultivation in 1954 was 6,156,000 feddan. The arable area is 7·5 million feddan. The aim of the Aswan High Dam project—the most daring programme for agricultural development in Egypt that has ever been put forward—is to bring all this land under irrigation, i.e., to increase the cultivated area by 22% (as compared with 1954). At its present rate of increase the population of Egypt will have grown by 22% in less than nine years. However, it is unlikely that the construction of the Aswan High Dam will be completed before the end of the 1960s. It is then evident that unless the natural rate of increase falls, further development projects will be required within the next ten years merely to maintain the present level of agricultural production per head.[1]

(*e*) The contribution of industrialisation towards absorbing the natural increase is also limited. The development of Egyptian industry is held up by various lacks—of capital, skilled workers, raw materials, etc. Even these problems may more easily be overcome than the most fundamental one—the domestic market, limited so long as the living standards and the consumption of the Egyptian fellah are low. In other words, so long as the problems listed as (*a*)–(*d*) remain unsolved the industrial development of Egypt will remain in straits. Hence it is not to be expected that by expansion, industry and associated urban professions will be able to absorb either the existing urban unemployed or urban natural increase, not to mention the rural population increases.[2]

The foregoing comments should not be taken to mean that agricultural and industrial development do not serve a valuable function in limiting the gap between natural increase and sources of employment in Egypt; on the contrary, both developments are essential for Egypt and hold much promise. The basic problem, however, cannot be solved without limiting the natural population increase.

The two possible ways of solving the problem are by *emigration* and by *birth control*. Before examining each of these, it may

[1] Cf. Issawi, *Egypt at Mid-Century*, pp. 78, 85–6, etc.
[2] For detailed treatment of this problem see K. Wheelock, *Nasser's New Egypt*, New York, 1960, Chapter VI.

be pertinent to enquire how much Egypt's heads of state are in fact interested in cutting down its population or arresting its increase. The answer is not unambiguous, but certain signs seem to suggest that in recent years a change of attitude has set in. The statesmen of the old régime often claimed that for political and defensive reasons a growing population was essential: 'The future of the small nations is obscure . . . our policy must be aimed towards an increase in the number of inhabitants' or 'In the struggle for survival, the strong wins and the small nations are strangled.' The conclusion was that marriage and natural increase are to be encouraged to strengthen military power.[1] Undoubtedly, such opinions, at least in part, originated among landowners and industrial leaders who were interested in cheap man-power. The military régime now in power has apparently come to the conclusion that its strength is not measured by quantity but quality, and it has been almost unanimously agreed that Egypt is overpopulated in so far as sources of employment are concerned.

There are many problems facing spontaneous emigration of Egyptian population surpluses. The difficult material conditions of the Egyptian fellahs, and their questionable state of health, have induced a state of apathy. They do not have the initiative to better their state and do not dare risk changing their homes. In the past the Sudanese Government several times tried to re-settle Egyptian fellahs along the Nile north of Khartoum. In the Gezira Scheme, too, canal-diggers were Egyptians, but not a single one of the thousands of these Sa'idis (Upper Egyptians) approached the Sudanese Government with a request for a settlement permit. It was so difficult to keep them there, even for the period under contract, that eventually Nigerian workers were brought in to do most of the work.[2] The Anglo-Egyptian agreement of 1936 (section 11, clause 4) permitted free migration from Egypt to the Sudan, considerations of public safety and health permitting. This clause has never been exploited by the Egyptian masses, although no obstacles were placed in their way by the British authorities in the Sudan. Beyond the boundaries of Egypt there was actually not a single colony of Egyptians

---

[1] 'Afifi, pp. 166–7; M. A. 'Alluba, *Mabadi' fi's-siyasa al-misriya*, Cairo, 1942, pp. 22, 228.

[2] See A. Toynbee, *Survey of International Affairs 1930*, London, 1931, pp. 211–12.

whose number exceeded a few hundred, except for the colony in Sudan, numbering several thousand (mainly irrigation officials and military personnel).

Clearly, then, if a large-scale emigration programme is envisaged it must be financed by the Government. It is highly unlikely that the Egyptian Government, concerned with the financing of momentous development projects (as well as equipping the armed forces), can assume such a heavy burden, either by providing funds or by organising the project. As to international bodies, the problem of resettlement of the Palestinian refugees still takes precedence. Moreover, such institutions tend not to take action in matters of 'population surpluses', unless there is a state of emergency and actual mortal danger (as with the Assyrians, Greeks, Turks, etc.).

Even assuming the Egyptian Government finds the necessary resources for financing such a project, the question still arises: Where are the emigrants to be resettled? Speaking economically, Egyptian fellahs could be brought to the Sudan or Iraq. However, political considerations rule out the possibility of large-scale resettlement in either of these two countries in the near future. Iraq is Egypt's principal rival in the Arab world, while the Sudan has feared in the past, and will undoubtedly continue to fear, an Egyptian 'fifth column' in her territory.[1] It is not surprising, then, that Issawi changed his opinion on the subject from one extreme to the other; in the first edition of his book he saw a 'vast emigration programme launched by the Government' as 'the only remedy for the existing overpopulation'. In the second edition he writes: 'In the present state of international relations, emigration offers few possibilities for Egypt'.[2] The possibility of resettling Egyptians outside the country arose after the merger with Syria and the establishment of the United Arab Republic. Indeed, there are extensive areas of Syria which would be suitable. However, the splitting-up of the U.A.R. in 1961 precluded even this slight chance, at least for years to come. Another unpredictable factor is the Egyptian fellah's reaction to transportation from his home to a foreign dwelling-place.

[1] See Mekki Abbas, *The Sudan Question*, London, 1952, p. 92.
[2] Charles Issawi, *Egypt, An Economic and Social Analysis*, London, 1947, p. 202; *Egypt at Mid-Century*, p. 242.

While economic and political considerations stand in the way of emigration from Egypt, the question of *birth control* depends largely on social and cultural factors. After the revolution in Egypt the Government made a number of efforts to launch a propaganda campaign for birth control, but in all cases the programme petered out after its first impetus. On 11 September 1953 the Egyptian Medical Association staged a symposium at the University of Alexandria on the subject of population, and the majority of the participants came to the conclusion that birth control is the only solution to the problem of overpopulation. After some time there was a public debate on the subject, and many articles supporting that view were published. A year later, the Minister for Social Affairs, Colonel Husain ash-Shafi'i, announced: 'Not only am I in favour of birth control, but I also believe it to be a social necessity.'[1] On 22 December 1955 the semi-official newspaper *al-Gumhuriya* printed a detailed article on the dangers of the rapid natural population increase in Egypt, and drew the conclusion that there is only one solution—birth control. This time the enterprise reached a new stage with the establishment of 'birth control centres', whose purpose it was to guide the populace in family planning. Several such centres were set up, mainly in the towns.[2] In May 1962 'Abd an-Nasir again stressed the necessity of family planning in his long programmatic speech.

The question of the attitude of Islam and of the Egyptian Muslim theologians is obviously of interest. Apparently, it is a common belief among the Egyptian masses that their religion forbids such control and that men of religion oppose it.[3] However, the 'ulama do not take a unanimous view on this question, and the opposition of religious functionaries is by no means as extreme as that of the Catholics. Some have expressed total opposition to all measures taken to prevent pregnancy, referring to the text in the Koran saying, 'Murder not your children for fear lest ye be reduced to poverty; we will provide for you and them',[4] and on many hadiths whose message is 'Be fruitful

[1] *al-Ahram*, 12 September 1953; 15 September 1954.
[2] Nada Tomiche, 'En Egypte: Le gouvernement devant le problème démographique' *Orient*, July 1957, pp. 108–9; Gharzuzi, p. 55.
[3] This was the almost unanimous opinion of many Egyptian fellahs interviewed by the author at the end of 1956.
[4] Koran, VI 151; XVII 31; etc.

and multiply'. When the debate was reopened in 1956 the Shaikh al-Azhar 'Abd ar-Rahman Taj proclaimed that birth control was a social sin, forbidden by the edicts of religion.[1] Others (such as al-Hudaibi, former head of the Muslim Brotherhood) have approved of the prevention of pregnancy for purely medical reasons, opposing it when economic factors operated. Yet other important theologians have stated that the Muslim religion has nothing whatsoever against prevention of pregnancy. As early as 1936 the movement for birth control succeeded in obtaining a fatwa from the Mufti of Egypt, permitting the use of preventive measures, and in 1952 the former rector of al-Azhar announced that he was in favour of birth control. Among the influential supporters of the new government policy were Shaikh Hasan al-Baquri, Minister of Waqf, and a group of officials of the Ministry of Waqf. They gave notice of their support of the policy of birth control in the newspaper *al-Gumhuriya*. It is notable that the chief opposition to the views voiced at the symposium came from the Association of Catholic Youth, and not from Muslim circles.[2]

Religious factors aside, any programme for birth control has to contend with the ignorance of the fellah, his desire for many children as working hands, the social status and security of large families, and the woman's fear of divorce. Apparently some classes of townsmen have reached the conclusion that it is to their advantage to raise a small number of children, but they still hesitate to put their decision into practice.[3] Undoubtedly, a rise in the level of education and social evolution will help the Egyptian population to overcome many of its misgivings about birth control, just as other nations overcame theirs; but it is not to be expected that the process will be rapid.

Second in importance to Egypt, in terms of pressure of the population on economic resources, is Lebanon. Here the problem is far less severe than in Egypt, and the difficulties standing in the way of its solution are less cogent. The Lebanese problem is closer to solution because: (*a*) the natural increase is slower there than in Egypt; and (*b*) the density of popula-

[1] *al-Ahram*, 23 April 1956.

[2] *al-Ahram*, 16 and 19 September 1953; *al-Gumhuriya*, 2 January 1956; see also Khalid M. Khalid, *Min huna nabda'*, Nazareth, 1959, pp. 139–44.

[3] This was, for example, the position of many townsmen whom the author met at the end of 1956.

31

tion is about one-half the figure for Egypt. These two aspects are in part the consequence of large-scale emigration of Lebanese to various parts of the world, which has continued over the past hundred years. According to statements appearing in *al-Hayat* on 30 April 1957 and based on official data, the number of Lebanese living abroad was 1,100,000 (about equal to the number of inhabitants of Lebanon), of whom half a million were in the United States and Canada, another half million in South and Central America, and the rest in Africa and Egypt.[1] Moreover, Lebanon is the Arab country with the highest percentage of persons not engaged in agriculture (including the rearing of livestock). Industry is relatively well developed, and there are satisfactory conditions of trade. The Lebanese have no qualms about emigration; they have wide-flung connections and good sources for financing further emigration. Not all countries are as ready to receive the Lebanese nowadays as they were two generations ago, but there are still many (among them, the oil states of the Middle East) which Lebanese businessmen and professionals may enter. The annual number of emigrants was

2,725	... ...	...	in 1952
3,315	... ...	...	in 1953
8,287	... ...	...	in 1954
4,555	... ...	...	in 1955

Because of the relatively high level of education and the urban nature of much of the Lebanese population, it may be expected that control of the birth rate will proceed more quickly than in Egypt. Worthy of note, however, is the large proportion of Catholics among the population. In the highly developed Maronite village of Hadeth el-Jobbe, Touma reports that no measures for preventing pregnancy are taken, and the birth rate, as well as the rate of population increase, are enormous.[2]

Concerning the possibilities of developing the economic resources of Lebanon, estimates vary widely. Some American experts believe that the area of Lebanese land under cultivation

---

[1] Other sources report slightly different numbers, but basically close to those given by *al-Hayat*. See, for instance, *Middle East Record 1960 (MER* in later references), Jerusalem, 1962, p. 364.

[2] Toufic Touma, *Un Village de montagne au Liban (Hadeth el-Jobbé)*, Paris–La Haye, 1958, p. 86.

could be increased one and a half to two fold, and irrigated areas by a factor of 2·5. Others have said that the whole of the cultivated area is cropped, and that there was no uncultivated land which could be brought into cultivation.[1]

---

[1] Bonne in *MEJ* 1951, p. 54; D. Warriner, *Land and Poverty in the Middle East*, London, 1948, p. 81.

II

WOMEN AND THE FAMILY

A. WOMEN

1. *STATUS OF THE WOMAN IN MUSLIM ARAB SOCIETY*

Characteristic of Arab society in the Middle East is the different status of men and women. Unlike many other societies, and particularly modern Western society, women are in a greatly inferior position both materially and spiritually, and discrimination is apparent in all spheres of life. The birth of a son is cause for celebration; not so that of a daughter. A mother of daughters only is condemned to a divorce that is sanctioned by society. Even in childhood, boys have a preferential status. Complete propriety is expected of a married woman, but not of her husband. It is the accepted opinion that the woman's function is to serve her husband. This attitude is largely social in origin, and its main causes in the villages are the strong influence of nomadic tribal society and concepts. The situation in cities, which deteriorated from the tenth to the nineteenth century, was due in part to the fact that female slaves were a fundamental element of society during this period. Female slaves in the harems were naturally irksome to the free urban woman.

It would be quite wrong to imagine that the Islamic religion is the only factor responsible for the debased position of women in the Arab East. On the contrary, in comparison with the situation which had previously prevailed, Islam improved both their standing and attitudes towards them. Muhammad opposed the practice of female infanticide; he placed a limit on the number of women whom a man may marry, setting it

34

at four; and he settled part of inheritances on daughters (who, apparently, had previously had no share). However, although Islam was an improvement over the Jahiliya, its approach in the light of twentieth-century conditions appears conservative and backward. 'And so, though Islam softened some of the harshest features of the old law, it yet has set a permanent seal of subjection on the female sex by stereotyping a system of marriage which at bottom is nothing else than the old marriage of dominion.'[1] Even this flat statement is not entirely true of all circumstances in which women's position is inferior. In some matters Islam plays no part, and the situation stems from social conditions alone (e.g., absence of women in social life), or from customs actually opposed to Muslim teachings (e.g., in inheritance). In other matters, such as divorce, Islam remains the fundamental cause for the inferior position of women. Thus no generalisations can be drawn, and each problem must be treated separately.

Certainly, Islam gives preference to the male,[2] and this approach still influences the attitude of modern Muslims. The fact that in some matters Islam assesses one man as equal to two women (in apportioning inheritances, in giving evidence, etc.) is undoubtedly an important reason for the general debasement of the Muslim Arab woman. Islam compels a woman to obey her husband, and in some places custom demands the most severe and extreme enforcement of this religious edict. For example, there is a practice in Egypt known as *bait at-ta'a* ('house of obedience'); if a woman disobeys her husband and leaves him he may call in police assistance to bring her back and imprison her until she becomes tractable. Abolition of this custom is one of the important clauses of a proposed new Egyptian law of personal status under consideration since 1960.[3]

There are two matters in which Islam continues to exercise a negative influence to this day—divorce and polygamy. In neither case did Islam worsen the situation that had prevailed in pre-Islamic times; concerning polygamy, it brought about

[1] W. Robertson Smith, *Kinship and Marriage in Early Arabia*, London, 1907, p. 121. See also pp. 65–6, 115 ff.
[2] Koran II 228; IV 34.
[3] Dorriya Shafiq, *al-Mar'a al-misriya min al-fara'ina ila'l-yawm*, Cairo, 1955, pp. 43–4; *al-Ahram*, 3 August 1960.

a certain degree of improvement. However, by endowing the practices of that age with the stamp of religious approval, Islam was responsible for the subsequent spread of customs impeding social development.

The Koran does not compel a man who divorces his wife to give any explanation or justification for his action; he may divorce her at will, simply by uttering the divorce formula. The Hanafi school of law, which predominated in Arab countries under Turkish rule, was even more extreme than others, ruling that utterance of any word similar to the term for divorce, *talaq*, in any circumstances whatsoever, was to be understood as a binding decision for divorce. On the other hand, a woman could plead for divorce or separation at law on two counts alone—either that the bride price had not been paid or that her husband was found to have a deformity incapacitating him for intercourse.

Prohibition of divorce proceedings when taken by the wife and their almost unbounded sanction when taken by the husband are, of course, highly significant causes of the inferior position of the woman.[1] Their influence is not limited to legal proceedings alone; in everyday life the continual threat of divorce is a depressing and debasing part of the Muslim woman's existence. At the same time there is a great difference between Egypt, whose divorce rate has recently become the world's highest (apart from Zanzibar and the Virgin Islands), and the other Arab countries, in which certain social restrictions on divorce are stronger, but where polygamy is more frequent. The survey of five Muslim villages of Palestine carried out in the 1940s showed that more than 30% of all women over the age of 33 had been married more than once. In Egypt divorce is commoner in the city than in the village, and more prevalent in the major cities than in the provincial towns (in complete contrast to the state of polygamy). In 1950, for instance, divorces for the whole of Egypt accounted for 27·4% of all marriages, while local figures were 44·2% for Cairo, 37·6% for Alexandria, and 35·9% for Suez. The divorce rate

[1] Payment of the bride price is, of course, a certain restraint on divorce; however, ways and means of overcoming this obstacle are practised in some regions of the Middle East. See J. N. D. Anderson, *Islamic Law in the Modern World*, London, 1959, pp. 52–3.

is lower in the Fertile Crescent countries, but the same difference between city and country is observed: in Syria in 1958 the country-wide rate of divorce was 7·9% of all marriages; the figure for Damascus was 19·0%. In Arab Palestine, too, the rate is higher in Westernised towns than in traditional society, and higher among the educated than the lower classes.

A possible explanation of the high divorce rate is the ease with which divorce may be accomplished, and the manner in which marriage is arranged, without appreciable intervention on the part of the couple concerned. A second cause is the higher standard of education, culture, and social development among men than among women. A young Arab man has great difficulties in finding a compatible wife. Naturally, the high divorce rate is responsible for severe economic and social problems.

The Koran (IV, 3) permits a man to have four wives simultaneously (not including female slaves), while a woman must live in complete 'monandry'. In most cases polygamy (like divorce) is the consequence of barrenness or lack of sons; however, in certain social groups (among beduin shaikhs and village notables, for example) polygamy, with the likelihood of a consequent large number of sons, is a sign of affluence and social prestige. In the Gezira Scheme in the Sudan 54% of all tenants had two wives, as against only 20% of those who did not lease land and whose economic and social standing were lower.[1] Obviously, because of the bride price, polygamy is feasible only for the prosperous, and thus in modern times there are many who do not attach much significance to this privilege of the Muslim religion. However, polygamy is quite frequent at the two extremities of the social scale—among the very wealthy, who can afford more than one wife, and the very poor, who require a second wife as a labour force. Beduins and villagers tend sometimes to invest all their savings in a second wife. Among the families living in Chibayish of Southern Iraq investigated by Dr Salim, 28% of all men were married to more than one woman. The average figure for the tribal provinces of Southern Iraq in 1947 was 12·6% (Muntafik) and 12·2% (Diwaniya). In Artas, the village surveyed by

[1] A. Gaitskell, *Gezira, A Story of Development in the Sudan*, London, 1959, p. 314.

Granqvist, 10·7% of all men had more than one wife.[1] The same (10·6%) is true of the five Arab villages of Palestine studied in the early 1940s. The percentage of polygamous marriages for villages in the province of Baghdad was 8·5% in 1947, as against 4·4% for the city of Baghdad in the same year, and only 2·8% for Cairo in 1937.

Those who belie the importance of polygamy also quote symptoms of its decline. A decline is clearly indicated by Granqvist's figures for the village of Artas. Rosenfeld, who studied marriage customs over five generations in Tur'an in Palestine, found that of the dead, 10·9% of all Muslim men had practised polygamy, while among the living the percentage was less even than 5·5%.[2] In Egypt there was a decline over the decade 1927–37 from 4·8 to 3·5%, in Cairo from 3·8 to 2·8%. But in contrast, and perhaps to a corresponding degree, the rate of divorce has risen, mainly among the lower classes.[3]

The negative influence of Muslim legislation is not reflected in the question of *inheritance of daughters*. The Koran (IV, 11) prescribed that a daughter was to inherit one-half the share due to a son and in so doing it theoretically ameliorated the woman's status. In fact, however, the practice in many countries has been to ignore or circumvent this precept; this has happened over a number of periods and is the current practice. It has been argued that Islamic inheritance laws were based on a tribal way of life, appropriate to owners of cattle and other movable possessions which can easily be divided up; but they are difficult to implement among people whose property is partly or mainly in land.[4] This explanation is insufficient, however, as is clear from the example of the beduins, whose daughters do not inherit at all.

---

[1] H. Granqvist, *Marriage Conditions in a Palestinian Village*, Vol. II, Helsinki, 1935, p. 205.

[2] H. Rosenfeld, 'An Analysis of Marriage and Marriage Statistics for a Moslem and Christian Arab Village', *International Archives of Ethnography (IAE)*, Leiden, 1957, Vol. XLVIII, No. 1, p. 53.

[3] At the beginning of the century serious European observers had the impression that in Egypt marriage to two wives is commoner than monogamy. See F. Schwally, *Beiträge zur Kenntnis des Lebens der mohammedanischen Städter, Fellachen und Beduinen im heutigen Ägypten*, Heidelberg, 1912, pp. 20, 34. On the correlation between decline of polygamy and increase of divorces see R. F. Woodsmall, *Der Aufstieg der mohammedanischen Frau*, Zürich–Leipzig, 1938, p. 148, as well as Granqvist, p. 271.

[4] R. Levy, *The Social Structure of Islam*, Cambridge, 1957, p. 246.

An obvious explanation is that the family is anxious to prevent loss of property at all costs. (An inheriting daughter would take her portion with her on marriage.) The zeal for keeping family property intact is so great that not only the beduins (who do not always adhere to Muslim law in other matters anyway) but also fellahs of many regions infringe the Muslim inheritance laws. In Egypt a daughter's share is frequently left with her brothers, and subsequently her husband considers it beneath his dignity to claim it. In Palestine brothers would compensate a sister with gifts when she left the family home to marry. In a recent article, Mariam Zarour notes that the women of Ramallah do not inherit land, of their own free will as it were. In order to cut daughters out of their inheritance and prevent land from leaving the family, the fellahs of Transjordan used to sign over part of the land in the name of one of the sons when registering all their lands.[1]

It may be noted that members of other communities, who were subject to Muslim inheritance laws at various periods, also ignored the ruling that a daughter should inherit half as much as a son. The Maronites, for example, were subject to Muslim laws from 1841; they did allow a daughter to inherit in accordance with the law (not disinheriting her entirely unless there were also sons in the family), but on her marriage they withdrew the share. In the Greek Orthodox village of al-Munsif, too, girls do not inherit.[2]

Egyptian landowners and urban property-owners used another device for circumventing the law—conversion of their possessions to family *waqf* (an institution similar to trusts, more fully explained in Chapter IV). By these means they could specify exactly who was to benefit from the income from these possessions, without being constrained to follow Muslim inheritance laws. In order to prevent part of the property, or the income from it, from reaching a married daughter's family, many of the founders of *waqf* denied daughters any share in

[1] J. Nahas, *Situation économique et sociale du fellah égyptien*, Paris, 1901, pp. 74–5; I. Canaan, 'Unwritten Laws affecting the Arab Woman of Palestine', *Journal of the Palestine Oriental Society*, Vol. XI, 1931, p. 194; Rosenfeld in *IAE*, p. 34; Granqvist, p. 256; Mariam Zarour, 'Ramallah: My Home Town', *MEJ*, Autumn 1953, p. 437; A. Konikoff, *Transjordan, An Economic Survey*, Jerusalem, 1946, p. 38.
[2] I. Aouad, *Le Droit privé des Maronites 1697–1841*, Paris, 1933, Titre II; Gulick, p. 128.

its income. Others were less extreme, and merely specified in
the *waqf* document that on marriage a daughter relinquishes
her share. Yet others deprived the offspring of daughters of
their share in the *waqf* income. In some cases, the share of a
wife was subject to the condition that she would not remarry
after her husband's death.[1]

The current severity of the problem may be judged by an
article by the well-known woman author, Bint ash-Shati',
recently published in *al-Ahram*. She writes:

I request those women who call for changes in the inheritance
laws not to claim that Muslim legislation robs us by granting us only
a half share—a half share, let it be said, to which no obligation is
attached. Those who rob us are the men who transgress the law,
giving preference to males. They receive all, by either fictitious sale
or other stratagems, in order that a daughter may be prevented
from taking her parents' bequest to an alien husband. Thus they
disobey a divine and sanctified law. Would it not be fitter to demand
protection of the woman's right to inherit according to religious
law, by setting up restrictions to defend her from the stratagems of
her robbers?[2]

In summary we may say, first, that discrimination against the
woman as heiress in the Arab countries is not the consequence
of a Muslim inheritance law but the opposite—a consequence
of its neglect; and second, that the law is broken because it is
contrary to existing social structure, based (as will be seen) on
the patriarchal, patrilinear, and patrilocal family.

Largely similar to the inheritance rights of daughters are their
rights to the *bride price* (*mahr*). Before Islamic times the bride
price was delivered after marriage to the woman's guardian.
Islam specified that the bride price was her own property.
However, in rural districts and among many tribes the bride
price customarily belongs to the bride's father (or other
guardian, e.g., her brother on the decease of her father), and
he may do what he chooses with it. Frequently he does, in fact,

[1] In a survey of landed property in Egypt and Muslim *waqf* in Palestine the
author encountered scores of cases of *waqfs* whose founders imposed such conditions.

[2] *al-Ahram*, 16 July 1960. Virtually the same was said by the Lebanese Mrs Nour
Hamade at the Teheran Congress of Muslim Women held in 1932. See H. Massé,
Le Deuxième Congrès Musulman Général des Femmes d'Orient, Paris, 1933, p. 98.

spend the bride price on jewellery or furniture for his daughter, which then becomes her property; but in many cases it is spent for his own needs. In certain regions of Arab Palestine a marriage contract is called *imlak*, that is, transfer of property. In Egypt, too, marriage is widely regarded as a 'sale' of the daughter, whose family determines her 'price' (bride price). In Upper Egypt it used to be customary for a bride's father to use the money in order to live in idleness for a number of years, to buy another plot of land, or to marry a second wife.[1] It should again be emphasised that these phenomena are part of the general social structure and have sociological explanations. The bride price is looked upon as compensation to the family or tribe for loss of a reproducing force to another family or tribe. It is in any case evident that in this respect too, discrimination against a woman, her subjection to men, and lack of independence are not rooted in Islam.

Again, the custom of veiling does not originate in religious Muslim law. The instructions of Islam are not specific and unambiguous, and the custom itself is limited to certain classes.

Explicit instructions to wear a veil are found in the twenty-third Sura (Chapter) of the Koran, where they are directed towards the wives of Muhammad only. However, some commentators have read a similar directive to all Muslim women in other verses of the same Sura. One commentator of the ninth and tenth centuries, at-Tabari, explained that a difference must be maintained between freeborn women (veiled) and female slaves (who expose their faces). And indeed it is the abundance of slave girls, particularly since the 'Abassid period, which gave rise to the custom of confining women of the upper classes in the *harim* (harem).[2] In the Sudan exposure of the face and head is still considered the mark of the female slave or woman of slave origin.[3] The custom became established and

---

[1] For Arab Palestine and Transjordan see J. A. Jaussen, *Coutumes des Arabes au pays de Moab*, Paris, 1908, p. 49; idem, *Coutumes Palestiniennes—I Naplouse et son district*, Paris, 1927, pp. 57-9, 77 n.; Canaan, pp. 177, 180; Rosenfeld in *IAE*, pp. 47 ff. For Syria see Chatila, pp. 194, 196; J. Weulersse, *Paysans de Syrie et du Proche Orient*, Paris, 1946, pp. 220-1; for Southern Iraq—Salim, pp. 78, 108; for Egypt— G. Legrain, *Fellah de Karnak*, Paris, 1902, pp. 317-19; Blackman, p. 92; Tomiche, p. 118.

[2] Levy, pp. 124-9. Also N. Abbot, 'Woman', in R. N. Anshen (ed.), *Mid-East: World Center*, New York, 1956, p. 200.

[3] J. S. Trimingham, *Islam in the Sudan*, London, 1949, p. 24.

continued among urban women (until the nineteenth century), but not among beduin and fellah women, who are not generally veiled. However, Egyptian village women of some districts do wear a veil, and do not work in the fields. Veiling of women in Upper Egypt is more common among the better-to-do fellahs than among those of the lower classes; it signifies a respectable position, and its neglect is considered a sign of degradation in peasant society.[1] Evidence that veiling is rather a social custom than a religious edict is found in the fact that in most cities of the Arab East Christian women also used to cover their faces. Christian women of Beirut, for example, ceased wearing veils only in 1890, and those of Nablus were still veiled in the 1920s.[2]

More widespread is the custom of confining the Arab woman to prevent her from coming into contact with men who are not members of her family. This again is unconnected with Islam, having started only some 300 years after Muhammad. Until then, it was even customary for women to pray in mosques together with men. Since then, segregation of women from men's company has assumed great importance. Women are not allowed to share in any communal activity or to assume any public position, and they never appear in men's company.[3] (Beduin women are an exception; their desert way of life does not permit of separation from men in the manner practised in settled communities. Another exception: in the Sudan there are two women who head local groups of the Mirghaniya sect.)[4] This isolation is the main reason why urban women do not participate in economic life and are dependent on men for their resources. Obviously active participation in non-material spheres of life too (which once was very strong) declined in traditional society, and reinstatement set in only towards

[1] 'Ali Pasha Mubarak, *al-Khitat at-tawfiqiya al-jadida*, Cairo, 1887-9, VIII, 28, 51, 105; IX, 88; XI, 64; XIII, 69; XIV, 121; Blackman, pp. 37-8; Boktor, p. 63.

[2] R. Thoumin, *Géographie humaine de la Syrie Centrale*, Tours, 1936, p. 320; Jaussen, *Naplouse*, p. 43. Similarly, Jewish and Coptic women covered their faces in nineteenth-century Egypt—cf. L. A. Frankl, *Aus Egypten*, Vienna, 1860, p. 131; T. Neumann, *Das moderne Ägypten*, Leipzig, 1893, p. 30.

[3] The stringent separation of the sexes is responsible for widespread homosexuality in the Arab East, particularly in those countries where separation is most strictly observed, as in Saudi Arabia and Yemen. See Lipsky, p. 304; Fayein, pp. 160, 194, 202-3.

[4] Jaussen, *Moab*, p. 44; Lipsky, pp. 52, 78; Trimingham, p. 234.

the end of the nineteenth century. The participation of women in politics is a new phenomenon of the twentieth century.

2. *THE MOVEMENT FOR THE EMANCIPATION OF WOMEN*

In the foregoing pages the main phenomena exhibiting inferiority and servitude of women in traditional Arab society have been discussed. In the last generation, however, the Arab countries of the Middle East have witnessed certain changes in women's social, legal, and political status. The background to these changes is fundamentally the closer contact of the Middle East with the West. Western countries ruled in the Middle East and Arabs visited the West, took to its learning, read its literature, saw its films, etc. Many educated Middle Eastern people found the status of the Western woman to be an integral part of the culture they emulated. The cinema, which became the most common form of recreation among all classes in the Middle East, exhibited the Western woman's way of life, which had hitherto been unknown to them. Furthermore, there were internal processes in the Middle East which initiated changes in the woman's position. Urbanisation, the formation of a working class (of men and women), extension of the transport system, variety of luxury goods available to the upper classes— all these helped to bring women out of isolation. Finally, the extensive growth of the educational system and spread of knowledge among men and women alike are to be noted. They played an essential part in modifying woman's status and in stirring up movements and trends for woman's emancipation.

The chief movements and trends will now be summarised.

The first trend which appeared in the Middle East set itself the sole aim of extending the *education* of girls. Its chief exponents were 'A'isha Taimur (1840–1902) and Malak Hifni Nasif (1886–1918), known by her pen-name Bahithat al-Badiya. They did not deviate in the slightest respect from the established framework of Muslim law and custom. Malak Hifni Nasif even opposed unveiling, which was already being urged.

As mentioned, some of the features marking the inferiority and servitude of the Middle Eastern Arab women were to be found in Muslim attitudes (the superiority of the male), Muslim laws (divorce and polygamy), or customs which commentators and doctors of religious law justified by reference to Islam (veiling and enclosure of women). Thus those intending to carry out reform in these matters encountered certain difficulties: first, religious law, which is the only law of personal status in the Arab countries. For example, a Muslim has no choice but to be judged by a qadi in matters of marriage and divorce, according to *shari'a* law. Second, the extreme opposition of the orthodox religious functionaries who still enjoy prestige and influence. Third, the problem which every reformer of woman's status must face—that of examining his conscience and reformulating his own personal relation to Islam.

In Kemalist Turkey a radical solution was devised: the legal validity of the *shari'a* was abrogated, and Swiss civil law, including laws of personal status, was adopted. The Government encouraged unveiling by propaganda and the creation of a public opinion in its favour, and sometimes by force. Religion and State were separated, the influence and status of religious functionaries was restricted, and the Kemalist movement accepted secularism as one of its basic tenets. None of the Arab countries followed Turkey's example; in none of them was there even a movement which put forward such a programme.

The second trend of Arab reformers approached the problem with principles generally termed 'Modernism'. The main aim of the 'Modernists' was to defend Islam, whose foundations were being shaken under the influence of Western culture. They recognised Muhammad and the Koran only, and attempted to ignore or completely denied later developments. By interpretation of the Koran they tried to prove that it is not incompatible with the spirit of modern Western civilisation. When they encountered difficulties they claimed that the spirit of the *shari'a* and not its letter are to be followed, especially in religious precepts concerning relations of public interest between men. Finally, they called for a renewal of *ijtihad* (the right of individual interpretation, by analogous reasoning), which had been abolished by orthodox Islam after the formation of the four schools of law recognised ever since.

There are hundreds of articles, pamphlets, and books by Arab Modernists on the problem of woman. Only the main trends in this literature are briefly surveyed here. The first line of thought again demanded an extension of the educational system for girls; its exponents remained loyal to the Koran, but tried to reinterpret it in the light of their aim to improve woman's status. The father of Modernism, Muhammad 'Abduh (1849–1905), commented on the continuation of the verse in the Koran permitting marriage to four women ('But if ye fear that ye cannot act equitably (towards so many, marry) one (only) ... '). He interpreted this as forbidding polygamy, for, he reasoned, it is impossible for a man to behave with complete justice towards all four of his wives (and in verse 129 of the same sura it is explicitly written that 'Ye can by no means carry yourselves equally between women ...').[1]

Exactly the same objection to polygamy was raised by Qasim Amin (1865–1908), a pupil of Muhammad 'Abduh, who directed his interests and literary activities to the problem of woman, and wrote two books on the subject: *tahrir al-mar'a* ('Woman's Emancipation', 1900) and *al-mar'a al-jadida* ('The New Woman', 1902). He added the further objection that since polygamy is in any case a privilege rather than a duty, secular authorities may ban it if, as in modern times, it is harmful to society. Similarly, he tried to show that the *shari'a* does not insist on veiling, and he made a plea for a gradual return to the true laws of modesty in matters of dress, as given in the Koran. He also called for greater social contact between the sexes, limitation of grounds for divorce, and the concession of the right of divorce to women—all, however, within the framework of the *shari'a*.

Shortly after the death of Amin, the Iraqi author Jamil az-Zahawi caused an uproar when he sent an article to the Egyptian newspaper *al-Mu'ayyad* (1 July 1910) opposing Muslim divorce procedures. He, too, demanded equal rights for the woman in divorce proceedings and announced that he preferred the Shi'a laws (requiring the presence of a *mujtahid* to validate divorce) and Wahabi law (which does not recognise

[1] Koran IV 3, 129. C. C. Adams, *Islam and Modernism in Egypt*, London, 1933, pp. 230–9.

45

simultaneous 'triple divorce'). He also spoke against the veil. The newspaper withdrew its support and published many articles in reply, and Zahawi was dismissed from his post as lecturer on law at Baghdad. Previously he had been active in the establishment of schools for girls in Iraq, and after his dismissal he participated in the movement for women in Lebanon.[1]

Representatives of the second branch of Modernism also tried to bridge the gap between claims for the emancipation of the woman and Islam, but their way lay in the creation of a spiritual Islam, ignoring the development of Muslim law. It is interesting that the principal exponents of this movement are not Egyptians (as were those of the first branch) but rather the Lebanese Druze woman Nazira Zain ad-Din and the Tunisian socialist at-Tahir al-Haddad. The principal work of the former, *as-sufur wa'l-hijab* ('Unveiling and the Veil') appeared in Beirut in 1928, and that of the latter, *imra'atuna fi'sh-shari'a wa'l-mujtama'* ('Our Women in Religious Law and Society') was published in Tunis in 1930. Nazira Zain ad-Din accepted the *shari'a* only in so far as it clearly and unambiguously confirms the teaching of the Koran itself, and she demanded the right of *ijtihad*. Haddad believed that the precepts of Islam are to be understood in the context of society at the time they appeared, and not as absolute and unchangeable. He claimed that Muhammad had indeed wanted to be more sweeping in his precepts, but was forced to compromise with the conditions of his age. Thus one should behave in accordance with the spirit rather than the letter of the *shari'a*. Haddad, then, considered only those verses of the Koran which support his beliefs. In the verses and edicts of the Koran specifying the superiority of the male both authors read a compromise with the backwardness of contemporary 'barbarian' ways, and in the verses which speak of equality of the sexes, the true spirit. Problems of polygamy and divorce are explained by both in terms of the difficulty of eliminating deeply rooted and established customs. Really, Muhammad strove to achieve monogamy and hated divorce. Of course, Nazira Zain ad-Din and Haddad were both in favour of unveiling and of closer social

[1] *Revue du Monde Musulman*, XII (1910), pp. 465-77. Cf. J. Berque, *Les Arabes d'hier à demain*, Paris, 1960, pp. 162-3.

contact between the sexes, but it was not so hard to harmonise these claims with Islam.[1]

Trends of a more extreme ideological nature did not arise in the Arab countries. Even the contemporary author Khalid Muhammad Khalid, and the vigorous leader of the woman's movement in Egypt today, Dorriya Shafiq, base their writings on Muhammad 'Abduh and Qasim Amin and use their methods. The movement for the emancipation of women in the Arab countries has since taken the form of organised women's associations, whose activities have a social nature rather than an ideological interest. Since the First World War scores of such women's organisations have been founded in all the Arab countries. Particular impetus came from Huda Sha-'rawi, wife of one of the three founders of the Wafd and daughter of one of the richest landowning families of Egypt. In 1923 she founded 'The Egyptian Federation of Women' (*al-ittihad an-nisa'i al-misri*), and demonstratively removed her veil. The demands of Huda Sha'rawi included raising the age at which girls may marry (to 16) and reforming the marriage and divorce laws. The activities of the women's organisations were not limited to the reform of legislation on personal status. They called for an improvement in the position of women and equality of the sexes in all spheres of social, economic, and political life. Many groups concerned themselves with educational and philanthropic activities for the advancement of woman. Since the Second World War there has been more and more emphasis on granting women political rights, particularly the suffrage. The struggle of women's organisations has often involved demonstrations, collisions, and imprisonment, such as those that occurred in the early 'thirties in Damascus after the unveiling of a large group of women, and in the 1950s in Egypt as a result of strikes and demonstrations conducted by the *Bint an-Nil* organisation of Dorriya Shafiq.[2]

Women's associations have held many congresses, including inter-Arab, inter-Muslim, and general Eastern; they have also participated in international congresses of women's movements.

[1] The works of Zain ad-Din and Haddad have been dealt with in detail in Rudi Paret, *Zur Frauenfrage in der arabisch-islamischen Welt*, Stuttgart, 1934.

[2] See Dorriya Shafiq, *al-Mar'a al-misriya*, passim; Berque, *Les Arabes*, p. 165. On women's organisations in Iraq, and for bibliography on the women's movement in Arab countries, see *OM*, 1948, pp. 108–12.

The decisions of the Inter-Arab Women's Conference of 21 December 1944 are a very clear example of the demands and activities of the whole movement:[1]

(*a*) *Political Rights.* The Arab Governments were called upon to work towards the political equality of men and women, and especially to grant both active and passive election rights by a gradual process, until complete equality is achieved. They were further called upon to replace men by women in positions for which women were better suited.

(*b*) *Citizenship and Legal Rights.* Laws of personal status were to be amended, the aims being to limit divorce rights; to place children of both sexes with their mother until adolescence; to lessen the subjection of women, to restrict polygamy and permit it only with a *qadi*'s approval; to compensate wives for the misuse of divorce laws; to raise the portion of a husband's salary which may be sequestrated for payment of alimony; to fix the marriageable age for daughters at a minimum of 16 in all Arab countries and to ensure that this law is observed; to establish equal treatment of men and women in criminal law; and to nullify the legality of all contracts and transactions which discriminate against the rights of wives or daughters in inheritance.

(*c*) *Culture and Education.* In this clause, several general demands were made of the Arab Governments for the spread and extension of education, and also special demands relating to women: instruction of small children by woman teachers; coeducation at an early age; administration of girls' education by women; training in the care of the sick and first aid instruction in girls' secondary schools.

(*d*) *Protection of the Health of Mother and Child.* This clause included demands for setting up clinics and low-priced restaurants, and reform of prison rules; enforcement of medical checks before marriage; foundation of centres for treatment of infants and mobile units for the guidance of pregnant women, and the establishment of maternity homes and hospitals for the treatment of venereal diseases in village areas; legislation for the protection of working women during pregnancy and after giving birth. The clause also included various points on

[1] Dorriya Shafiq and Ibrahim 'Abduh, *Tatawwur an-nahda an-nisa'iya fi misr*, Cairo, 1945, pp. 145–51.

48

the care of abandoned children and reform of legislation for working youth.

(*e*) *Protection of Morality*. Abolition of state-controlled prostitution; prohibition of work by girls in public houses, closing down of gambling establishments, and general attention to the social situation prevailing after the war.

(*f*) *Encouragement of Economic Co-operation among the Arab Countries*. Granting female candidates access to all positions; and payment of equal salaries to men and women for equal work.

Participants in the women's movements discussed here came from a narrow stratum of the upper and middle classes, and did not include the city masses, far less the villagers. Their influence on the policy-makers of modern Arab states is not, however, to be underestimated. Furthermore, while many changes in the status of women have been imposed by legislation from above, there has also been a certain change of values among Arab women themselves. These two factors together have brought about the actual changes in woman's status, which will now be discussed.

3. *CHANGES IN WOMAN'S POSITION IN SOCIETY AND THE STATE*

The first trend in the movement for the emancipation of women had as its central motif the extension of the education of girls, and the claim has continued ever since. In fact, fundamental changes have taken place in the last generation.[1] In nearly all Arab countries the percentage of girls out of the total pupil body has risen considerably at all stages of schooling. It is instructive to consider the period between the World Wars (from 1913–14 to 1944–5) in Egypt, reflecting the change of a generation. In this period the percentage of girls in all schools rose from 14 to 40%. The number of girls in elementary schools rose by a factor of 15, in trade schools and teachers' colleges by a factor of at least 10 and in secondary schools by a

[1] The following figures are based on R. D. Matthews and M. Akrawi, *Education in Arab countries of the Near East*, Washington, 1949; *Statistical Yearbook of the United Nations;* UNESCO, *Compulsory Education in the Arab States*, 1956, pp. 67–70; and Cohen, pp. 185–209.

factor of 6. In 1913–14 there were no women at all in establishments of higher education—which were not in fact open to
them until 1927; however, by 1944–5 the number of women
students had already reached 1,040, and in 1957–8 there were
7,766, i.e., 12·2% of all university students. Even in conservative Iraq the fraction of girls in elementary schools rose from a
fifth to a quarter over the twenty-five years from 1930 to 1955;
in Transjordan, from 1922–3 to 1945–6 the proportion of girls
to all pupils went up from 10 to 20%, and in 1955 their share
had reached 31·4%. In the Iraqi universities there were 1,215
women studying in 1955 (22·3%). In Syria and Lebanon, too,
there was a large absolute increase, but not a relative one,
since these countries had foreign schools which undertook the
education of girls (particularly Christians), and one of the first
functions of the independent governments was to extend the
educational system in its entirety. The number of girls attending
elementary schools in Syria doubled between 1944 and 1954,
and the number of women students rose over the same period
from 69 to 934 (18·6% of all students at the Syrian University).
Obviously, this development in the field of Arab education is
more striking in the city and less so in the village, where the
force of custom is stronger.

Despite the considerable increase in the number of girls
attending school, illiteracy among women is still very common.
According to the census of 1947 in Egypt, for instance, the
percentage of females (over the age of 5) who could read and
write was only 12·7% (as against 10·0% in 1937 and 4·7% in
1927, and 32·8% for males in 1947). Nevertheless, in the last
generation there has been an outstandingly large number of
women of note in literature and writing.

Changes in the urban woman's position in economic life
have been incomparably slower, involving many more obstacles
than the spread of education among women. Education did, in
fact, open the door to thousands of teachers (it being customary
for women to teach girls, men boys). There was slower progress
in the trend towards nursing as a profession, and on the whole
men are still in the majority among attendants of the sick in
hospitals. The same is true of office work. The first female
lawyers and doctors have made their appearance, mainly in
Egypt, but so far in very small numbers.

Members of the upper and middle classes enter such professions. The economic independence of women of the poorer classes has not undergone clearly defined change. There are still few women of these classes who have work involving contact with the public, e.g., as charwomen, shopkeepers, waitresses, etc. Home crafts have always been carried on by women, but marketing has remained in the hands of men. Female labour used to be common enough in the traditional industries of Syria and Lebanon (particularly the silk industry in Lebanon), comprising 43% of all the labour force in 1913. Decline of such industries has resulted in an actual decrease in the employment of women; in 1937 they constituted 34% of all workers in the traditional crafts and 19% of all workers in modern industry. According to data of the Lebanese Government, women made up 23·3% of all industrial workers in 1950.[1] According to a 1954 industrial census in Iraq, only 13·7% of all industrial workers were women in that year. Lower figures apply to Egypt; the censuses of 1927, 1937, and 1947 give percentages of women out of all workers in industry as being in the range of 7·5–7·9% (57,000 in 1947), and according to an industrial census of 1937, only 3%.

It is notable that the concentrated grouping of women in several large-scale concerns during the Second World War evidently had considerable effects on their social life. Of particular relevance in this connection is an article by M. K. Munib, describing the life of women at a large textile mill in al-Mahalla al-Kubra; in 1946 there were 2,000 women engaged in work at the mill, in addition to several thousand who worked for the mill in their homes (in the preparation of spools, etc.). According to the author, women worked in separate departments from men, but contact between the sexes was freer than is customarily permitted in Egypt. Furthermore, most of the women were independent bread-winners of complete families (generally landless and unemployed families of nearby villages).

Economic independence on the part of women is, then, on

[1] Data are taken from K. Grunwald, 'Hati'us shel Surya ve-Levanon', *Hamizrah Hehadash*, V, pp. 245, 253. A decrease in the share of women among workers in the older industries has been noted also by the authors of Patai's *Jordan*, p. 156. However, in recent years there may have been a renewed increase in the percentage of women out of all workers in modern industries; see IBRD, *The Economic Development of Syria*, Baltimore, 1955, p. 375.

the increase, if slowly. The various countries differ somewhat: in Egypt it is customary for women to cease work on marriage, whereas in Syria and Lebanon they occasionally continue earning after marriage.

Since the First World War the participation of women in political activities has spread. Almost all political parties of the Arab countries have had women's committees (generally headed by the wives of the party leaders), but few women rose to political leadership by their own efforts. The members of these committees were drawn from a limited group, and their activity was variable. More and more, however, women have taken part in the struggle of nationalistic movements against foreign rule.

Obviously, these changes in the level of education and in economic and political spheres have had a marked influence on customs; in particular, they have helped to hasten the unveiling of the urban woman. This process has not yet been completed, but is at any rate going forward gradually. At first women tended to go unveiled only in remote places; later, in the immediate environment of their homes too. They were quicker to behave freely among non-Arab foreigners than among Arab men. Upper-class women preceded the masses,[1] and younger women preceded their elders. A transitional state is found among many young women, who have taken to wearing a veil of light and semi-transparent material. The unveiling has progressed more quickly in the cities than in backward provinces: Cairo is ahead of Tanta, Aleppo and Baghdad are ahead of Hamah and Najaf. Generalising, Egypt is ahead of other Arab countries. A sign of the change is the fact that the wife of King Fu'ad (1917–36) appeared veiled in public, while

[1] From a survey conducted among secondary-school girls of Alexandria it appears that in this generation the extent of emancipation of women is directly proportional to the socio-economic standing of the family, i.e., the greater the income of a girl's family, the more freedom she has. In the previous generation the daughters of middle-class families had been more emancipated than those of upper classes. See M. Berger, 'The Middle Class in the Arab World', in W. Z. Laqueur (ed.), *The Middle East in Transition*, London, 1958, pp. 70–1. For a very similar trend among Arabs in Palestine see J. Waschitz, *Ha'aravim Be'eretz Yisrael*, Merhavia, 1947, p. 222. On Iraq, D. G. Adams says: 'In recent years the generalization that seclusion is greatest among the urban wealthy has been less true in the largest cities, although it is still true in the towns' (*Iraq's People and Resources*, p. 24 n.).

the wives of King Faruq (1936–52) exposed their faces. Unveiling has been delayed in countries in which Muslims were in conflict with members of other communities (e.g., in Palestine and in India); here the veil was the symbol of the traditional values of Islam. Eye-witness reports give the impression that in Saudi Arabia there has been little progress in unveiling and releasing women from their seclusion. The Government has actually placed obstacles in the way of attempted reform.[1]

Naturally, religious functionaries and traditional public opinion are against unveiling; their opposition to this has been more virulent than to other innovations, such as freedom of women to travel in trains and buses, to do their own shopping, to vary their dress and hair-style according to fashion, to attend the cinema in mixed company, and so on. All these habits have spread year by year. Only in one respect has there been almost no change—social recreation in mixed company. There is hardly a place or social class in the Arab Middle East where social activities are conducted among an adult population of freely intermingling men and women not of the same family. In the Christian villages of Lebanon, however, young people's social life is mixed, and the social activities of some universities and modern movements, particularly left-wing, are also shared by men and women.[2]

Many factors—the social changes described above, contact with the West and formation of states on a Western pattern, and the movement for women's emancipation—have brought about reform of the laws of personal status in all the Arab countries of the Middle East. Reform in all matters connected with the status of the Muslim woman started in 1917 with the Ottoman 'Law of Family Rights', which remained valid after the First World War, with only slight modifications, in Syria, Lebanon, Palestine, and Transjordan (since 1927). In Egypt there was some parallel reform in laws of 1920 and 1929, and similar laws were passed in the Sudan. A special Lebanese law was enacted in 1948 to deal with personal status questions in

[1] R. H. Sanger, *The Arabian Peninsula*, New York, 1954, pp. 13–15, 68–9, 93–4.
[2] Gulick, pp. 101–2; Touma, pp. 119–21. But not in Lebanese Muslim villages (see Fuller, p. 48), and generally not in towns such as Ramallah (Zarour, p. 437) or even Beirut, with a large Christian population (Saïd Chehabe-ed-Dine, *Géographie humaine de Beyrouth*, Beirut, 1960, pp. 291, 293).

the Druze community; this law involved some fundamental changes in keeping with the more liberal tradition and laws of that community towards its women. In 1951 further amendments appeared in Jordan in the 'Jordanian Law of Family Rights'. In 1953 the 'Syrian Law of Personal Status' came into effect, valid for the 'Alawi, Shi'i, and Isma'ili communities too; by virtue of the same law the Druzes were henceforth to be ruled by the contents of the Lebanese law of personal status of Druzes. In Iraq a new law of personal status went into effect in 1959, and in 1960 a draft law of personal status was published for the U.A.R. which should have been effective for all religious communities. However, to date (October 1962) this project has still not been put into operation.[1]

None of these reforms (except the Druze law) diverged in any respect from the *shari'a*, the Muslim law. To make them possible, the legislator did not bind himself to any particular school of law (*madhhab*); rather, in each question, he picked the rulings of that particular one which happened to be closest to his aim, or even mixed elements of several schools. In isolated cases only were there real innovations, i.e., rulings which could not be based on those of any of the existing schools; but even then, ways were found to fit the new ideas into the framework of Islam, sometimes by returning to early Sunni interpretations.

One of the first questions considered in law was the age of marriage. Islam prescribes no lower limit, and any innovation might be regarded as infidelity and disbelief in Islam, particularly as Muhammad himself wed one of his wives when she was very young. As a condition for marriage, the Ottoman law, then, stipulated that a young man must be at least 18 and his bride at least 17, but empowered judges to approve marriage at a younger age on the ground that the couple was mature enough; in no event was the marriage of girls younger than 9 or boys younger than 12 allowed. In Egypt regulations of 1923 and 1931 stipulated that marriages were not to be registered

---

[1] For details on these laws see J. N. D. Anderson, 'Recent Developments in Shari'a Law', *Muslim World* (*MW* in later references), 1951, pp. 113–26; 271–88; Idem, 'The Personal Law of the Druse Community', *Die Welt des Islams* (*WI*), 1953, pp. 1–9, 83–94; Idem, 'The Jordanian Law of Family Rights', *MW*, 1952, pp. 190–206; Idem, 'The Syrian Law of Personal Status', *BSOAS*, 1955, pp. 34–49; Y. Linant de Bellefonds, 'Le Code du statut personnel Irakien du 30 décembre 1959', *Studia Islamica*, XIII, 1960; *al-Ahram*, 3 August 1960.

if the young man and woman were under the ages of 18 and 16 respectively, but if such marriages were nevertheless performed they were not annulled.[1] Since 1951 a judge in Jordan cannot validate a marriage if either of the couple is under the age of 15 (and in Syria if the boy is younger than 15 or the girl younger than 13). The 1948 Druze law was more stringent, setting the minimal age at 16 for boys and 15 for girls, and further ruling that the *qadi* must give his approval in a medical certificate. The 1959 Iraqi law places the minimal age at 18 for both sexes, but empowers the *qadi* to ratify the marriage of couples over the age of 16. The Syrian and Jordanian laws, as well as the draft law of the U.A.R. of 1960, also include the instruction that the *qadi* may refuse to consent to a marriage in which the age difference between the partners is too great. However, the lack of birth certificates has made it very easy to circumvent all these regulations, and hence the demand on the part of women's organisations for their effective implementation.

A more difficult question, from the legal viewpoint, is that of polygamy. Clause 38 of the Ottoman Family Law gives legal effect to conditions that a woman writes into her marriage contract, forbidding her husband to marry a second wife and requiring that, if he does so, either she or the second wife be considered divorced. This clause has been implemented in Jordanian and Syrian legislation. An attempt to extend the idea to Egypt has so far been unsuccessful. A committee, appointed to bring forward amendments to the law of personal status, made certain recommendations in 1926: to validate such conditions drawn up by a woman in her marriage contract; to permit marriage to a second wife only with the local *qadi*'s permission; and to instruct these judges not to give their permission unless it has been proved that the claimant can behave with propriety towards his wives and can support them both while still fulfilling his other financial obligations. King Fu'ad placed a veto on these recommendations, although they had governmental approval, and thus they were not included in the 1929 law. Similar proposals from the Ministry of Social Affairs were again defeated in 1943. On the other hand, Syrian

---

[1] To prohibit registration of a certain action, and thereby elude its legality in court, was one of the important methods of introducing reform without affecting the shari'a.

legislation of 1953 ruled that the *qadi* may withhold his consent to marriage to a second wife if it has been proved that the husband cannot support both wives. Similarly, the 1959 Iraqi law of personal status laid it down that marriage to more than one wife is forbidden without the *qadi*'s consent, and that consent is to be given only when justified: when the husband can support more than one wife, and when the *qadi* is convinced that he will treat all wives equitably. According to the new proposal for a law of personal status in the U.A.R., marriage to a second wife will be considered damaging to the first wife and may serve as grounds for divorce. The 1948 Druze law forbade polygamy altogether, in keeping with Druze tradition.

There has been extensive and diverse reform of divorce law. Its aim has been to restrict the unlimited right of a husband to divorce his wife, and to enable her to obtain divorce at law. As early as 1915, the Ottoman Sultan issued two orders (*irada*) specifying that a woman would thereafter be able to obtain divorce in a law court either if her husband had abandoned her and it was impossible to exact money from him for her upkeep or if her husband suffered from some disability which would be harmful to the continuance of marriage. The 1917 Ottoman law extended a wife's rights to include cases in which her husband had been absent for four years or had behaved with cruelty or disturbed domestic peace, after arbitration by the court. Similar regulations came into effect in the Sudan in 1916, and in Egypt in 1920 and 1929, with further extension of a woman's right to divorce (if abandoned for a year, and in cases of cruelty, without arbitration). The 1951 Jordanian law was similar to the Egyptian (while requiring arbitration in cases of cruelty) and so too, broadly speaking, was the Syrian law of 1953 and the 1959 Iraqi law.

As to a husband's right to divorce his wife, the 1917 Ottoman law stipulated that repudiation of a wife under the influence of intoxication or intimidation, or by hints whose meaning is unclear, is not valid. The 1929 Egyptian law followed the same ideas, adding to the restrictions on divorce by the husband, and ruling in particular that triple divorce at one and the same time is not recognised by law.[1] The 1935 Sudanese regulations

---

[1] If a Muslim divorces his wife three times he cannot marry her again until she has first married another man and been divorced by him.

were identical, and in general lines so, too, were the Jordanian law of 1951, the Syrian law of 1953 (which went further, ruling that a woman divorced without due cause and able to prove that this has caused her material damage may claim compensation), and the Iraqi law of 1959. In 1943, and again in 1945, the Egyptian Ministry of Social Affairs drafted a bill under whose terms a man who divorced his wife or registered divorce without the local *qadi*'s consent would be punishable, the *qadi* being instructed not to agree to divorce without examining the reasons and making an attempt to reconcile the couple. But these proposals were not accepted. The new U.A.R. Bill on personal status rules that divorce is valid only when witnessed by a *qadi* and according to a *qadi*'s decision. The 1948 Druze law stated that divorce required a *qadi*'s consent, and added that a man might not remarry a woman he had previously divorced.

Over the past ten years some of the Arab countries have begun to grant women political rights. The first to do so was Syria, whose election law of 1949 conferred active (but not passive) election rights on women with elementary school certificates. Lebanon followed with an amended election law of February 1953 granting women full election rights, without limitation to the literate or any other group. According to this law, the participation of men in elections is compulsory, while that of women is a right. Syria has meanwhile (May 1959) granted full election rights to women. The most recent election law of Egypt also gives women full election rights (while compulsory voting is required for men). In July 1957 Egypt became the first Arab country in which two women were elected to parliament (the National Assembly). Iraq was the first Arab country where a woman held a ministerial post; on 14 July 1959 Dr Naziha ad-Dulaimi was appointed Minister of Rural Affairs.

B. THE FAMILY

In the traditional society of the Middle East the family is the economic and property-owning unit. The family as a whole, rather than any of its individual members, is owner of those possessions which constitute the basis of the family's maintenance. The son of a family naturally continues in his father's footsteps in the traditional family occupation. The family is also the fundamental social unit; the participation of an individual in wider groups, such as a religious sect or even a political party, is through his family only. The family has overwhelming importance in traditional Middle Eastern society, and has hardly been weakened as a result of the urbanising trend, economic changes, or spread of education. What, then, are the special characteristics of the Middle Eastern Arab family, and how are they changing? There are three main characteristics: (*a*) the extended family structure; (*b*) patriarchal rule (and associated patrilinearity and patrilocality); and (*c*) preference for marriage within the family (endogamy) unless this conflicts with religious morality.

1. *THE EXTENDED FAMILY*

The traditional Middle Eastern family structure is the extended family (*ahl, dar*). That is, one household unites the father of the family, his wife or wives, his unmarried daughters, his unmarried sons, and married sons with their wives and children. This family lives in a single house or in apartments closely grouped or attached to one another, sometimes around a large common courtyard. Beduins live in a number of tents set up in a close group. This is still the form of family structure which predominates in most tribal and rural areas of the Middle East, if not in the cities. The most detailed statistics on this subject were published in the survey of five Arab villages of Palestine in 1944. In 29·2% of all households of these villages married sons lived together with one or both of their parents. Many cases, however, are not included in this number, not because the married sons left their parents' home, but because of the death of the parents. A further look into one of the villages showed that only a third of all sons left their parents' home after marriage. The typical form of the extended family is evidently less common in Egypt than in the Fertile Crescent countries, because in Egypt the average life-span of the father is lower—i.e., he often dies before his sons marry.

Wherever the extended family exists, it is also the unit of

family property. The possessions of the extended family belong to it as a whole, and all its members work together on the farm or in the family business. The father of the family supervises family possessions, directs the farm or business, and finances his sons' expenses. The triple significance of the extended family as a unit of property, economy, and dwelling has inter-connections: the requirements of farming landed property and the efforts to prevent its division are the main reasons for unit housing of the extended family. That family structure is, then, preserved more among large landowners than among smaller ones, more among landed fellahs than among peasant tenants and agricultural labourers.[1] The scope of the extended family depends largely on the manner in which its property is kept. For example, Ammar points out that a widow moves to live with her brother's family whenever she transfers her land to his keeping or allows him to farm it. Since married sons own no property so long as their father remains alive, they live and work with him; after his death the sons continue to live to-gether if they go on farming the family land collectively, and separate only after the land has been divided up among them.

For as long as the extended family exists, its importance as a social unit surpasses that of the biological family (parents and young children); however, in recent times, and particularly in the present generation, a striking change has set in: married sons tend to move off to their own homes, and the unit of housing and property has dropped to two generations only—the biological or conjugal family—as is customary in Western European society. Many Middle Eastern mansions with their extensive courtyards, which in the nineteenth century were the homes of extended families numbering thirty or forty persons, no longer house such families; their owners let them to institu-tions or split them up into apartments.[2]

The causes of this change are numerous. First, the city has new earning prospects which enable sons to break away from

---

[1] Ammar, pp. 42-4; Weulersse, pp. 119, 217-18; Chatila, p. 50; Jaussen, *Naplouse*, p. 126. It is interesting that when speaking of the extended family Miss Fuller gives examples of landed families, whereas when passing to a description of the 'immediate family' she quotes tenants and workers (Fuller, pp. 63-4).

[2] K. El Daghestani, 'The Evolution of the Moslem Family in the Middle Eastern Countries', *International Social Science Bulletin* (*ISSB*), Vol. V (1953), No. 4, p. 684; see also Berque, *Les Arabes*, p. 87; Chehabe ed-Dine, pp. 296, 299, 339.

their dependence on the family property and traditional family occupation and to become financially independent. Disagreement among brothers or between father and sons has always been common within the extended family; with the recent advance of economic potentialities, there have been more and more cases of sons leaving their home whenever quarrels broke out. Also, the spread of education among both sons and daughters has introduced new concepts counter to the traditional way of life, and favouring aspirations to independence. There is greater opposition to the division of the family into the customary two worlds—of men and women. That measure of independence which the woman achieved has spurred her to rebel against her mother-in-law's rule, subjecting the women of the family.

The movement away from the extended family has varied in strength among classes and regions. It depended on the potential sources of economic independence available to the younger generation, and on housing conditions which would enable new families to leave the old pattern of life. In the last generation the problem has intensified in certain Middle Eastern cities. Members of the middle classes have undergone greater changes than their upper-class counterparts, who are held back by fear of fragmentation of their property and loss of social standing; more change has occurred in the town than in the country, more in cities than in provincial towns. The movement had a greater impact on villages under urban influences and trends of modern life than on more backward villages.

Thus, for example, the extended family was the predominating economic and social unit in Chibayish in Southern Iraq, in the isolated Maronite village of Hadeth el-Jobbe neighbouring the peak of Mount Lebanon, and in the Israeli Arab village of Tayyiba in 1954. Even in Ramallah, with its large Christian population, the move from the extended to the conjugal family was only slight. On the other hand, in the Christian village of al-Munsif, between Beirut and Tripoli in Lebanon (many of whose inhabitants work in the city, some emigrated to America and returned), Gulick found in 1952 that the conjugal family predominated and only two families were extended. A 1952–3 survey of 1,903 families in Beirut counted 4,926 unmarried sons as against 142 married sons, indicating that the number of married sons who remained in their father's homes was very low.[1]

2. *PATRIARCHAL RULE*

A second fundamental characteristic of the Middle Eastern Arab family is the existence of patriarchal rule: the father is the master of the immediate family and head of the extended family. He is the absolute ruler of all its members. This rule derives from the fact that as head of the household he owns all the family possessions; so long as he lives, neither his sons nor other members of the family have any property of their own. Furthermore, he oversees the family labour force, be it in agriculture or in an urban family business. In traditional circles sons generally have no resources or other means of sustinence; being thus compelled to work on their father's estate or in his business, they are totally dependent on him. Moreover, any attempt to rebel against his rule may endanger their share in the inheritance.

Patriarchal rule is particularly strong in villages and traditional towns. Obviously it is weakened by fragmentation of the extended family, notably in cities undergoing modernisation. Significant, however, is the almost total absence of patriarchal rule in beduin society. This point was already stressed eighty years ago by Robertson Smith. A characteristic of beduin society is the 'extreme weakness of internally exercised authority in agnatic sections'. Only in times of strife and war does the authority of the head of the extended family, or head of several extended families, assert itself.[2]

A prominent feature of patriarchal rule is that young men and women do not make their own decisions in the matter of marriage. Parents arrange the marriages and even choose the partner, and daughters and sons are compelled to comply. The practice persists to this day among all classes. Various suggestions have been made in explanation: since a girl marries at a very young age, her parents can better select a suitable

---

[1] Salim, p. 78; H. Rosenfeld, 'Temuroth bamivneh hahevrati shel hakfar ha'aravi Tayyiba', *Mibifnim*, April 1956, p. 459; Gulick, pp. 60, 109–10; Zarour, p. 436; C. W. Churchill, *The City of Beirut*, Beirut, 1954, pp. 32–3.
[2] R. F. Murphy and L. Kasdan, 'The Structure of Parallel Cousin Marriage', *American Anthropologist*, 1959, p. 20.

partner for her; since the bride will live within her husband's (extended) family, it would be unacceptable for that family, i.e., the father and mother of the groom, not to have their say in the choice of a bride; and finally, as urban women are veiled, a young man cannot in any case choose his wife through acquaintance, and it is thus preferable that his parents, knowing the family, should do so in his place. However, there is a more basic reason for this custom. A son is dependent on his father for obtaining the bride price, and therefore his father has the last word in choosing bride and wedding date. The daughter, as noted earlier, is still widely considered to be family property, or more exactly, her father's property, often deprived even of a bride price. In return, he is bound to defend his daughter's honour (and hence the family name) whenever she is treated improperly. It is, then, obvious that decisions about her marriage are his.[1]

In this as in all other practices of traditional society, changes are now making their appearance in various parts of the Middle East and in various classes of its population. The number of cases in which the couple becomes acquainted before marriage is growing. In the Lebanese village of Munsif investigated by Gulick, matters have reached such a point that marriage is possible even without parental consent (although it remains customary to request formal agreement), and the accepted practice is now that marriage is based on the free choice of the parties concerned, within the framework of existing laws of endogamy. However, bride prices are not recognised in Munsif —a fact which was undoubtedly important in this development.[2] Generally, the practice is still that the father or family arranges the marriage of sons and daughters; if this is irksome to sons it is far more frustrating to daughters, and is a funda-

[1] See Salim, p. 78; Rosenfeld, *Tayyiba*, p. 463; Jaussen, *Naplouse*, p. 123. It may be noted that only one school of law, the Hanafi, allows a Muslim woman to make her marriage contract on her own, on condition that she chooses a husband who is her equal in social standing. All other schools require that she be contracted in marriage by her guardian (see Anderson, *Islamic Law*, pp. 43-4, 47).

[2] Gulick, p. 82, and similarly Touma, pp. 118 ff. In Beirut too the practice of paying a bride price is disappearing (Chehabe ed-Dine, p. 292). Among the Muslims of Israel, an active movement is afoot against the high level of bride prices, and the first marriages without any payment have been carried out. In Kuwait the Government has recently intervened to limit bride prices, which had soared to fantastic heights (*az-Zaman*, Iraq, 14 May 1960).

mental cause of complications in married women's sexual life.[1]

The rule of the head of the family over his wife and even his adult sons finds its expression in a code of behaviour patterns, particularly strict in Egypt and especially in Egyptian villages. But even in an Egyptian village (30 km. from Cairo) which is considered to be a guardian of traditional forms, its inhabitants being of the 'Arab race', the following comments have been made by A. Lichtenstadter, who lived there for five months in 1950:

Under the influence of 'modern' Western ideas, friction may arise between father and son. Through contact with his contemporaries outside his own circle, through school and newspapers, the young man increasingly becomes aware of his father's restricting supervision and resents his dependence and the restraint on his freedom of action and decision in his work and private life. The older man finds it difficult to relinquish the customary domination over his son, even though in theory he may realise that it is outmoded and that 'modern' life and 'modern' youth demand fewer restrictions and more ceding of responsibility.[2]

Together with patriarchal rule, the Middle Eastern Arab family is characterised by two further traits. First, it is patrilineal, that is, each individual belongs to his father's rather than his mother's line. In Chibayish of Southern Iraq it is customary to call the father's family by the name *ahli* (my family) and that of the mother by the name *ahl ummi* (my mother's family). In the event of a quarrel between the families of the two parents each individual must support his father's side, even when an uncle on his mother's side is involved. On marriage the woman rather than the man joins a new family (and in theory takes on a new allegiance). Hence the attempts to deprive daughters of their share in the inheritance, mentioned earlier; hence also the totally different status of uncles on the paternal and maternal sides in matters of inheritance, in matters connected with chastity of daughters of a brother or sister, the adoption of orphans, and so on. Finally, the patrilineal doctrine explains the difference between cousins on the paternal and maternal

[1] See R. Makarius, *La Jeunesse intellectuelle d'Égypte au lendemain de la deuxième guerre mondiale*, The Hague, 1960, p. 53 n.

[2] I. Lichtenstadter, 'An Arab Egyptian Family', *MEJ*, Autumn 1952, p. 385. For code of behaviour in Egyptian villages see Ammar, pp. 50–3. For Syria and Palestine see Chatila, p. 42; Jaussen, *Naplouse*, p. 87.

sides over their desirability as partners in marriage to a girl. (In this connection, more will be said in the following section on endogamy.)

The Middle Eastern Arab family is also characterised by patrilocality. That is to say, a young couple generally lives in the husband's home and belongs to his extended family, rather than in the home of his wife's family. Patrilocality fits in with the rest of the characteristics of the Middle Eastern Arab family described here—rule and supremacy of the male who, to all intents and purposes, 'buys' his wife, and kinship to the paternal rather than to the maternal family. All these require that a married couple live within the husband's family.

The southernmost region of Upper Egypt, however, is to a certain extent an exception. Here it is customary for the husband to live in the home of his wife's family for the first years of marriage (in the village of Silwa, described by Ammar, for one year). This is undoubtedly associated with the fact that the Nubians and Beja, inhabitants of Northern Sudan, still retain some remnants of a matriarchate—for example, the family is matrilineal.[1]

3. *ENDOGAMY*

In the traditional Middle Eastern Arab family there is a clear inclination towards endogamy, i.e., marriage between relatives of the father (members of a single *hamula*)[2] and, when possible, between cousins (son and daughter of two brothers). The Arab *hamula*, with its endogamic tendency, is in total contrast to the clan in most African tribes, where exogamy (marriage to women of other clans) is the rule. The endogamic trend is still fairly general, and authors have stressed its prevalence in various classes of desert, village, and urban populations. Nevertheless, distinct differences do exist among these groups.

In beduin society and among a few specific groupings of fellahs the custom of marriage between cousins has become so engrained that a young man has rights over his female cousin and may claim compensation if he waives them. Among the

[1] Ammar, pp. 197 ff.; H. A. Winkler, *Ägyptische Volkskunde*, Stuttgart, 1936, pp. 204–16; G. W. Murray, *Sons of Ishmael*, London, 1935, pp. 54–6; Trimingham, pp. 179–80.

[2] On the *hamula* ('clan') see below, Chapter IV.

Banu Asad tribe, settled in the village of Chibayish in Southern Iraq, this right covered all daughters of the 'clan' (*fakhdh*— the local term for a *hamula*). The right is called *an-nahwa*, and in modern times led to serious complications; it had been improperly applied, for extortion, and after one particularly severe case, about twenty years ago, the practice was abolished. Nevertheless, in 1953 Dr Salim found that 38·4% of the women belonging to the families he studied were their husbands' cousins; 51·2% were members of the same *fakhdh* as their husbands, and 62·2% were members of the same maximal lineage as their husbands. Similar findings are reported by Berque from the Egyptian village of Fisha in the province of Minufiya: marriage of cousins in 36·2% of all marriages; marriage not of cousins but of persons living in a single quarter of the village in 48·6%; together, marriage within a quarter (which is identical with the *hamula*) in 84·4% of all marriages. Barth has found that 50% of all marriages in certain Kurdish villages were between cousins.[1]

However, such high figures are not found everywhere. Rosenfeld has drawn up a table summarising data for Artas (studied by Granqvist), the villages of Ramla (the Village Survey of 1944), and Tur'an (Rosenfeld). According to this table, the percentage of marriages between cousins out of all marriages was not much more than 13% in Artas and in Tur-'an, while marriage within the *hamula* accounted for 33·7% of all marriages in Artas, 55·8% in the Ramla villages, and 31·5% among the Muslims of Tur'an.[2]

An author who wrote on marriage among Syrian Muslims was of the impression that the custom of marriage between cousins and within a family is more common among notable village families than among the simple fellahs; it is more common in villages than in towns; and in towns, too, the custom is mainly restricted to well-to-do and prominent families, less prevalent among the middle classes, and least of all among the masses. It is commoner in the provincial towns than in the cities.[3]

If these impressions are correct they support the opinion that

[1] Salim, pp. 121–2; J. Berque, 'Sur la structure sociale de quelques villages égyptiens', *Annales Économies—Sociétés—Civilisations*, 1955, p. 205; F. Barth, 'Father's Brother's Daughter Marriage in Kurdistan', *Southwestern Journal of Anthropology* (*SWJA*), Vol. 10, No. 2, p. 167.

[2] Rosenfeld in *IAE*, p. 46.   [3] Chatila, pp. 91–8.

marriage of cousins is actuated mainly by the desire to retain family property intact. Others claim that the practice serves to strengthen and consolidate the family in the face of quarrels between its various factions.[1] A number of authors summarise the causes of marriage within the father's family, and particularly between cousins, as follows: (1) a young woman marrying a relative on her father's side can go on living in the same house, if the family structure is extended; (2) since her parents and her husband's parents belong to the same family, the dilemma of split loyalties does not arise; (3) the parents on both sides can rest assured that bride and groom are well suited by social background and lineage; (4) on marriage of cousins, the bride price is much lower than the sum customarily paid by the groom's family to outsiders;[2] (5) by the same stroke, the bride's father, of course, loses. He is consoled by the fact that his son-in-law is his nephew, loyal to him and his family, ready to support him morally and materially, unlike a strange son-in-law, whose loyalties are with his own family; (6) the daughter's inheritance remains within the family if she marries a cousin, and her children will remain within the extended family to which she and her husband belong.[3] All these explanations, however, do not give a complete answer to the question: Why was this custom preserved much more among Arabs than in other societies? Whatever the answer, we note that more care is taken to ensure that a daughter marries some relative than that a son chooses a member of the family group for his wife.

Evidence from various regions and classes of the Arab Middle East proves that endogamy within the extended family or *hamula* has decreased. In the process of tribal settlement, traditional endogamic customs of beduin society have been lost, as the example of Chibayish demonstrates. The greater economic independence of the younger generation, the rise in

[1] For this discussion see Barth, p. 171, and Rosenfeld in *IAE*, pp. 38-40.

[2] In Chibayish a tenth to a fifth only (Salim, p. 120). In Silwan near Jerusalem it was no more than a tenth (Jaussen, *Naplouse*, pp. 267-8).

[3] Patai, *Jordan*, p. 284; Barth, pp. 167-8; Fuller, pp. 53-4, 65. Barth notes, with some justice, that the preservation of a daughter's inheritance within the family may be a factor only in those regions where it is, in fact, customary to let the daughter keep her inheritance in accordance with Muslim law (see above). Robertson Smith (p. 163) explains the priority rights of a male cousin as a remnant of Tibetan polyandry which existed in early Arabia: the woman was shared by a group of related men.

the standard of education, decreasing domination of parents, particularly over choice of a partner in marriage for their son or daughter, and a general change in frame of mind—all these trends are against endogamy. They do not, however, entirely cancel out the two economic reasons for endogamy—low bride price and preservation of the inheritance in the family. (On the other hand, as noted, the latter problem is generally solved by depriving daughters of their share altogether.)

Endogamy is a meaningful concept beyond the family and *hamula* too. Various authors have stressed the marked tendency towards marriage within the village (village endogamy). In the five Palestinian villages studied in 1944, among 73·5% of all marriages, man and wife were members of the same village, and in the village of Tayyiba in the Israel Triangle Rosenfeld found that the percentage was 80%. However, village endogamy does not necessarily signify a consciousness of territorial ties. In Chibayish, for example, where intra-village marriages constituted 82·3% of all marriages, all villagers are members of a single tribe (Banu Asad), while Munsif, where Gulick found village rather than *hamula* endogamy, is a kind of Greek Orthodox island in a sea of Maronite neighbours. Of course, there is a high natural likelihood that members of any particular village will become acquainted. When there are reasons for strong ties with neighbouring villages or towns the percentage of village endogamy often falls distinctly; for example, in Artas in Palestine marriage within the village accounted for only 57·6% of all marriages.

Thus, as ties with the outside world and particularly with towns strengthen, there is a drop in village endogamy (and hence also in family and *hamula* endogamy). In this connection it is instructive to examine the figures of Gulick for marriages between 1860 and 1952. In the thirty-four marriages of 1860–89, not one person of another village was concerned. In 1890–1919 there were three inter-village marriages out of a total of forty-four in all—i.e., one per decade. In more recent times the percentage of marriages out of the village has risen as follows:

1920–9	9%
1930–9	33%
1940–9	39%
1950–2	71%

Incidentally, the same table indicates that in Munsif, among all marriages out of the village, interfaith (i.e., non-Greek Orthodox) marriages are the commonest. Clearly, urbanisation and trends towards modernity are responsible for this, as other authors have pointed out in connection with their studies of the city. However, there is no doubt that Munsif is unusual in this respect, and religious endogamy is still the rule in most rural areas, and to some extent in the cities too. There are no statistics on this subject.

Finally, there is the question of endogamy within a social class. It will be seen that, apart from special regions, an aristocracy of lineage does not exist in the Muslim countries of the Middle East. While Islam is opposed to favouring one man over another on the grounds of lineage (as is customary in tribal Arab society), Muslim law, as it became codified in the first centuries of Islam, did accept the principle of equal social status between man and wife. This principle has even been embodied in modern laws of personal status, as follows (Clause 45 of the Ottoman Family Law): 'It is a condition of marriage that a man suit his wife by economic standing, profession, and so on. Suitability of profession may be judged by whether his business or work is similar, in terms of social standing, to that of his wife's guardian at marriage.'[1] This clause, with more or less the same wording, became part of the legislation on personal status in the Arab states.[2]

It is difficult to assess the influence of this law as distinct from the custom which is, in any case, accepted—that marriage should be between members of the same social circle. Be that as it may, there are clear indications that marriage tends to be arranged within a single social class, particularly the class of large landowners. Chatila notes that whereas in the smaller towns members of this class marry within the family group, in the cities 'men of the upper classes marry women of the same social set, but not of the same family'.[3] Marriage within the families of the largest landowners was a very frequent occur-

---

[1] Translated from the Arabic and Hebrew versions in S. D. Goitein and A. Ben Shemesh, *Muslim Law in Israel*, Jerusalem, 1957.

[2] For the Syrian Family Law see Chatila, pp. 89–90. In later legislation this principle was abolished; for example, in Iraq in 1959 (Linant de Bellefonds, pp. 95–6).

[3] Chatila, p. 92.

rence in pre-revolution Egypt. Some examples of the best-known families follow: the mother and wife of Fu'ad Siraj ad-Din are of the Badrawi-'Ashur family. The latter family is also connected by marriage with the al-Atrabi and al-Maghazi families, again former estate-owners. The family of ash-Sharif of Ibyar (Gharbiya) is related to the Mahmud family of ar-Rahmaniya (Buhaira), and the Tarazi family of Asyut is related to the 'Amr family. All the important families of large landowning Copts in Upper Egypt, Minya and Fayyum—Khayyat, Ibsakhrun, Buqtur, Bishara-Andra'us, Bushra Hanna, Doss, Shenouda, Fanus, Wisa and Salih—are interrelated by marriage.[1] By marriage between landowners, it has sometimes been possible to unite stretches of landed property which would otherwise have broken up because of divided inheritances.

[1] Information based on reports and obituaries in *al-Ahram* of the 1940s and 1950s. Also J. E. Blattner (ed.), *Who's Who in Egypt and the Near East*, Cairo, 1950.

III

RELIGIOUS AND ETHNIC COMMUNITIES

A. SURVEY OF RELIGIOUS AND ETHNIC GROUPS[1]

1. *THE RELIGIOUS COMMUNITY IN MIDDLE EASTERN SOCIETY*

Most of the inhabitants of the Arab Middle East are Sunni Muslims by religion and speak Arabic. In his book on minorities, however, A. Hourani estimates that members of other religious groups or persons speaking other languages constitute more than a quarter of the population of these countries.[2] The conclusion remains valid even if some of his more out-of-date data are corrected, and also if the population of Sudan, the Arabian Peninsula, and Libya (not included in Hourani's estimate) are added.

Apart from the Sunni Muslim population, there are more than twenty religious communities (*tawa'if*; singular *ta'ifa*) which may be included under the headings of Islam, Christianity, or Judaism, or which developed from monotheistic religions, the pagan faiths of the Southern Sudanese tribes being excluded.

This plurality of religious communities has many causes:

(*a*) It was in the Middle East that the three monotheistic religions and their main schisms all made their appearance.

---

[1] The racial distribution of the population of the Arab Middle East is not discussed here. Racial differences, in so far as they have been preserved, have no importance in the consciousness of most of the inhabitants of the region. In cases of prominent racial features, such as those found in the Sudan, for example, the matter is brought up in the discussion of the communal structure of the different countries.

[2] A. H. Hourani, *Minorities in the Arab World*, London, 1947, p. 13.

There were also various attempts to adapt these religions to the beliefs with which they came in contact (paganism, the religions of Persia and India, and Greek philosophy), which in some cases resulted in the formation of a new sect or religion.

(*b*) Disagreements of a tribal, regional, or social nature often gave rise to sects; political division and religious schism developed concomitantly.[1] Division of this kind occurred within Islam and Christianity.

(*c*) The Middle East has periodically been a centre or objective of nomads, particularly those of Arab and Central Asian tribes. The many conquests from the North and from the Mediterranean left in their traces a population of variegated religion and language, which persists to this day.

(*d*) The Arab Middle East has at times served as an asylum for the members of religious sects who fled persecution in neighbouring territories. This, too, has led to an increase in the number of religious communities found in Arab countries.

Note may be made of two factors restraining the Sunni Muslim majority from engulfing other religious sects (and from replacing their languages by Arabic). It is to their credit that most of the communities which ever sprang up in the Middle East have been preserved.

(*e*) The first restraining factor is geopolitical, and is due to the existence of mountainous and desert country, the absence of satisfactory communications, and the resulting long-term isolation of many regions from a central authority. For these reasons, the central government used not to be in control of extensive regions, and various communities were in fact autonomous, having little contact with the towns, coastal areas, and riversides, highly populated by Sunni Muslims. Obviously, this factor operated more in the Fertile Crescent countries and in Sudan than in Egypt; and indeed the number of minority groups in Egypt is small.

(*f*) The second restraining factor is religious. The basic attitude of Islam towards monotheistic religions (*ahl al-kitab*) is tolerant; they must be allowed to maintain their religion, even if they are not first-class citizens in a Muslim state. These principles were generally put into effect, and apart from isolated, generally short periods of persecution, there were no

[1] See Bernard Lewis, *The Arabs in History*, London, 1950, pp. 70-4, 99 ff.

attempts to massacre the Christians and Jews or forcibly to Islamise them. There was, of course, a continual gradual process of Islamisation among certain religious communities, but in most cases it did not assume an extreme form.

The tolerance of Islam did more than just help monotheistic religions to maintain their identity; it played a role in the preservation of the basic importance of the *religious community as a social unit* in the Middle East. The social and political value of the religious unit remained even after Western rationalism had permeated the Middle East and an attitude of indifference towards the precepts of religion had become widely prevalent. In other words, weakening of the religious way of life did not imply that the Middle Eastern man was any the less conscious of his part in a religious community having definite social and political functions.

In explanation of this phenomenon, it is to be noted that Islam does not differentiate between religion and state. The head of a Muslim state had both religious and political functions, and Muslim religious precepts have formed an integral part of the law of the state throughout its development and to this very day. At the same time the Muslim state has tolerated the presence of other monotheistic religions within it. Hence there was no choice but to permit members of these religions to administer their community affairs according to their own religious edicts.

Under the Ottoman Empire this principle of autonomy found expression in the *Millet* system (the Turkish form of the Arabic word *milla* meaning both nation and religious community). According to this system, the Christian and Jewish communities were allowed autonomy in law (after 1856 only with respect to laws of personal status) and the administration of the affairs of the community, including supervision of communal possessions, education, etc. Moreover, the leaders of the various communities were their official representatives before the authorities. Such autonomy was not in theory granted to heterodox Muslim communities, but in practice it did prevail in some isolated territorial centres in which those communities were strong enough to maintain autonomy. In such regions, for example, they had their own law courts, in which judgement was passed according to their customs and religious precepts, while in other regions they were forced to seek judgement in Muslim law courts.

Most of the religious communities were closely knit units; their many social and political roles linked the members of a community, scattered though they might be throughout the Ottoman Empire. The communal consciousness of inhabitants of the Middle East became stronger in the nineteenth century, because foreign powers assumed protectorship of the various religious groups, siding with them in their disputes with other groups or with Ottoman governments, or sometimes even stimulating such disputes for political purposes. The Maronites had a traditional tie with France, the Druzes with Britain, the Greek Orthodox with Russia, etc. These ties strengthened the religious community as a political unit and thereby intensified the community spirit of its members.

The solidarity of the religious community was due to yet another specifically Middle Eastern cause: the late development of the middle classes, modern intelligentsia and proletariat who would be readier than the traditional classes to replace their religious faith by a new allegiance on a national or class basis.

Because of these factors, the religious communities retained their social and political functions to a considerable degree, even after the Ottoman Empire was replaced by independent national States in the Arab Middle East. *Jurisdiction in matters of personal status* (marriage, divorce, and all related affairs, adoption and guardianship, heritages and wills, *waqf*, etc.) was left to the special religious law courts, not affiliated to the system of civil jurisdiction—the *shari'a* law courts for Muslims, and the ecclesiastical or rabbinical law courts for Christian and Jewish communities. In all States of the Arab Peninsula in which the number of Christian and Jewish communities is small, matters of personal status are judged according to *shari'a* law. In Saudi Arabia religious law is applied even more widely; the *shari'a* court also deals with civil, mercantile, and criminal cases.[1] The situation is similar in the Yemen and in Oman. In

---

[1] A. M. Sālim, 'Nizam al-qada' wa't-tashri' fi'l-mamlaka al-'arabiya as-sa'udiya', *L'Egypte Contemporaine*, October 1959, pp. 6, 28, etc. It is to be noted, though, that in recent years civil legislation is also on the increase. (See Sālim, *passim*, and Anderson, *Islamic Law*, pp. 83–4.)

Iraq the religious law courts were sanctioned to deal with matters of personal status by virtue of the 1927 Constitution (Clauses 75–80), and no changes have been introduced since then. In Jordan the juridical authority of *shari'a* law courts is based on the appropriate Ottoman law of 1913, that of other religious law courts on a law of 1938. Also in the Sudan, the youngest of the Arab states, the transitional legislation of 1955 split the judicial into civil and religious branches.

In the period between the two World Wars repeated efforts to limit the juridical authority of the religious law courts in Lebanon and Syria met with opposition on the part of the leaders of the religious communities. A new Lebanese law of 2 April 1951 again left jurisdiction in all matters of personal status (engagement, marriage, divorce, bride price, adoption, guardianship, heritages, bequests, wills, *waqf*, etc.) in the hands of the religious courts. A general strike of lawyers in Lebanon at the end of that year, calling for repeal of the statute and one civil legal system for all communities, was again opposed by all the heads of the religious communities; they managed to frustrate a parliamentary attempt to reach a compromise by which the power of religious courts would be limited.[1] During the period between the two World Wars Egypt was the scene of various attempts to limit the authority of religious law courts, all of which failed because of minority-group opposition. However, after the military revolt, Egypt was the first and to date the only country in the whole Middle East (including Israel) to abolish religious courts. As of 1 January 1956, the settlement of all claims was transferred to civil courts.[2] The civil courts, however, pass judgement on matters of personal status according to religious law.

[1] For the Lebanese law of 1930 and chronological survey of communal jurisdiction in Lebanon see P. Rondot, *Les Institutions politiques du Liban*, Paris, 1947, pp. 74–5, 129–33; for Syria see Hourani, pp. 75–7. Developments in 1951 according to *Hamizrah Hehadash*, III, pp. 274–5, 378.

[2] Law No. 462 of 1955 (24 September 1955). The main criticism of the law raised by representatives of the minority groups was that Muslim judges would now judge Christians according to Christian precepts, while Christian judges would not be transferred to the new courts. There is also discrimination in that a Christian may become a Muslim during the hearing of a case and be judged according to Islamic law, but not the opposite. In this connection, see also P. Rondot, 'Minorities in the Arab Orient Today', *Middle Eastern Affairs* (*ME Aff* in later references), 1959, p. 222. In Turkey religious courts were abolished after the Kemalist revolution.

The religious community has maintained not only its juridical authority but also some fundamental rights in the realm of political rule. This is clear in countries such as Yemen, in which the spiritual leader of the Zaidi community is at the same time the political leader of the country, or Saudi Arabia, in which the history of the ruling royal line is closely aligned with the ascendancy of Wahabism, or Libya, whose king is the head of the Sanusi order. In Egypt and the Fertile Crescent countries too the fundamental importance of religion and the religious community is an accepted fact in political life. Islam was the official religion of Egypt, both according to the old constitution of 1923 (Clause 149) and the temporary one of 1956 (Clause 3). The same is true of Iraq according to the old constitution of 1925 (Clause 13) and the new temporary one of 1958 (Clause 4); so also in Libya as of 1951 (Clause 5), and in Jordan as of 1952 (Clause 2). The Syrian constitution of 1950 set down in its preface that the majority of Syrians are believers in Islam, and the Government thus also proclaims its adherence to the faith. In Clause 3 it is written that: (1) the religion of the president of the republic is Islam; (2) Muslim law will form the basis of legislation. This was a compromise between the original wording of the legislatory committee which set forth Islam as the State religion and the demands of the Christians and freethinking Muslims, who demanded that this clause be omitted.[1] According to the temporary constitution of the U.A.R. of March 1958, the provisions concerning a state religion or the president's religion were repealed, to be reintroduced into the National Charter of the U.A.R. (Egypt) in May 1962. In the Sudan a compromise similar to that of Syria ('the Islamic religion will serve as the foundation of the country's legislation') apparently solved the same dilemma early in 1957.[2] There is no such clause in the Lebanese constitution, but the president is always a Maronite, by tradition. In Egypt it has become traditional to elect one Copt to the Government, and in a like fashion, one Palestinian Christian is customarily a member of the Jordanian Government. Proportional representation by religious communities (but not by

[1] P. Rondot, *Les Chrétiens d'Orient*, Paris, 1955, pp. 228–9; *Hamizrah Hehadash*, II, pp. 54–5.
[2] *Hamizrah Hehadash*, VIII, p. 218.

linguistic groups) is set down in the election laws of Iraq, Jordan, Syria, and Lebanon.

The religious community also has great importance as a social framework. First, philanthropic societies, youth movements, women's organisations, and other non-political groupings are generally organised on a community basis. In Lebanon there are even political and semi-military organisations which are centred on the various communities, in practice if not in theory. Secondly, the group life of youth and adults in the cities is to a very great extent kept within the community framework. Recent developments in this connection will be discussed at a later point.

It is apparent, then, that in almost all the Middle Eastern countries the religious community still preserves its weighty social and political role. There are even factors working to strengthen this role—e.g., movements such as the 'Muslim Brotherhood', representing a reaction to liberalism which is made to appear as the ideology of the Western Powers, and so on. Other factors operate in the reverse direction: urbanisation, leading to the formation of ties of loyalty among members of a professional group or even a social class; and extension of education, which strengthens national consciousness, based on a common language.

2. *THE RELIGIOUS COMMUNITIES*[1]

1. *Muslims and Related Communities.* The majority of all Muslims in the Middle East are Sunnis, and theirs is the largest of all the religious communities in that region. However, it is not homogeneous as regards customs, views, and religious practices.

The Sunnis are divided into four schools of law (*madhhab*, pl. *madhahib*) which were established in the eighth and ninth centuries of the Christian era and are all recognised as belonging to orthodox Islam. The four are:

[1] This survey does not aim to describe the beliefs of Islam and Christianity in any detail. Rather, the framework of the communal structure in the Middle East is sketched out, that the reader may gain a general orientation. Social characteristics of the main religious communities are discussed separately in the section on the communal structure of the different countries.

(*a*) The *Hanafi*, accepted in Turkey and thus predominant in official religious establishments in all Middle Eastern countries which have been under Turkish rule, and in cities which were influenced by that rule. Among the population, Hanafis are widely found in Turkey and also in Syria and Iraq.

(*b*) The *Shafi'i*, whose members are found among the inhabitants of Lower Egypt, the peasants of Israel, Syria (beduins) and Iraq (Kurds), and also in Hijaz and 'Asir in Saudi Arabia, among some of the inhabitants of Yemen, and in Aden.

(*c*) The *Maliki* of Upper Egypt, Sudan, Bahrain, Kuwait, and Libya.

(*d*) The *Hanbali*, now found in Saudi Arabia and in a few parts of the Arabian Peninsula.

The differences among these schools are not fundamental, and the division no longer has any importance in the consciousness of Muslims. Modern legislation is based on one or another of the schools of law, choice depending on where the provisions are most suitable to modern life.

Among Sunni (and Shi'i) Muslims there is also a popular form of the Islamic religion which has its roots in Muslim mysticism, Sufism (*tasawwuf*), and which has over the years become organised in orders of dervishes (*tariqas*). This popular religion scorns or even defies the ossified official law and places its emphasis on love of God and adherence to Him by exercises in which His name is repeated (*dhikr*), trances, and monastic asceticism. Saint worship became the most important aspect of their orders, and some dervishes practised sorcery and lived as beggars. The *tariqas* came into collision with the official Islam, but at times managed to reach long-lived compromises. They strayed less far from orthodoxy in the Arab Middle East than in Turkey, India, and North Africa, and in cities less than in villages. The *tariqas* provided a social framework for the village population, for the lower classes, and especially for city artisans. There are no reliable figures on the extent of influence and number of members of the dervish orders. Their influence has probably decreased in recent generations. Berque found clear signs of such a trend in his investigations of the Egyptian village of Sirs al-Layan. In general, however, the problem has not been sufficiently studied. It is certain that in the Sudan the influence of the *tariqas* in public life and even in politics is great.[1]

The *Wahhabi movement* was founded in the eighteenth century as a reaction to the saint-worship and deviations of the dervishes, and in opposition to the Sunni religious sages, who did not speak out against these deviations. This is a puritanical movement calling for a return to the original Islam of the Koran and Sunna; it grew out of the Hanbali school, the most conservative of Sunni Islam, negating all innovations (*bid'a*). The movement started among Beduin Najdi tribes; it was able to expand because of political support afforded by the princes of the line of Saud who eventually conquered most of the Arabian Peninsula. As a result, and in consequence of Wahhabi control of the cities of Mecca and Medina, to which pilgrimages are conducted from all parts of the Muslim world, the Wahhabis became less extreme and the differences between them and the rest of the Sunni Muslims became obscured. Today, Wahhabism is accepted among the inhabitants of Najd and al-Hasa in Saudi Arabia. Wahhabis are found also in Trucial Oman, in Qatar, and at other points along the eastern coast of the Arabian Peninsula.

Under the direct or indirect influence of Wahhabism, two further movements appeared in the middle of the nineteenth century, which also purposed to bring about reform in Islam. These movements, comprising even now a considerable sector of the population of two Arab countries, are the *Sanusiya* and *Mirghaniya* (or *Khatmiya*). From the viewpoint of their principles, these movements were closer to orthodox Islam than was Wahhabism (at least in its earlier forms), while their organisation was similar to that of the Sufi *tariqas*. They purposed to Islamise primitive tribes, and both movements occupied themselves with this activity, each in its own region. The common place of origin of the two movements was Hijaz. The Sanusi branch was founded by Muhammad Ibn 'Ali as-Sanusi, and made its centre at the Oases of Cyrenaica. It became known in

[1] Berque (*Structure sociale*, p. 211) found that in several of the villages of Minufiya, about a fifth of all the men took part in *tariqa* activities. On Sirs al-Layan see J. Berque, *Histoire Sociale d'un village égyptien au XXème siècle*, The Hague, 1957, pp. 37–42. On activities of *tariqas* in other Egyptian villages see Ammar, pp. 187–8, 215; Winkler, *Bauern*, p. 137. On the Sudan see Trimingham, *passim*.

Libya as an order fighting foreign rule—first against the French and later the Italians. The present head of the order is the King of Libya, and the order is influential among the majority of Cyrenaicans. The Mirghani branch was founded by Muhammad 'Uthman al-Amir Ghani and operated in East Africa and the Sudan. Its influence remains great in Eastern Sudan, and the movement is among the most decisive political factors in that country.

Principles similar in part to those of Wahhabism (although not, evidently, directly derived from that movement) were adopted also by the *Mahdiya* movement, founded in the 1880s in the Sudan in protest against the oppression of Sudan under foreign rule. This movement, which sprang from among the Sufi *tariqas*, later became their adversary and, on accession to rule, their suppressor.

As was the rule among the Wahhabis, the followers of the Mahdi were forbidden by their leader, Muhammad Ahmad, to engage in activities such as smoking, music, the sorcery of dervishes, saint worship, etc. But a further principle was added—belief in the Mahdi, the messiah, which had been widespread among the Muslim masses of Africa. During its reign the movement abolished the *madhhabs*, claimed *jihad* (holy war) as one of its basic beliefs, and changed the *Shahada* (profession of faith), thus to all intents and purposes leaving Sunni Islam. But after its fall the movement gradually became more moderate, and now may be considered orthodox in all respects. The movement is not to be found outside the Sudan, but there it fulfils an important political role. The *Ansar*, followers of the son of the Mahdi, are mainly found in Central and Western Sudan (Kordofan and Darfur).

All these movements either branched out from Sunni Islam relatively lately or developed within it. On the other hand, the great split between Sunna and Shi'a took place in the first century of Islam. The origins of the split are to be found in the political rivalry between 'Ali, the fourth Caliph and cousin and son-in-law of Muhammad, whose capital was at Kufa in Iraq and his supporters Iraqis, and Mu'awiya of the family of Umayya, an aristocratic family of Mecca, who moved his capital to Syria. After the political fall of 'Ali his supporters founded a religious sect which found many sympathisers among

79

the Mawali (clients of an Arab tribe) and non-Arabs who had become Islamised; the sect voiced their social struggle against the ruling aristocracy. In place of the Caliph of Sunni Islam, Shi'i Islam adopted the institution of the *Imam*, passing by heredity in the family of the prophet. The Imam was supposed to possess divine qualities. He can never be wrong. Devotion to the Imam (*wilaya*) has been added by the Shi'a as a sixth pillar of Islam. The Koran has a deep allegorical meaning that only the Imam can comprehend. The *mujtahids*, the religious sages of the Shi'a, have much wider authority than do the Sunni *'ulama*. Among other things, they have the right of individual interpretation of the religious law (*ijtihad*). Two other principles which differentiate Sunna and Shi'a are *taqiya*—the right of the Shi'is to conceal their beliefs in times of persecution—and *mut'a*—temporary marriage. Also notable is the practice of mourning the death of Husain, expressed by the custom of *ta'ziya*—acting out the agonies of 'Ali and his sons, Hasan and Husain, every year on the day of 'Ashura (the 10th of the month of Muharram).

The various sects of the Shi'a are divided on the issue of who is the last in the line of Imams. The closest to the Sunna in its principles is the *Zaidiya* sect, which claims that the line of Imams has still not ended. It does not invest the Imam with superhuman power. His succession is not hereditary; the Imam must be of the family of the prophet, a learned man, and a warrior having the ability and power to win and maintain the position of Imam. The sect predominates in the Yemen, where the Zaidi Imam heads the state. The number of Zaidis in Yemen is about two and a quarter million.

The largest subdivision of the Shi'is is the *Imamis*, who recognise twelve Imams. The last of them was Muhammad al-Mahdi, who disappeared about the year 873. They believe he is still in hiding, and await his eventual return. Imami Shi'a is the official religion in Persia. In the Arab countries of the Middle East it is represented mainly by Iraq (where about half the population are Imami Shi'is). Here the Shi'a holy places are to be found, notably at Najaf (near old Kufa, traditionally believed to be the burying-place of 'Ali), Karbala (Mashhad Husain, the grave of Husain, son of 'Ali), Samarra, and al-Kadhimiya. Also members of the sect are 230,000

Mutawalis (in Arabic: *Matawila*) of Lebanon, comprising a fifth of the population of that country. In the island of Bahrain Imami Shi'is make up more than half the population, i.e., over 50,000 persons (according to the 1950 census, in which they were not counted separately, and according to their fraction in the 1941 census). A few Shi'is are also found in Oman and Muscat, and a further 15,000 in Syria, chiefly in the northern provinces of Homs and Aleppo.

The third and most extreme sect of the Shi'is represented today in the Arab Middle East is the *Isma'iliya*, which splintered off from the Shi'is in the middle of the eighth century because of a controversy on the question of the rightful successor to the sixth Imam. The Isma'iliya extended the principle of esoteric interpretation of the Koran, and thus took on many elements of neoplatonism. Missionaries of the sect, from the select few to whom the secrets of the religion were revealed by degrees, spread these opinions throughout the 'Abbassid Empire. The Fatimid line was thus established, on the one hand, while, on the other, Isma'iliya gave rise to two popular revolutionary movements—that of the Carmathians, which in the tenth and eleventh centuries founded a republic in the province of al-Hasa of the Arabian Peninsula, and that of the 'Assassins', notorious for their terrorism in the eleventh and twelfth centuries (one of their centres being Syria). Today there are some 60,000 Isma'ilis in the province of al-Hasa in Saudi Arabia (constituting an eighth of the population) and 40,000 in Syria, mainly in Hamah province, where they are 13% of the population. They also reached the region of Latakia after their wars with the 'Alawis. About 50,000 are to be found in Yemen.

The extremist branches of the Isma'iliya have gone so far from Islam that at least some of them can hardly be called Muslims. This is true of those sects in which Isma'iliya forms one, but not necessarily the only, element. Two such communities of the Arab Middle East on whom the stamp of Isma'iliya is deeply impressed, yet which are not within the Islamic framework, are the 'Alawis and the Druzes.

The *'Alawis*, who are also known as Nusairis, are inhabitants of the mountainous region east of Latakia in Syria, called Jabal an-Nusairiya. It is not expressly known how the religion was formed or when; however, by the eleventh century it was to be found in its present form. From the Isma'iliya the 'Alawis took over the neoplatonic concept of emanation, the importance of the number seven (the Godhead has seven incarnations). However, the 'Alawi god is threefold: 'Ali = *ma'na* (meaning essence); Muhammad = *hijab* (veil), and Salman al-Farisi = *bab* (gate). There are those who see in this remnants of Christian influences, others who believe that the former pagan all-Syrian religion is here preserved (sun–moon–sky). Like the Isma'iliya, the 'Alawi religion is secret, revealed only to the *khassa* (the select few) stage by stage. The 'Alawis celebrate the seasons of the year as well as the Muslim holy days. In Syria they numbered 410,000 in 1955, i.e., more than 10% of the whole population; they live chiefly in the province of Latakia, where they constitute over 62% of the inhabitants. There are also 'Alawis in Turkey and particularly in Hatay (formerly Alexandretta); here, according to French sources, their number reached 62,000 in 1936 (28% of the population). Several thousand live in Northern Lebanon.

The *Druze* sect was founded in the eleventh century around the personality of the Fatimid Caliph al-Hākim, to whose followers he was the personification of the deity. Ad-Darazi and another follower brought together a band of believers at Wadi at-Taim on the slopes of Mount Hermon. Al-Hākim died in mysterious circumstances, and his followers claim that he will appear as the Mahdi at some later time. The Druzes have a mystical belief in one god. From the godhead there are five emanations, which have materialised in human form, like the deity, a number of times. The influence of the Isma'iliya is apparent, among other things, in the importance which the Druzes attach to the number seven (seven commandments replacing the five pillars of Islam, for instance), in their acceptance of the principle of *taqiya* (secrecy of the religion), and in the structure of the sect which is divided into the *'uqqal* (singular: *'aqil*), to which the secrets are revealed, and the *juhha* (*jahil*), from whom they are hidden.

The legal status of the Druze woman is more advanced than that of women in the Muslim and 'Alawi communities. In general, the Druzes have fewer holy days and religious edicts than Muslims and Christians. They have almost no prayers and rites. They hold services in a small primitive building called

82

the *khilwa*. The number of Druzes in Syria was, according to the official estimates for 1955 quoted above, 118,000 (3·1% of the total population). Most of them are concentrated at Jabal ad-Druz, where they constitute 90% of all inhabitants. In Lebanon the figure was 90,000, i.e., 6–6·5%, according to official population estimates of the middle 'fifties. (In Israel there are some 20,000 Druzes, and a few thousand more are settled in America.)

Finally, the remnants of the Khawarij should be noted; these opposed the Sunna and Shi'a alike in the first period of Islam and claimed that the Imam is to be chosen without regard for his familial origin. One of their principal branches, the *Abadiya*, is still to be found in certain parts of North Africa, Libya (several tens of thousands in Tripolitania), and in the principality of Oman on the shores of the Persian Gulf, where it is recognised as the official religion, followed by most of the half-million inhabitants.

2. *Christians*. The middle of this century found approximately 3,050,000 Christians in all the Arab Middle East, divided among the countries as follows:

Egypt	1,500,000	being about	8·0%	of the population
Lebanon	680,000	,,	,, 53·0%	,,	,,
Syria	450,000	,,	,, 13·5%	,,	,
Sudan	200,000	,,	,, 2·5%	,,	,,
Iraq	150,000	,,	,, 3·0%	,,	,,
Jordan	120,000	,,	,, 10·0%	,,	,,
Libya	50,000	,,	,, 4·5%	,,	,,

Possibly a further few thousand should be added for the Arabian Peninsula, but there are no reliable estimates. While most of these Christians speak Arabic, another language has been retained for common usage or for prayer among some communities. Moreover, in some countries the Christians of certain denominations may be distinguished from their Muslim neighbours by differences in the social structure of their community. From reliable vital statistics according to community, it appears that the rate of natural increase is lower among Christians than among Muslims. The status of women is higher among the Christians. The urban element is generally more prominent. The standard of education is higher (especially among women, as a result of missionary activity) and the proportion of Christians among clerical workers, professionals, journalists, etc., is greater than the proportion in the total population. This last point has at times led to friction with the Muslims in their efforts to enter these fields, as their standard of education has risen in recent generations. However, in all these respects there are differences which depend on the particular community and country under consideration.

The number of Christian denominations is very large, considering the limited number of members of that faith. The reason is that nearly all groups split twice: once when the various national sects left the Orthodox Church because of doctrinal divergencies or disputes of another nature, and a second time when part of each newly formed sect gave its allegiance to the Roman Pope, the rest remaining independent. In fact, however, there are only three large Christian communities in the Arab Middle East, whose adherents make up two-thirds of all the Christians: the Copts in Egypt, the Maronites in Lebanon, and the Greek Orthodox found in various countries.

The Greek Orthodox community (in Arabic: *Rum Ortho-dhoks*) is the Eastern Orthodox Church formed from the four original Eastern sees. In the 1950s there were 150,000 of them in Syria, 126,000 in Lebanon, and 50,000–70,000 in Jordan. There is no basis for estimating their number in Iraq. In Egypt they may be placed at about 100,000, half of Greek origin (before the recent exodus of the Greeks). The community is led by the patriarchs: 'of Antioch', centred at Damascus; 'of Alexandria', in Cairo; and 'of Jerusalem'. The patriarchate of Antioch is almost exclusively Arab; that of Alexandria has both Arab and Greek elements; in Jerusalem the higher priesthood is all Greek. In the last generation this has proved a cause of dispute between the low Arab element and the higher priesthood.

The first schism of the Orthodox Church gave rise to *Nestorianism*. The church of this community is called the 'Eastern Church' or 'Assyrian Church'. The division, which occurred in 431, was caused by the opinion that Jesus had two personifications—the divine (the Logos) and the human. The sect was a large one (its emissaries reaching even China) until Timur Leng (Tamerlane) slew many of its members in the fourteenth

84

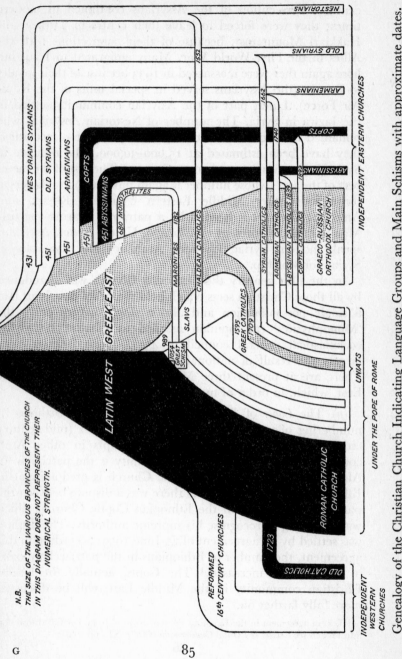

Genealogy of the Christian Church Indicating Language Groups and Main Schisms with approximate dates.
(From C. T. Bridgeman, *Religious Communities in the Christian East*, The Nile Mission Press, n.p., n.d.)

N.B.
THE SIZE OF THE VARIOUS BRANCHES OF THE CHURCH
IN THIS DIAGRAM DOES NOT REPRESENT THEIR
NUMERICAL STRENGTH.

century. Persecution of the Assyrians continued in modern times; they were forced to leave their centre in Turkey (the Hakkiari Mountains), because of their connections with the Allies in the First World War. Many emigrated to Iraq, but here again they were massacred in 1933 because of their loyalty to Britain (the Assyrians served in special units of the Royal Air Force). Later, part of the Assyrian community settled in the Jazira in Syria. The number of Nestorian Assyrians who remained in Iraq is not known with any degree of accuracy: they have been estimated at 15,000–30,000. The number in Syria (Jazira) was around 10,000 in 1950. The rest of the members of the sect (whose number is again unknown) are dispersed throughout other Middle Eastern countries, Russia, and America. The sect is headed by a patriarch bearing the title Mar Shimun, at present of Chicago, United States. Assyrians speak modern Syriac (modern Aramaic) and use classical Syriac for worship.

In the fifth century the Orthodox Church was abandoned by all those Christian sects which held the belief that Jesus had a single personification and also a single nature only—the 'Monophysites' (an opinion assailed at Chalcedon by the ecclesiastical general council of 451). These factions were largely the result of national revolts against Byzantine rule. There are at present three Monophysite sects in the Middle East, which, in order of numerical importance, are:

(*a*) The *Copts* of Egypt (also called 'Coptic Orthodox'), numbering 985,000 persons at the 1937 census (mid-century estimate—1,200,000). There are few Copts in other Arab countries. At the head of the community is the patriarch 'of Alexandria', in Cairo. The Coptic Church is predominant in Ethiopia also. For many years there was a dispute between the patriarch in Egypt and the Ethiopian Coptic Church, which was unwilling to recognise his supreme authority. The dispute was settled by an agreement of 25 June 1959; according to this agreement, the number of Ethiopians in the patriarchal board of electors was increased.[1] The Copts, actually the largest Christian community in the Middle East, will be discussed more fully farther on.

---

[1] Text of agreement in the Egyptian Press of 29 June 1959. For full translation into French see *Cahiers de l'Orient Contemporain* (*COC*), XL, pp. 286–7.

(*b*) The *Armenian* (or Gregorian) community, numbering about 110,000 in Syria (mainly in Aleppo), 65,000 in Lebanon (mainly Beirut), 15,000 in Egypt, and 12,000 in Iraq.[1] The Armenian community is led by patriarchs subject to the 'Catholicos' of all the Armenians, of Etchmiadzin in Soviet Armenia. Armenian is the language of worship, and generally also of common usage.

(*c*) The *Syrian* community (or 'Jacobites'), having 45,000 followers in Syria in the 'fifties (almost all in the Jazira), 12,000 in Iraq,[2] and 4,500 in the Lebanon. At its head is the patriarch of Antioch, living in Homs. The language of prayer is Syriac; this is also the spoken language for part of the community.

In the year A.D. 1054 Christianity split into the Catholic (Latin) Church in the West, and the Orthodox (Greek) Church in the East. The schism was the outcome of long-term national, linguistic, and cultural divergencies, as well as of theological and religious disputes. In the Middle East there was at first no Latin Catholic community; such a group came into existence only over the generations following the Crusades, and under the influence of the mission and foreign communities in the Middle East. Hence the *Latin community* existing today is most variegated, composed of members of the native population, those belonging to monastic orders, and foreigners. The Pope appoints apostolic delegates at its various centres, and a patriarch (generally European) in Jerusalem. In 1950 the Latin community numbered 6,500 in Syria and 4,000 in Lebanon. In the 'forties the number for Palestine was 25,000, of whom 5,000 were Europeans; there are no reliable up-to-date figures for Jordan. According to the 1937 census, the figure for Egypt was 60,000, of whom 35,000 were Italians, 20,000 British and French, and 5,000 foreigners of other nationalities. From then until the middle of the century the

[1] All numbers are based on official figures for the middle of the century. However, the true number of Armenians may be smaller, since the extent of their return to the Soviet Union may have been under-estimated. For the same reason, no estimate for Jordan is feasible.

[2] This and some other figures for the size of communities have appeared without change in all estimates since the 1930s, when the first *Iraq Directory* (1936) was issued (p. 472). The 1960 *Directory of the Republic of Iraq* repeats the same figures (p. 423).

number of foreign members of the Latin Church has fallen by about one-half. In the Sudan the number of Catholics was estimated to be over 160,000 in 1955; in Iraq, 33,000 (the number appears exaggerated); and in Libya, 47,000 (Italians) in the 'fifties.

Over the ages, not only individuals but also whole communities or parts of them have embraced the Catholic faith. These have been granted the privilege of retaining a certain degree of autonomy, in matters of language and details of liturgy. These groups which have 'united' with the Catholic Church are known as *Uniates*.

The largest community, and the first to enter the Catholic Church as a whole, was that of the *Maronites*. Members of this group at first harboured the monothelite doctrine,[1] but as early as the days of the Crusades, they approached the Catholic Church and remained associated with it until final formal unification in the eighteenth century. Even afterwards, they were permitted to retain the ancient Syriac language for prayer, while for speech Arabic took first place. Unlike most Uniate communities, the Maronites did not split after unification; the whole community accepted the Pope's authority. Relations between the community and Rome were not actually always good, and only recently a serious quarrel broke out between the two sides. The patriarch 'of Antioch' heads the community from Lebanon. In 1950 the number of Maronites in Lebanon was of the order of 370,000, with a further 15,000 in Syria. In Palestine there were 5,000–6,000 Maronites in the 1940s, and in Egypt 3,000 in 1937. America and Africa account for a large number of Maronites, certainly no less than the number in the Middle East. The community has an important role in shaping the character of Lebanon.

The rest of the Uniates are communities which split from the different 'Orthodox' groups and which recognise the authority of the Pope. They have their autonomy, special customs, and, in general, their own language of prayer. Such Uniate communities are the Greek Catholic (the 'Melkites'), the Chaldean

---

[1] The essence of this doctrine is that Jesus had a 'single will'. It is a compromise between Orthodox and Monophysite beliefs. It was supported in the seventh century by the Emperor Heraclius in an attempt to unify Christianity under the threat of Islam.

(Assyrian) Catholic, the Coptic Catholic, the Armenian Catholic, and the Syrian Catholic. Their following according to country, quoted where figures were available, is as follows:

	Lebanon 1950	Syria 1950	Iraq 1936[1]	Egypt 1937 (census)	Palestine 1946
Greek Catholics	76,000	52,000	—	23,428	20,000
Chaldeans	1,300	5,200	98,000	121	—
Coptic Catholics	—	—.	—	35,706	—
Armenian Catholics	13,900	18,500	—	3,169	800
Syrian Catholics	5,800	18,500	25,000	1,383	300
Total	97,000	94,200	123,800	63,807	21,100

The percentage of the urban element is generally higher among the Uniates than among the parallel independent community. That is, the process of affiliation with Rome was stronger among urban Christians than among rural ones. Thus, for example, the Nestorians are hill-dwellers or settled farmers, while almost two-thirds of the Chaldeans live in Baghdad or Mosul. More than 30% of the Coptic Catholics are to be found in Cairo and Alexandria, as against 10% of the Coptic Ortho-dox. This fact explains to a very large degree the relatively good social and economic state of the Uniate communities (particularly the Greek Catholics of Lebanon, many of whom are concentrated at Zahla).[2]

The number of Catholics in the Middle East may, then, be summarised as follows: about 400,000 Maronites, 400,000 Uniates, 250,000 Latins—in all, over a million persons.

The *Protestant* communities in the Arab Middle East appeared in consequence of missionary activities (especially English and American) in the nineteenth and twentieth centuries; there was no local Reformation in the East. These communities are extremely divided. The number of Protestants in Egypt was 78,203 according to the 1937 census, of whom 65,034 were

[1] *Iraq Directory* (1936), pp. 467, 469. The 1960 *Directory of the Republic of Iraq* has again the same figure for Syrian Catholics (p. 425) and a slightly lower one (86,500) for Chaldeans (p. 429).

[2] Rondot, *Les Institutions politiques du Liban*, pp. 35–6; Cf. N. Moutran, *La Syrie de demain*, Paris, 1916, pp. 368–90—a detailed account of this community by one of its members.

Copts,[1] and 13,169 others (mainly British). In the Sudan an official estimate of 1955 put the number of Protestants at 31,000; in Syria (1950), 13,000; in Lebanon, (1950) 12,500; in Palestine (the 1940s), 12,000–15,000. Several thousand are also to be found in Iraq.

3. *Jews*. The number of Jews in the Arab states has undergone significant changes since the 1940s; some Jewish communities have largely or entirely disappeared as a result of emigration to various countries, particularly Israel. At the end of the 1940s the number of Jews in Arab countries of the Middle East was as follows (official figures, where available):

Iraq (1947 census)	118,000	
Egypt (1947 census)	65,639	(including about 6,000 Karaites)
Syria (official estimate of 1944)	30,038	
Lebanon (official estimate of 1946)	5,830	
Libya (estimate of 1948)	35,000	
Yemen	60,000–70,000	
Aden (1946 census)	7,290	

There are also a few hundred Jews in the Arabian Peninsula and Sudan. As to the present number of Jews in the Arab countries, there are estimates which differ greatly one from another; at all events, the main communities (of Iraq, Egypt, and Yemen) have been reduced to a few thousand only.

4. *Other Communities*. The *Yazidis* are a small sect whose language is Kurdic. They have a special religion, uniting elements of ancient paganism, principles of the Zaradusht (Zoroastrian) religion of fire-worship (dualism); of Judaism (dietary laws); of Nestorian Christianity (baptism); of Islam (pilgrimages); of *tasawwuf* (homage to Shaikhs); and of Shi'i sects (secrecy). The 'malak tawus', Satan, is of special importance in that religion, being of a positive nature. The Yazidis' centre is at Shaikh 'Adi, north of Mosul; in Iraq they are also found in the Jabal Sinjar region. There were 32,437 Yazidis in Iraq (according to the 1947 census) and a further 3,000 in Syria. Yazidis are also found in Persia, Turkey, and Soviet Armenia. They total about 60,000–70,000.

[1] The percentage of Protestants among all Copts rose from 5·5% in 1927 to 6·0% in 1937. Their increase was at the expense of the Orthodox, who also lost to the Catholics. See Rondot, *Les Chrétiens d'Orient*, pp. 150–1.

In the Yazidi region of Iraq, Jabal Sinjar, there is a second sect of a similar nature—the *Shabak*, also Kurdish-speaking. The influence of extremist Shi'i sects ('Ali Ilahi) is felt among the Shabak sects. They number about 12,000 persons.

The *Mandaeans* (also Sabi'a or Subba) have a religion compounded of Jewish, Christian, and Muslim elements. Baptism plays an important role, and hence their name: 'Christians of John the Baptist.' They dwell in Southern Iraq. They speak Arabic, but for liturgy have a special language (a dialect of Aramaic). In the 1947 census 6,597 Mandaeans were counted.

Apart from their colony in Israel, the *Baha'is* are nowadays found in Iraq (Baha' Allah, the founder of the sect, was active for a number of years in the middle of the last century, in Baghdad and Sulaimaniya), in Egypt, and dotted over other countries. They are estimated at 2,000 in Iraq. The ethics of behaviour of Baha'is show Christian influences; the religion has no theological system, liturgy, or priestly hierarchy.

Finally, the *paganism* of the Sudan, with its animistic beliefs, is to be noted. The number of pagans is estimated to be more than a third of the population. Classification of the pagans is discussed under the communal structure of Sudan.

3. *LINGUISTIC GROUPS*

Arabic is the language of the majority of inhabitants of the Arab countries of the Middle East. Literary Arabic, not merely the classical but also the modern (the language of journalism, for example), is common to all Arab countries, apart from slight variations of terminology. For this reason there is close cultural and literary contact among persons of the educated class in the various Arab countries.

On the other hand, there are significant differences among the many dialects of spoken Arabic. All the dialects of Arabic spoken in the Arab Middle Eastern countries, except Libya, are included in the category of Eastern dialects; the borderline between the Eastern and the Western is customarily drawn from Sallum to Chad. The Eastern dialects are again divided into two main groups: one includes Egypt, Palestine, Syria, and Lebanon, and the other the Arabian Peninsula, the Syrian desert, and Iraq. Within each of these two groups there are further differences from country to country and even from district to district. The Egyptian dialect is known throughout the Arab world (at least in the cities) as a result of the growing circulation of Egyptian films.

The similarities and differences between any two dialects are not determined only by the geographical distance between the regions concerned; social factors also have their say in shaping the dialects, each having its own special peculiarities. In almost every country dialects specific to the beduin, the fellah, and the town dwellers may be distinguished. The dialects of the large cities (especially Jerusalem, Damascus, Beirut, and Aleppo) differ among themselves less than each differs from the vernacular of the fellahs in the neighbourhood; for example, the dialect of Omdurman has become the common language of all Sudanese cities. This is not true of Iraq, where the speech of both town dwellers and villagers was apparently influenced by the nomads of Northern Arabia. Differences of dialect have also been noted on comparing communities (for example, the Jews and the Muslims of Baghdad) and also between men and women (women tending more to retain special local idioms because of their lack of contact with inhabitants of other regions, and because of their illiteracy).

Other *Semitic Languages* include Syriac–Aramaic, used chiefly for liturgy among some of the Christian communities of the Fertile Crescent countries (the Chaldeans, Syrians, and to some extent the Maronites). Small groups of people speaking dialects of Syriac–Aramaic also remain among the Syrian and 'Assyrian' communities in Northern Iraq and Northern Syria, and among the inhabitants of some villages around Damascus. Between Hadhramaut and Oman some Southern Arabic dialects are still spoken.[1]

The largest contingent of people talking non-Semitic languages in the Arab countries is found in the Sudan, where much of the population speaks one or another *African* language.[2]

[1] Numerical estimates of the people speaking the various languages can be only very rough, not only because statistics are not reliable but also because in censuses population is classified according to religious community (in the tradition of the Millet system) and not by language.

[2] For classification of these languages we have used mainly J. H. Greenberg, 'Studies in African Linguistic Classification', *SWJA*, Vol. 6 (especially index and map on pp. 394–7).

The largest family of such languages in Sudan is that called *Eastern Sudanic*; it includes the following tongues: (*a*) Nubian, the spoken language of Nubia (in the Northern province from old Dongola to the Egyptian boundary at Wadi Halfa) and in various areas of the Nubian mountains (in Southern Kordofan); (*b*) the language of the Beir, in the Upper Nile, at the Ethiopian boundary; (*c*) the language spoken in the hills of Tabi, south of the Jazira; (*d*) Merarit, at Jabal Marra in Darfur; (*e*) Dagu, in Southern Darfur; (*f*) Nilotic, including the language of the large tribes of Dinka, Nuer, Shilluk, and Anuak; (*g*) Nilo-Hamitic, spoken by the Bari tribe of Sudan in the area of Juba, at the southern boundary.

A second large family of African languages is the *Hamito-Semitic* or *Afro-Asiatic*. This family includes (apart from the Semitic languages) the group known as the Cushite languages, whose northern branch is spoken by the Beja tribes in the province of Kasala. A second language of the same family is Berber, spoken by about 40,000 Berbers and 7,000 of the Tuareg tribe of Jabal Nefusa in Tripolitania and Fezzan in Libya (as well as part of the inhabitants of the Maghrib countries).[1]

There are various regions of the Sudan, particularly Kordofan and the province of the Blue Nile, where some languages of smaller families are spoken. It is worth noting that the original languages of the Sudan have been preserved more than the original religions; for example, the Nubians and Beja are Muslims, but do not speak Arabic. Non-Arabic languages are spoken by 45% of the Sudanese population, i.e., about 4½ millions. African languages are also spoken by the Negroes dispersed throughout the Arab East, particularly in Libya, Hijaz, Muscat, Qatar, and Kuwait. Their second language is generally Arabic.

While the Southern and Western regions are the meeting-ground of Arabic and African languages, the Northern and Eastern parts are in contact with *Turkish, Caucasian*, and *Indo-European* languages.

Turkish is spoken by about 30,000 of the Turkoman tribes, semi-settled in Northern Syria, and by an unknown number

[1] For linguistic groups in Libya see L. Dupree, 'The Non-Arab Ethnic Groups of Libya', *MEJ*, Winter 1958, pp. 30–8.

(no well-established figures being available) of Turks, inhabitants of the cities of Northern Syria. According to an official source of 1932, the number of Turks and Turkomans in Iraq was 75,685 (two-thirds Sunnis and one-third Shi'is).[1] Since then, their numbers may not have doubled as has the general population of Iraq. They are mainly settled in the northern provinces of Iraq. In the rest of the Arab countries there are a few hundred, or at most a few thousand, who speak Turkish. The 1947 census gave the number of Turkish nationals in Egypt as 5,375.

Various *Caucasian* dialects are spoken by the Circassians and the Chechens, resettled in the nineteenth century by the Ottoman Government on the border of the Syrian desert, after exile from their homes by the expanding Russian rule. Their religion is Muslim, partly Sunni and partly Shi'i. In recent generations they have spoken Arabic as well as their own language. They include both city dwellers and farmers. Circassians and Chechens were estimated to number about 40,000 at the middle of the century, one half in Syria, most of the other half in Jordan, and a few in Iraq.

The *Armenians* in the Arab countries continue to speak Armenian, an *Indo-European* language, but many of them have learned Arabic also. Most are refugees who came to those countries after the First World War because of persecution in Turkey. They settled in the cities of the Fertile Crescent (mainly in Aleppo and Beirut, in their own special quarters) and in Egypt, where Armenian nuclei had been present even earlier. They engaged chiefly in commerce, manual trades, and the free professions. The Armenians did not adapt themselves to the political and social structure of the Arab countries (for example, retaining their own political parties), and in recent years a movement to return to Soviet Armenia has arisen among them. The numbers for the Gregorian and Armenian–Catholic sects in Syria, Lebanon, Egypt, and Iraq (together with a few thousand in Israel and Jordan) add up to about 250,000 (a tenth of all the Armenians in the world); of these, more than half live in Syria, and most of the rest in Lebanon.

Persians are found in Iraq, mainly in the sacred Shi'i cities

[1] *Statistical Handbook of Middle Eastern Countries*, Jerusalem, 1944, p. 79 (and p. 162, for source).

and in the principalities of the Persian Gulf, where for the most part they work in the oil industries and in commerce. (In some places, such as Bahrain, they have been conspicuous for the profits they amassed in business.)[1] Official Iraqi sources gave their number as 65,509 in 1932, and on this basis various authors have estimated that they now number some 80,000–120,000. The estimates for the principalities of the Persian Gulf also diverge widely, and only in Bahrain (many of whose inhabitants left because of political pressure) a figure from the 1950 census is available—6,934. In Kuwait, Qatar, Muscat-Oman, and Trucial Oman there are several thousand Persians.

The Persians may reasonably be followed by the *Indians* (speaking any of the languages of the Indian continent), who are also mainly inhabitants of the principalities of the Persian Gulf, though also found in Iraq, Hajaz, and Aden. In each of these places they number several thousands.

None of the five linguistic groups mentioned carries much weight in the Arab countries. In the Arab states of Asia there is only one large non-Arabic group, the *Kurdish* language. The Kurdish language is made up of a group of dialects close to Persian which differ considerably among themselves. It is spoken by the tribes settled in the mountainous regions on the borders between Persia and Iraq, between Persia, Turkey, and Soviet Armenia, and between Turkey and Syria (sometimes called Kurdistan). In recent years literature and journalism in Kurdish has developed; in Iraq it is written mainly with Arabic characters, in Syria with Latin characters, and in Russia with Cyrillic. Most of those speaking Kurdish dialects in the Arab countries—i.e., Iraq and Syria—are Sunni Muslim tribes, but there is also a minority group of Shi'i tribes and members of other religious groups also, particularly Yazidis. Estimates of the number of Kurds differ widely. According to the most reasonable evaluation, there were 800,000 in Iraq and 250,000 in Syria at the middle of the century—together more than a million, this being a third of all Kurdish-speaking people.

All the above linguistic groups belong to the original population of the countries now included under the name of Arab

[1] F. I. Qubain, 'Social Classes and Tensions in Bahrain', *MEJ*, Summer 1955, pp. 274–6.

States, or are communities which reached this region from neighbouring parts of Africa or Asia. One further group may be noted—the *Europeans* who have settled in Arab countries and may be divided on a national basis. Several hundreds or thousands of persons of European origin speaking European languages are to be found in each of the Arab countries of the Middle East, larger numbers being found only in Egypt and Libya. In these two countries a recent fall in the number of Europeans has been noted. The largest community is that of the *Italians* in Libya, whose number fell from 110,000 before the Second World War to 47,000 at mid-century.

In Egypt[1] the number of Italians was 23,667 in 1954, as against 52,462 according to the census of 1927. They are settled mainly in the two principal cities, and engage in manual trades and commerce. In Libya about half used to be farmers, but those who remained after the War were mainly merchants, artisans, and professionals in the large cities. In Egypt the largest community is that of the *Greeks*, whose members numbered 76,264 in 1927 and 48,272 in 1954. They also live in the large cities, notably in Alexandria, and their occupation is commerce. Unlike other foreigners, the Greeks were until recently dispersed in various provinces of Lower Egypt, where they engaged in shopkeeping and moneylending. As a result of the 1961 nationalisation laws, the Egyptian Greek community is disappearing, most of its members returning to Greece. The number of French and British was 23,735 in 1954 as against 58,501 in 1927.

B. THE COMMUNAL STRUCTURE OF THE ARAB COUNTRIES

1. *EGYPT*

The communal structure of Egypt is an extremely simple one: approximately 1,345,000 Copts (Orthodox, Catholics, and Protestants) constituted 7·1% of the total population, and

---

[1] All Egyptian data refer to nationality rather than the more relevant linguistic grouping, on which there is no available information. Data for 1954 according to *al-Ahram*, 1 June 1954.

140,000 foreigners, 0·7%.[1] More than 90% of the inhabitants are Arabic-speaking Sunni Muslims.

The geographical distribution of the *Coptic community* displays a certain degree of territorial concentration. Half of the Copts are concentrated in three provinces of Upper Egypt (which contain less than one-fifth of the entire population of Egypt): Asyut, where they make up 21% of the population; Minya (18%), and Suhag (Girga) (15·5%). In the Nile Delta, on the other hand, the Copts make up only 1–3% of the total population. The concentration of Copts in the four large towns of Lower Egypt has increased over the past generation, as shown by the following figures:

Percentage of Copts in Total Population of Four Largest Towns

	Cairo	Alexandria	Isma'iliya	Suez	All Egypt
1927	8·9	4·1	4·1	3·4	6·7
1947	10·8	7·6	8·0	7·9	7·1

The Copts, therefore, have both a rural and an urban population. Although their share in Egypt's rural population (approximately 5%, according to the 1937 Egyptian census) is somewhat lower than their share in the general population, more than half the Coptic population earns its living from agriculture. This is in complete contrast to the other Christian and foreign groups in Egypt, whose farming population is insignificant. In the past many Government clerks, especially those engaged in surveying and finance, were Copts. At the beginning of this century Copts constituted 45% of the Egyptian civil service (and 97·8% of the tax collectors or 'sarrafs').[2] The situation has since changed fundamentally, and the 1937 census shows that the Copts were only 9·1% of all Egyptian civil service personnel.

This development is due partly to a bridging of the gap between the levels of education of Copts and Muslims in Egypt. Although a certain difference still reveals itself in the sphere of education, there is very little difference in other aspects of social conditions. For example, the proportion of blind individuals (according to the 1937 census) was 2·7% for both the

[1] According to the 1947 census. The number of foreigners includes Turkish nationals but not nationals of the Arab countries (totalling 5,900). Details of the 1960 census have not yet been published.

[2] Official figures quoted by K. Mikhail, *Copts and Moslems under British Control*, London, 1911, p. 44.

Muslims and the Orthodox Copts, while it did not exceed 1%
for the rest of the Christian population.

In their laws and customs, too, the Copts and Muslims have
more in common than they have differences. Although the
Copts, like other Christians, do not abstain from alcohol, they
circumcise their sons, as do the Muslims (this applies mainly
to the rural areas, not to Cairo). The Copts also refrain from
eating pork, and their womenfolk are veiled in places where
Muslim women observe this practice. Coptic marriage and
funeral customs are similar to those of the Muslims (the Copts
permit marriage of relatives, in contrast to other ancient
churches). Copts and Muslims pay visits to the same saints'
tombs, which are often shared by the two communities.[1]
According to Egyptian law, the Copts also inherit and will their
property according to the Muslim *shari'a* laws if they are
Egyptian subjects. Only since 1944 have they been allowed to
transfer their property by inheritance according to the ancient
laws of the Coptic community if all the heirs agree to a settlement on these lines.

The common belief that Copts have external characteristics
which enable them to be distinguished easily from Muslims is
completely erroneous. Although he exaggerated slightly, Lord
Cromer was essentially correct in saying that 'the only difference
between Copt and Muslim is that the former is an Egyptian
who worships in a Christian church, whilst the latter is an
Egyptian who worships in a Mohammedan mosque'.[2]

The *foreign subjects* (most of whom speak European languages)
are almost all concentrated in the two cities of Cairo and
Alexandria, principally the latter. In 1947, 43·5% of them
resided in Alexandria and 38·5% in Cairo. The various foreign
communities differ in their economic structure, but there are
also numerous similarities among them. Their geographical
distribution indicates that they are not engaged in agriculture
to any considerable degree: according to the 1937 census, only
1·9% of the foreign subjects supported themselves by farming.
This does not mean that they have no connection with agriculture. Despite the fact that in the twentieth century they have

[1] Mubarak, XI, 70; Blackman, pp. 248, 258.
[2] Earl of Cromer, *Modern Egypt*, London, 1908, Vol. II, pp. 205-6. See also
Boktor, pp. 46-7 (the author is a Copt).

never constituted more than 2% of Egypt's population, they
have had possession of considerable areas of the country's
arable land. This is clearly shown by the following table:

Foreign Landownership in Egypt

	Percentage of foreign citizens in the total population	Farm land in foreign hands, as percentage of total area of land in private hands
1917	1·6	13·0
1927	1·6	9·0
1937	1·2	7·4
1947	0·7	5·9

Foreign-owned land continued to decrease after 1947, and
the process was speeded up by the agrarian reform, as over
90% of the land owned by foreign citizens was in large estates
of 50 feddan and over. On the other hand, foreign subjects
have continued until recently to play an important role in
urban trade and commerce.[1] About a third of all directors of
joint-stock companies in Egypt were Europeans, and, according
to the 1937 census, more than half the gainfully employed
Europeans were engaged in commerce, banking, finance, and
industry. But in these spheres too the foreigners' share has
dropped, particularly after the 'Egyptianisation' and nationalisation of the last few years. Summing up, it can be said that
this part of the Egyptian population, which played a decisive
role in the country's economy until the Second World War, has
since lost this dominant position, and has also suffered a
numerical decline both relatively and absolutely.[2]

2. THE SUDAN

According to an estimate based on various sources, the population of the Sudan is divided by principal religious communities,
approximately as follows:

Arabic-speaking Muslims	55%
Non-Arabic-speaking Muslims	10%
Non-Arabic-speaking Pagans	35%

[1] See Issawi, *Egypt at Mid-Century*, pp. 63, 206–8.
[2] It should, however, be noted that the quantitative decline is due partly to
changes of nationality and not all to emigration of foreign nationals.

The Sudanese *Muslims* are divided into a large number of religious orders (*tariqas*). Fierce internal conflict, which has taken on great political significance, exists between the Khatmiya or Mirghaniya and the Mahdiya. Supporters of the Mirghaniya are found among the inhabitants of Kasala province in the East, especially the Shukriya and Bani 'Amir tribes, and in addition it has considerable influence in North Kordofan and the Northern province. The Mahdiya's influence has remained strong among the Baggara in West Kordofan, Darfur (particularly among the Negro tribes there), and the Jazira. But its influence declined markedly after the Mahdi rebellion was quelled and the Sudan conquered by Britain and Egypt. Many Sudanese have returned to their previous loyalties to the tribe, which had been weakened by the Mahdiya.

In addition, the Muslims are divided between *Arabic*-speaking and those speaking various *African* languages. The Arabic-speaking Muslims constitute more than one-half of the Sudan's population. They are in turn divided into camel-raising tribes (*ahl al-ibil*), cattle-raising tribes (*baggara*), peasants, and town dwellers. Muslims who speak various African languages can be divided into the following three main groups:

(*a*) The Nubians, who live along the banks of the Nile from Debba to the Egyptian border. They are also called Barabra or Danaqla (after one of the tribes). They live by agriculture, but many of them have migrated to the towns of Egypt and Sudan, where they work as servants, watchmen, and cooks.

(*b*) The Beja—the nomadic tribe of the region between the Nile and the 'Atbara and the Red Sea. Their tribal organisation is weaker than that of the Arabs, and they usually roam in small family groups. Another important difference between the Beja and the Arab beduin is that the former have no stringent blood vengeance laws and do not practise the payment of blood money. The projects for cotton cultivation in Kasala province are leading to their gradual settlement on the land.

(*c*) Various groups of Muslim Negroes, particularly in Central and Western Sudan.

The principal groups of *pagans* in South Sudan are—from north to south—the tribes of the Nuba mountains and the Funj region (south of the Jazira), the Nilotes (Shilluk, Nuer, Dinka, etc.), the Nilo-Hamites (such as the Bari, in the vicinity of Juba), and the south-western group of tribes (Zande, etc.). Their common peculiarities, apart from the fundamental difference between their religious beliefs and Islam, are:

(1) Territorial concentration. Roughly the entire area situated south of latitude 12° is pagan, apart from the west, where Islam has penetrated farther southwards. Thus pagans form the majority of the inhabitants of the Upper Nile province and Equatoria (including Bahr el-Ghazal and Mongalla). They are also found in South Kordofan and the southern part of the Blue Nile province.

(2) Language. All the pagans speak African languages, and none speak Arabic, while all the Muslims speak Arabic—apart from the three groups noted above, whose members do not form more than 10% of the Sudan's population.

(3) Race. In contradistinction to the Muslim region, the pagans of the south have not intermarried to any extent, and thus they have maintained their specific racial characteristics.

(4) In the southern pagan regions there is not a single urban settlement with a population of over 25,000 people.

However, this does not mean that the assemblage of southern pagans is homogeneous; on the contrary, the various groups which fall under this category display fundamental differences of language, race, occupation, social structure, and way of life.

The largest group from among the southern pagans is the *Nilotes*.[1] They number almost a million persons, over 90% of whom belong to the Nuer, Dinka, and Shilluk tribes. This group has a common language with various dialects, but the members of the two largest groups—the Dinka and the Nuer—understand one another. In addition, they have certain common racial characteristics: the Nilotes are, on the average, the tallest people in the world, with unusually long legs, long heads, and

---

[1] The following according to A. Butt, *The Nilotes of the Anglo-Egyptian Sudan and Uganda*, London, 1952. See also C. G. Seligman, *Pagan Tribes of the Nilotic Sudan*, London, 1932, Chapter I; E. E. Evans-Pritchard, *The Nuer*, London, 1940, Chapter I.

thin, flexible bodies. Cattle play a major role in their economic, religious, and social life, and form the principal source of income for all tribes except the Anuak. They do not cultivate any market crops, and engage in very little trade. Another common social trait is exogamy, or marriage only outside the clan. Sons marry their father's widow (but not their own mother) or a dead brother's widow. The relationship is based on blood ties and territorial units. In every tribe one clan is acknowledged as the ruler. The Nilotes do not wear clothes; they believe in ghosts, totems, witches, and rainmakers.

A complete contrast to the Nilotes in many respects is provided by the *Zande* and the *south-western tribes*, which total about a quarter of a million persons. They are short of stature, with broad heads, and speak a language which is an eastern branch of the Niger–Congo family of languages, and has no other representative in the Sudan.[1] They are farmers, and have never owned cattle, although they are skilful hunters.

The *Nilo-Hamites* form a transition group between the two groups mentioned above. The *tribes of the Nuba mountains and the Funj region* are extremely diverse groups which show very marked basic differences from one another.

3. *THE ARABIAN PENINSULA*

The following conclusions can be drawn from the table on page 104:

(1) There are no large linguistic minorities in the Arabian Peninsula. The largest linguistic minority is the Persians, but even their share in the general population does not reach any sizeable proportion (except for Kuwait, but there is no certainty that the estimates are correct). The total proportion of the non-Arabic-speaking population in the Arabian Peninsula does not exceed 3 or 4%.

(2) The proportion of non-Muslims in the population of the Arabian Peninsula is even smaller, since a large part of the Persians, Indians, and other foreigners are also Muslims.

(3) Throughout most of the countries of the Peninsula the Sunni Muslims form a decisive majority. There are almost no

---

[1] Greenberg in *SWJA*, Vol. 5, No. 2.

non-Sunni Muslims in Najd and Qatar (Wahhabi countries), in Hijaz, 'Asir, and Aden (though the Aden colony does contain a small Shi'i and Isma'ili minority), and in Trucial Oman (but in this country the Sunnis are themselves divided into different sects).

(4) Two countries contain a sizeable Shi'i minority (more than 10%): Kuwait and al-Hasa province of Saudi Arabia bordering on Kuwait.

(5) The Sunni Muslims do not form a majority in all the countries of the Peninsula. They are a minority in three countries: in Muscat and Oman (an Abadi majority); in Bahrain (a Shi'i–Imami majority); and in Yemen (a Zaidi majority).

Abadiya is the religion of the main sections of the two clans in Oman, Hinawi and Ghafiri (other branches of these two clans being Sunni Muslims). The Abadi tribes of the interior mountains of Oman were the main force behind the revolt of 1915, which resulted in a certain degree of autonomy under the rule of an elected Imam.[1]

The *Imami Shi'is* of Bahrain live in settlements of their own and do not intermingle with the rest of the population. Though they constitute the majority of the population, they have the character of a 'minority', since, as in Iraq and Lebanon, they form the poorest and lowest classes of society. They are all occupied in agriculture or other physical labour, while the Sunnis have no connection with agriculture except as landowners. These points, and the fact that the ruling family is Sunni, form the background to the tension between the two communities. The Isma'ilis, like the Shi'i Muslims, are members of the lower classes in Eastern Saudi Arabia, being engaged as labourers and artisans. They were thus among the first to be employed by the Aramco Petroleum Works.[2]

The *Zaidis* of Yemen are the largest non-Sunni community in the Arabian Peninsula. According to Lambardi's figures, they form 55% of the population, and they are concentrated in an almost completely defined geographical area: the

---

[1] L. Massignon (ed.), *Annuaire du monde musulman 1954*, Paris, 1955, pp. 40–2; La Documentation française, *L'évolution politique des états de la peninsule arabe*, 2e partie, No. 1042, 22 December 1948, p. 17.

[2] Qubain, pp. 271–3; Lipsky, pp. 63, 90, 160.

The Communal Structure of the Arabian Peninsula

Country	Province	Sunni Muslims			Shi'i Muslims			Abadiya	Non-Arabs		
		Hanbalis and Wahhabis	Shafi'is	Malikis	Zaidis	Imamis	Isma'ilis		Persians	Indians	Others
Saudi Arabia	Najd	Almost 100% Wahhabis									
	al-Hasa	80%		Small minority			About 12%				
	Hijaz		About 90%							Sizeable numbers	
	'Asir		Almost 100%								
Yemen			About 45% in south and coast		About 55% in hills and north		About 1%				
Aden (colony)			Large majority			About 6%				About 11.5%	About 11%
Aden (protectorate)			Almost 100%								
Muscat and Oman		20–25%				About 10%		About 60%	2.5%	2.5%	2.5%
Trucial Oman		About 50%		About 25%					2.5%	2.5%	
Qatar		More than 90% Wahhabis							About 5%	A few	
Kuwait				80%		Approx. 20% (Persians)			20% (Shi'is)	A few	
Bahrain				44%		51.5% (incl. Persians)			6.3% (Shi'is)	2.5%	2%

The table has been compiled on the basis of data taken from the 1954 *Annuaire du Monde Musulman*, other sources serving for comparison. Most figures are estimates of the authors of the Yearbook, and must be accepted as such with reservations.

104

mountainous regions, except for the southernmost areas. Thus Zaidis are all the inhabitants of the province (*liwa*) of San'a, except those living in the western areas; the province of Hajja, except for the plains; one northern district (*qada*) of the southern province of Ibb; and all the northernmost province of the country, Sa'da. Shafi'is, on the other hand, form an absolute majority in the southern province of Ibb, and are all the inhabitants of the southern province of Ta'izz and the coastal province Hudaida. While all the higher officials are Zaidis (since the ruler is a Zaidi), a large part of the important urban merchants of the lowlands and coast are Shafi'is. The Shafi'is maintain the contacts with the outside Muslim and Arab world. This difference forms the background to many political movements in Yemen.[1]

4. *IRAQ*

The communal structure of Iraq, as described in the following table, is based on official figures for 1932:

Communities in Iraq as Percentages of the Total Population

Language	Sunnis	Shi'is	Christians	Jews	Others	Total
Arabic	20·5	53·0	2·0	3·0		78·5
Kurdish	13·5				1·0	14·5
Turkish	2·0	1·0				3·0
Persian		2·0				2·0
Syriac			2·0			2·0
Total	36·0	56·0	4·0	3·0	1·0	100·0

Comments on the Table:

(a) The numbers have been rounded off.

(b) The 'others' are mostly Yazidis.

(c) The Christians have been divided arbitrarily between speakers of Arabic and Syriac; the official figures do not classify the 'local Christians'.

(d) Since the 'thirties there have been two main processes affecting the numerical relationships of the communities: the migration of some of the Nestorian Assyrians, and the departure of most of the Jews. As a result, the proportion of the Christians has decreased to 3%, and of the Jews to less than ½%, with appropriate increases in the proportions of the other communities.

[1] Lambardi, pp. 143–62; La Documentation française, *Le Yemen*, No. 2141, 18 February 1956; J. Heyworth-Dunne, 'The Yemen', *ME Aff.*, February 1958, pp. 53–4.

In addition to the Arabic-speaking Sunnis, therefore, there are in Iraq two large communities—the Arabic-speaking Shi'is and the Sunnis who speak Kurdish dialects (Kurds).

The *Shi'is* of Iraq are concentrated in the six southernmost provinces of the country—Karbala, Hilla, Kut, Diwaniya, Muntafik, and 'Amara, where three-quarters of all the Shi'is of Iraq are found and where this group makes up 98% of all the inhabitants. They are also the majority in the province of Basra, though there is a large Sunni minority in the city of Basra. The Shi'is form more than 25% of the population in the province of Baghdad, where two of the Shi'i holy places, Samarra and Kadhimain, are located. Because of this geographical division, some generalisations may be made about the Shi'is of Iraq:

(1) The Shi'i population of Iraq is mostly tribal, since in the southern provinces mentioned (except Karbala) the tribal population forms more than two-thirds, and in 'Amara and Muntafik even more than four-fifths, of all the inhabitants.[1]

(2) The proportion of Shi'is among the urban population is smaller than their share of the total population, since the three largest cities—Baghdad, Mosul, and Basra—are mostly Sunni, and Kirkuk is completely Sunni, while the three Shi'i towns—Najaf, Kadhimain, and Karbala—are much smaller.

These facts obviously influence the general social level of the Shi'i population. The provinces of Diwaniya, 'Amara, Hilla, and Karbala are those with the smallest number of schools in proportion to their population, and the provinces of Diwaniya and 'Amara also have the lowest number of government doctors and health workers in proportion to the population.[2]

To all this may be added that Iraq, like the other countries of the Fertile Crescent, was part of the Sunni Ottoman Empire until the First World War. Afterwards a Sunni king was crowned, and he founded the dynasty which reigned until 1958. There are also tribes, especially the tribes of Muntafik, in which the tribesmen are Shi'is, while the shaikhs (of the Sa'dun

---

[1] See E. Dowson, *An Inquiry into Land Tenure and Related Questions*, London and Baghdad, 1932, p. 12.

[2] *Iraq Directory* (1936), pp. 412–13; H. Al Witry, *Health Services in Iraq*, Jerusalem, 1944, p. 27; *Directory of the Republic of Iraq 1960*, pp. 486–9, 622–30.

family) are Sunnis. It is not surprising, therefore, that the Shi'is have a smaller share in the Government, the Army, and urban occupations in general than their proportion of the population would warrant. It must be pointed out, however, that the social gap between the Sunnis and Shi'is is gradually narrowing, as the result of the extension of the educational system during the past few years and as a result of the process of urbanisation, which is drawing many Shi'is from the southern provinces to the cities, and especially to Baghdad.

A special characteristic of Shi'i society in Iraq is the more important status and influence of the *mujtahids* among the Shi'i population than that of the Sunni *'ulama* among the Sunnis. It was the opposition of the Shi'i community that was mainly responsible for the fact that the new law on personal status drawn up as early as in 1947 was not passed until the military revolt.

Mut'a (temporary marriage) is practised only at holy places and among the Ma'dan (marsh dwellers). The new law of personal status passed in 1959 does not recognise this type of marriage.[1]

The *Kurds* form the majority of the population in the provinces of Sulaimaniya, Kirkuk, and Arbil, and they also inhabit part of the province of Mosul. In general, we can describe as Kurdish-dominated territory that part of Iraq situated northeast of a line drawn in a north-westerly direction from Mandali (in the province of Diyala on the Persian border) south-west of Kifri and Kirkuk to Mosul, and from there along the highway and railroad to the Syrian border.[2]

The chief concentration of non-Kurds in this region is to be found in a number of towns having a Turkish-speaking population, Kirkuk with its mixed population, and Mosul, Arabic in character. As a matter of fact, except for Sulaimaniya (which is also only a small city), there are practically no Kurdish urban concentrations. During the last generation Kurds have indeed migrated to the largest cities as labourers, some of them in

[1] Linant de Bellefonds, pp. 82-3, 88; Salim, pp. 98-9; Adams, *Iraq's People and Resources*, pp. 24, 86.

[2] On the distribution of Iraq's Kurdish population, as well as the peculiarities of its nomadism, see League of Nations, *Report Submitted to the Council by the Commission Instituted by the Council Resolution of September 30th, 1924*, C. 400, M. 147, 1925, VII, pp. 38-43, 55, and Map No. 6.

the oil industry, but the overwhelming majority of the Kurds is occupied in sheep-raising and agriculture. All manners of living, from nomadism to fixed settlement, are to be found among the Kurds; however, the nomads among them have a much smaller range than the Arab beduins of the lowlands, since they raise sheep rather than camels.

The number of sedentary peasants is constantly growing. There are few Kurdish craftsmen either in the villages or in the cities, and even fewer merchants. In some Kurdish regions families of a nobility which is divided into well-defined ranks have preserved their traditional status.[1]

The Kurds are organised in tribes ruled by an *agha*. As in the rest of Iraq, in recent decades the Kurds have gone through a process of disintegration of the tribal organisation. In the course of land registration the tribal heads became large landowners and some of them moved to the city. Some of the lands passed into the hands of urban businessmen.[2]

In addition to the *agha*, the Kurdish tribes also have a *shaikh*, a religious leader. But the official orthodox religion has only a small influence among the tribes. The laws regulating their lives are generally the laws of tribal tradition. The Sufi orders have also won a great deal of influence among the Kurds.[3]

In their attitude to women, the Kurds are freer than the Arabs. Kurdish women are not veiled, and may appear in the company of men. There are cases of a woman being the head of a Kurdish tribe. Polygamy is very rare, and is limited to tribal heads.[4]

5. *SYRIA*

The communal structure of Syria may be best illustrated by means of the following table, in which the chief religious communities are classified, first according to their proportions in the different provinces of Syria, and, following that, according to the languages they speak.

[1] P. Rondot, 'Les Tribus montagnards de l'Asie antérieur', *Bulletin d'Etudes Orientales de l'Institut Français de Damas*, Vol. VI, 1936, pp. 30, 40; B. Nikitine, *Les Kurdes*, Paris, 1956, pp. 57, 63–4, 128–9.

[2] Dowson, p. 20.

[3] Rondot, 'Les Tribus montagnards', p. 43; Nikitine, pp. 211–19. See also C. J. Edmonds, 'The Kurds of Iraq', *MEJ*, Winter 1957, pp. 52–5.

[4] See Nikitine, pp. 97–101.

Syrian Communities according to Provinces and Languages (in percentages)

Province	Sunnis	Isma'ilis and Shi'is	'Alawis	Druzes	Greek Orthodox	Armenian Orthodox and Catholic	Other Christians	Others (Jews, Yazidis)	Total
Euphrates	98·0				0·1	1·1	0·8		100
Hawran	92·5		0·4		2·6	0·1	4·4		100
Damascus	82·7	0·1	0·7	2·5	3·9	3·2	4·7	2·2	100
Aleppo	82·4	1·0	0·3	0·2	1·1	8·9	4·3	1·8	100
Jazira	67·9	0·2	0·1		0·2	6·8	22·4	2·4	100
Homs	66·3	1·3	10·4		9·4	1·4	11·2		100
Hamah	64·6	13·2	9·5		11·0	0·4	1·3		100
Latakia	18·9	1·8	62·1		12·8	1·3	3·1		100
Jabal ad-Druz	1·8			87·6	5·7	0·7	4·2		100
Total	68·7	1·5	11·5	3·0	4·7	4·2	5·2	1·2	100
Arabic	57·4	1·5	11·5	3·0	4·7	0·2	3·1	1·1	82·5
Kurdish	8·3						0·1	0·1	8·5
Armenian						4·0			4·0
Turkish	3·0								3·0
Syriac							2·0		2·0

Comments on the Table:

(*a*) Percentages higher than the average for Syria as a whole are emphasised by heavy type; these numbers indicate geographical concentrations of each group.

(*b*) The numbers in the lower part of the table (languages) are percentages of the total population. The sum of all the numbers for each community therefore gives its percentage of the total population (registered in the line dividing the two parts of the table).

(*c*) Since no statistics concerning the linguistic distribution of the population have been published, the figures in the lower part can be accepted only as estimates.

(*d*) The percentages in the upper part are based on figures published before the emigration of a part of the Armenians to Soviet Armenia. It is possible, therefore, that the percentage of Armenians has decreased since then and that the percentages of the other communities have risen accordingly.

(*e*) The 'others' are Jews (1·1%) and Yazidis (0·1%). The Jews speak Arabic and the Yazidis speak Kurdish. The Yazidis are found mainly in Jazira province, the Jews in Damascus and Aleppo. The percentages are based on the figures preceding the migration of some of the Jews.

(*f*) It is again to be noted that before 1960 no population census had been taken in Syria for many years. The official figures for the middle 'forties, upon which the table is based, are therefore only calculations of the statistical department of the Syrian Government.

The table shows that the provinces of Syria can be divided into three classes:

(1) Provinces in which the Sunnis form more than four-fifths of the population (Euphrates, Hawran, Damascus, and Aleppo). Only in the last-mentioned is there a sizeable religious minority—i.e., Armenians who settled in the city of Aleppo, most of them after the First World War.

(2) Provinces in which the Sunnis form about two-thirds of the population, and the religious minorities about a third. These provinces can again be divided into two classes: (*a*) Provinces in which Arabic-speaking Sunnis are a majority; these include Homs, where there is a large minority of 'Alawis, Greek Orthodox, and Syrian Orthodox; (*b*) Jazira, where most of the Sunnis are Kurds, and the Arab Sunnis a minority. Among the largest of the religious minorities in this province are the Syrian Orthodox, Armenians, and Nestorians, who settled here mostly after the massacre in Iraq. This province is therefore the most variegated of all the provinces of Syria from the point of view of communal structure.

(3) Provinces in which the Sunnis are a minority. These include Latakia, which has an 'Alawi majority, and Jabal ad-Druz, where the Druzes are a majority. (Both these provinces also contain large Greek Orthodox communities.) In fact, these two territorial concentrations of the 'Alawis and the Druzes are the most outstanding and important phenomenon in Syria's communal pattern.

Seventy-five per cent of all the *'Alawis* inhabit the province of Latakia in Syria.[1] Almost all the 'Alawis are peasants: the percentage of urban dwellers among them is the lowest of all the communities in the province. More than other peasants in the Arab countries they have preserved an organisation in tribes and sub-tribes (*'asha'ir*). The tribal ruler, the *agha* or *muqaddim*, possesses the right to exact from his subjects work without pay, military service, part of the bride price, gifts, and various forms of taxes. He is also judge and arbitrator. In addition to being a subject of his tribal ruler, the 'Alawi is also a serf of some landowner. These tribal rulers and landowners are sometimes one and the same, but many of the lands of the 'Alawi region are in the hands of large landowners from the city of Latakia, most of whom are Sunnis. Noting further that the 'Alawis are also compelled to make various payments to the religious leaders, the shaikhs, it is understandable that great poverty and illiteracy prevail among the members of this community. During the 1940s 'Alawi students constituted only 3% of all students in Syria at a time when the community formed 11·5% of the general population. The 'Alawi region lags behind the rest of the country in other social amenities as well. A listing of Syrian doctors by province indicates that the number of inhabitants per doctor is higher in Latakia than in any other province of Syria (if Damascus, Jabal ad-Druz, and Hawran are included as one unit). The nutritional state is lower and the percentage of those afflicted with trachoma higher among the 'Alawi than among other communities.[2] The 'Alawi woman, who, according to their religion, does not possess a soul, has a lower status than the women of most of the communities

---

[1] On the 'Alawi community and its social structure see J. Weulersse, *Le pays des Alaouites*, Tours, 1940, pp. 333–7.

[2] Ibid., p. 78; *Global Epidemiology*, pp. 141, 153.

of the Arab countries. But, together with these differences, there are many customs common to the 'Alawis and the Muslim Arab fellahs—abstention from pork, polygamy, marriage between paternal cousins, circumcision (at the age of 3 or 4), and others.

The territorial concentration of the *Druzes*[1] in Syria is higher than that of the 'Alawis, since their proportion to all the inhabitants of the province of Jabal ad-Druz is even higher than that of the 'Alawis in Latakia, while there are almost no Druzes in other provinces. As against this, about half the Druzes live outside Syria. All the Druze population in Jabal ad-Druz is rural in character, and not even the 'capital', as-Suwaida, can be called a city, having, as it does, far fewer than 25,000 inhabitants. In their other places of settlement too, almost no Druzes are town-dwellers, the overwhelming majority among them being peasants, and especially mountain peasants. As in other mountainous regions in the Arab countries, the Druze mountain shows a prevalence of small and middle-sized landed property, with large estates playing only a minor role. However, as a result of the lack of urbanisation and modernity, the Druzes have preserved the rule of the 'great families' and are strongly opposed to the imposition of central authority. As a result of persecutions and wars there is a strong feeling of communal solidarity, which has often taken on a clearly military form reflected in militant fanaticism. It may be that this is one of the reasons which has led many of the Druzes to choose the occupation of soldier, and their share in the Army is greater than their proportion of the general population. (This is, of course, also a heritage of the Mandatory period, since the French recruited members of minority groups for their armed forces, against the Arab National movements.)

The level of education among the Druzes is relatively high. In the province of Jabal ad-Druz the number of pupils (compared with the population as a whole), and the relative number of schools and teachers, are among the highest in Syria.[2] The legal status of the Druze woman is somewhat different from that of the Muslim woman. The Druzes forbid polygamy. This ban

---

[1] The following is based mainly on H. Blanc, *Hadruzim*, Jerusalem, 1958 (and sources mentioned in Blanc's extensive bibliography).

[2] IBRD, *The Economic Development of Syria*, pp. 457–9.

was written into the Syrian Personal Law of 1953. The same law stipulated that divorce had to receive the ratification of a *qadi*. It may also be pointed out that at various times in modern Druze history women have fulfilled central social and public roles. Another difference between Druze and Muslim social law is the Druze freedom of inheritance by will, which also received written form in the above-mentioned Personal Law, whereas Muslims are not permitted to bequeath more than one-third of their property by will.

In dress, food, and language habits there are no fundamental differences between Druzes and Muslims, although the Druzes of the Jabal can be recognised by their dialect, which is similar to that of southern Lebanon from which they came some generations ago.

6. *LEBANON*

Official statistics for the middle of the present century show the communal pattern of the Lebanese population (see Table on p. 114).

As in the case of Syria, it should be noted that the percentages are not based on any census, since none has been carried out since 1932. The reason for this is that since its formation after the First World War the state of Lebanon has done everything possible to preserve the inter-community equilibrium that was established at that time, and does not want to endanger this balance by a census. In 'Mount Lebanon', the original autonomous area, the Maronites form two-thirds of the total population and all the Christians together three-fourths. This situation changed following on the creation of the State of 'Greater Lebanon' by the annexation of the Sunni regions (Beirut, Tripoli) and Shi'i areas (South Lebanon, al-Biqa'). Additional changes followed the migration of Armenians into Lebanon (settling mainly in Beirut) and the refugees from Palestine, whose numbers and communal distribution are not reflected in the official figures. In the light of this last factor, and the greater natural increase of the Muslims, it is doubtful whether the Christians are still in the majority in Lebanon. But until the present time the absence of a new census has apparently served as an efficient means of preserving the balance between

The Inhabitants of Lebanon and its Provinces According to Community at the Middle of the Twentieth Century (in Percentages of the Population of Each District, Province, or of the Total Population)

District	Province	Sunnis	Shi'is	Druzes	Maronites	Greek Orthodox	Greek Catholics	Armenians Orthodox and Cath.	Other Christians	Others
	Beirut	34·4	7·5	1·6	8·0	11·2	3·2	23·8	7·7	2·6
Ba'abda					48·5					
al-Matn					51·2					
ash-Shuf				30·3	34·7					
'Alaih				45·7						
Kisrawan					85·8					
	Mount Lebanon	6·1	5·6	17·6	51·6	7·6	5·1	5·0	1·2	0·2
al-Kura						61·5				
Zaghurta					92·2					
al-Batrun					75·8					
'Akkar		47·3				25·0				
Tripoli		77·2								
	North Lebanon	39·8	0·4		36·2	19·1	0·9	0·5	0·5	2·6
Sidon		39·5	61·4							
Tyre			79·5							
Marj'uyun			66·2	33·6						
Hasbaya					66·2		17·0			
Jazzin										
	South Lebanon	11·5	58·0	2·6	14·3	3·1	8·5	0·8	0·9	0·3
Zahla						28·9	25·1			
Ba'ibek			67·5				30·9			
al-Harmal			60·2							
Rashaya				35·6						

114

Comments on the Table:

(*a*) For provinces numbers in **heavy type** indicate instances of percentages higher than the average for Lebanon as a whole, i.e., relative territorial concentration of a group.

(*b*) For the districts, the highest percentages only are listed.

(*c*) 'Others' are Jews (in Beirut) and 'Alawis (in North Lebanon, particularly 'Akkar and Tripoli).

the communities. This is reflected in public life, particularly in the following ways:[1]

(1) Every single position in Government and Parliament is reserved for a specific community: the Prime Minister must be a Sunni, the Speaker a Shi'i, etc.; this is in addition to proportional representation of the communities in Parliament, which also exists in other countries of the Middle East.

(2) According to the Constitution (paragraph 95), the different communities have the right to proportional representation in public administrative positions as well. The various communities have defended this right fervently, and this paragraph of the Constitution, introduced in 1926 as a temporary measure, has never been annulled.

That Lebanon is the only country in the Arab East not to have a Muslim majority is also indicated by its jurisdiction: Muslim law does not have first preference as in other Arab countries. For example, elsewhere a Christian may divorce his wife according to Muslim law as soon as he becomes a Muslim. In Lebanon he is judged according to Muslim law only in relation to acts that have taken place since his conversion, not retroactively.[2]

As the table on page 114 shows, no single community has a majority in Lebanon. The largest community, the Maronites, constitutes less than 30% of the population. But the table also shows that there is a great deal of geographical concentration of the main communities. Parallel to this, clear social differences between one community and another may be distinguished.

The *Sunni Muslims* are concentrated in the coastal cities.

---

[1] For the following see mainly Rondot, *Les Institutions politiques du Liban, passim.* See also C. G. Hess and H. L. Bodman, 'Confessionalism and Feudality in Lebanese Politics', *MEJ*, Winter 1954.

[2] Rondot, *The Minorities in the Arab Orient*, p. 225 and *passim*.

They form three-fourths of the inhabitants of Tripoli, and more than half of all the Sunnis of Lebanon dwell in the two largest cities. (There are also some Sunni fellahs whose settlements are scattered throughout the country.) In Beirut and Tripoli the Sunnis are numbered among the wealthiest businessmen and landowners. This fact, as well as the very high percentage of urban dwellers among the Lebanese Sunnis, is responsible for an educational level which is much higher than that of the Sunnis in other Arab countries, although still lower than that of the Christians.

The *Shi'i Muslims* (Mutawalis) of Lebanon, in contrast to some of the other Arab countries, have been recognised as a community distinct from the Sunnis since 1926. They form an absolute majority in the province of South Lebanon and in some of the districts in the province of al-Biqa'. They are village dwellers for the most part, and their society has preserved strong feudal characteristics, landowning families holding sway over wretched peasant serfs by means of private armed bands. In the cities where they are found (especially Tyre and Sidon) they also form the lowest strata. From the standpoint of level of education, and hence also from that of their share in the higher officialdom, they are the most backward community in Lebanon.

The characteristics of the *Druze* community were discussed earlier. In Lebanon the Druzes form a rural group concentrated in the southern part of Mount Lebanon and the regions of Hasbaya and Rashaya. In Lebanon, as in Syria, they have preserved to a large extent a quasi-feudal order in which the traditional aristocratic families dominate public life.

The *Greek Orthodox* are rather scattered, though there is a large concentration in the Kura district in the north and a sizeable community of wealthy businessmen in Beirut.

The *Greek Catholics* are found mainly in the southern and eastern parts of Lebanon. In comparison to other communities, their levels of education and wealth are among the highest in Lebanon.

The *Armenians* settled in Lebanon after the First World War, most of them in shanties in the suburbs of Beirut. They are for the most part craftsmen and small traders, but a good number of them have succeeded in rising in the social ladder by im-

116

proving their standard of living, entering the free professions and commerce.

The largest community in Lebanon, and the one which has to a great extent put its stamp on the character of the state, is the *Maronite* community. The Maronites form the majority of the population of Mount Lebanon, with their chief centre in the district of Kisrawan (north-east of Beirut). They also form a majority in two districts of North Lebanon. In these two provinces almost 80% of all the Maronites are concentrated. They are for the most part village-dwellers, the other Christian communities exceeding them numerically in the large cities. Until the nineteenth century the Maronite districts were ruled by noble families which maintained a régime of landed and military feudalism (differing from the form of feudalism prevalent in other regions of the Arab Middle East). They were headed by an *amir*, whose position passed by inheritance through the same family. After the collapse of their control and the liquidation of feudalism, an agrarian system was established in which agricultural land is *mulk* rather than *miri*—unlike the other countries of the Fertile Crescent. This system is also characterised by the existence of a sizeable class of small land-owning farmers. (Details see below, Ch. IV.)

The share of the Maronites among emigrants to America and other countries has been large, to some extent as a result of their ties with the Christian world (via the Vatican and France), which have been maintained for hundreds of years. All these factors have brought the Maronites a degree of prosperity and a level of culture above that of other communities. The level of illiteracy among the Maronites is lower than among most of the other communities.

Compared with the Copts of Egypt, the Maronites have preserved many more of the special laws and customs distinguishing them from the Muslims. This difference is reflected, for example, in legislation with regard to inheritance and bequests. While the Muslim laws of inheritance are effective for the Copts in Egypt, unless all the heirs agree to pass over them, a special law was enacted on 7 March 1929 in Lebanon, concerning non-Muslim Lebanese bequests, which appreciably increased (to at least half the property) the part that non-Muslims are permitted to bequeath freely. Previously Muslim

I

law, which since the middle of the nineteenth century had been effective for the Maronites also, had limited this part to one-third, in contradistinction to the special customs and laws of the Maronite community. In this matter Maronite law is similar to the Druze law, which, as noted earlier, has since 1948 regained the right of free bequest. It may be pointed out, however, that owing to neglect of the instructions of some of the Maronite law books, as well as disregard of the Muslim law, which has been effective for Maronites since 1841, the latter, like other communities in the Middle East, tend to discriminate against their married daughters in matters of inheritance.[1]

7. LIBYA AND JORDAN

In Libya and Jordan, both of them countries with relatively small populations, the Sunni Arab Muslims form 90% or more of the population. The communal structure of the two countries is a simple one, neither of them having any large non-Arab or non-Sunni Muslim community worthy of mention in this survey. The communal structure of Libya may be described roughly by means of the following table (in percentages):

Province	Sunni-Muslim Arabs		Abadi Berbers	Catholic Italians	Total
	Sanusis	Other Sunnis			
Tripolitania		60·5	3·7	4·2	68·4
Cyrenaica	26·6				26·6
Fezzan		5·0			5·0
Total	26·6	65·5	3·7	4·2	100·0

Jordan has two minorities: a linguistic one—Circassians—who number only a few thousand in all, and a religious minority—Christians of various sects. There are widely differing estimates of their numbers, and there are still no official figures based on a census. Estimates of their size vary from 7·5 to 12% of the general population.

[1] Aouad, pp. 206–19, 240–6, 305–8.

IV

ECOLOGICAL STRUCTURE

Most of the countries of the Arab East lack reliable information on all aspects of the distribution of inhabitants among beduins, semi-nomads, villagers, and townspeople. Clearly, beduins constitute a large proportion of the inhabitants of the Arabian Peninsula—a quarter to a third of the total population, according to various estimates; in Saudi Arabia they account for as much as one-half to two-thirds of the population (together with semi-nomads); in Libya nomads are about one-fifth of the population (in Cyrenaica, more than 50%); and unsettled tribes are prevalent in Sudan also, but there is no available material from which some figure may fairly be assessed. Estimates for the countries bordering on the Syrian Desert—Iraq, Syria, and Jordan—place the percentage of beduins at 6–10% in each of them; while in Egypt (0·25%, i.e., 50,000) and in Lebanon their number is insignificant.

From 20 to 30% of the population of every Middle Eastern country, with the exception of Lebanon, the Sudan, and the Arabian Peninsula, is urban (living in towns of 25,000 persons at least; lesser groupings fall into the category of large villages). In all the Middle East the majority of the population is rural. The countries bordering on the Syrian Desert and Libya, whose nomadic population is considerable, are about two-thirds rural, but this number includes many semi-nomadic elements, particularly in Iraq and Libya. Villagers in Egypt (including inhabitants of many townships of several thousand persons) constitute three-quarters of the population. In Lebanon alone the ecological structure is slightly different; here over one-third of the population is urban, less than two-thirds rural.

Before describing each of the three main ecological groupings of the Middle East a few introductory remarks are due on the relations among them in the scale of social values of Middle Eastern Arabs. Undoubtedly the beduin regards the villager with contempt and considers his status as inferior because he has neither lineage nor freedom. Fundamentally, this is also his view of townsfolk, although, in so far as there is contact between them, the beduin recognises that the townsman is more prosperous and that the town is the centre of power and government. The villager is generally afraid of the beduin and perhaps even ridicules him, but he is proud of any beduin origin he may have. He is suspicious of the townsman, and sometimes even hates him for his greater power. The townsman is contemptuous of both beduin and villager, because of their ignorance and primitive way of life, although again in many towns there are still families which take pride in their beduin past. Not surprisingly, these fundamental attitudes are steadily becoming blurred, as settlement of the beduins and urbanisation advance, and as townsmen's nationalistic feelings, particularly Socialist trends, become stronger.

A. THE BEDUINS[1]

1. *MATERIAL LIFE*

The material life of the beduin is, of course, adapted to the desert—the environment in which his society was formed, and its two main features are: (*a*) *camel raising*, and as a by-occupation, or in some tribes at a further stage of development, the raising of horses and sheep; and (*b*) *nomadism*, characterised by the typically beduin form of abode, the *tent*.

The camel is a versatile source of livelihood. The beduin rides it on his raids (*ghazw*) on caravans of other tribes and tribal settlements. At least in the past the camel was one of the principal sources of the beduin's income. It serves as a means of locomotion during his wanderings and as a beast of burden in his commercial caravans. Its milk and flesh are staples of his diet and are also marketed in settled regions, in exchange for grain, dates, etc. The camel's hair is woven to make the tent-

[1] The best general survey of the beduins and their society in modern times is R. Montagne, *La Civilisation du désert*, Paris, 1947. This survey has often been used below without explicit reference at each point.

flaps of his home; its dung is used to compound fuel material. These two products are also sold in the villages and towns of the Fertile Crescent.

The beduin's horse is mainly used for transport in battle, while sheep give him food (milk and meat) and wool. Sheep, horses, and the products are sold to villagers and townsfolk. Obviously then, contact with the permanently settled populace is essential for the beduin, be it contact by raids or by trade, as he is in need of the settler's agricultural produce, manufacture, and services.

The main livestock reared by a tribe determine its character, and on this basis beduins may be divided into the following classes:

(*a*) Camel-raisers, wandering far from settlements (and authorities); because of the nature of the camel, whose needs are modest, such tribes may sojourn in arid areas. These tribes are the strongest and fiercest, masters of the desert. They collect *khuwa* or *khawa* (tax of 'goodwill') from agricultural settlements in the oases and wadis, a tax which is paid in grain and dates, in exchange for protection.

(*b*) Closer to settlements there are camel-rearers who have also begun to occupy themselves with sheep grazing. Generally such beduins eventually split up, the sheep-rearers being edged towards settlements by the camel-rearers. Those who are mainly occupied with sheep use the camel only for transport and are slowly converted into full sheep-raisers.

(*c*) *Shwaya* (or *Shawiya*)—sheep-raisers. Their range of migration is more limited, and they are therefore more subject to external rule and must put up with the pastureland assigned them (*dira*). If this region is near rivers and marshes the beduins also tend to raise cattle (water buffalo, cows) and in part become *baqqara*.

(*d*) *Baqqara* (pronounced *baggara*). Their way of life is, in fact, intermediate between those of nomad and farmer. The *baqqara* build houses, living in their tents in spring and summer only, when they take their flocks far from settled areas. They remain beduins in spirit only. In the Sudan the Arab tribes which penetrated south of latitude 13° have taken over cattle-raising from the original Negro population, for camels cannot live in this region because of the flies. Most of these tribes are in part settled on the land.

Grazing land must be provided for camels and sheep, and hence the need to move from place to place in search of suitable pastures. The *migratory directions* of the main tribes of Northern Arabia and the Syrian Desert, throughout the year, are fixed by season:

In spring pastures are found in the steppes bordering the desert.

In summer tribes move to the hills as much as possible (to Salma in Arabia, south-east of Ha'il; the mountains of Syria and Lebanon; 'Ajlun in Jordan, etc.). Others transfer to the broad valleys and wadis of Arabia, where rainfall is high and the ground is covered with grass and bushes. They stay here in groups for an extended period, at a summer camp erected around springs and wells.

In autumn, with the onset of rain, they set out in caravans towards settlements for trade, in order to get in a supply of goods (grain, dates, cotton clothing, various tools), and if possible, to collect the *khuwa*. (Only shaikhs actually come into contact with the settlements.)

In winter they return to the desert in search of vegetation in addition to that which comes up after the first rains.

In other parts of the Middle East the directions and calendar of migration are determined by similar considerations, in accordance with the local conditions.

This is a hard life from a material viewpoint. Hunger is not rare, and people age rapidly. As against this, beduins are unrestricted; they are exempt from limitations imposed by a central authoritative body of the state; and they are not subject to what the beduin feels is the onerous life of the villager, which he despises and tries to avoid. The ideal of all beduins is the true beduin tribe, rearing its camels far from any settlement.

2. *SOCIAL ORGANISATION*[1]

The characteristic trait of beduin social organisation is that it is based only on *blood ties*, from its smallest unit to the broad

[1] Unless otherwise stated, the analysis in this section is based on material published in the following works—for Northern Arabia, the Syrian desert, and Trans-

federation of tribes. In the Syrian Desert and Northern Arabia
there are two such federations—the Qahtans, Southern Arabs
(Shammar), and descendants of Ma'add ('Anaiza). The fact
that the genealogies of these tribes are often imaginary does
not lessen their importance in the beduin's mind. The classification of beduin society into its units, and the names and sizes
of these units, differ widely from tribe to tribe and region to
region. The following are the main units into which their
society is generally divided:

(*a*) The extended patriarchal family, the basic unit of beduin
society. Its usual name in the Syrian Desert and in Israel is
ahl, but the names *'a'ila*, *bait*, and *ahl al-bait* are also applied in
Southern Iraq and Upper Egypt.

(*b*) A group of families which had a common father five to
seven generations ago is called a *hamula* in the Israeli Negev,
in Transjordan, and in the Syrian Desert. Other regions use
different terms, among them the *fakhdh* in Southern Iraq,
bait-byut in Cyrenaica, and even *qabila* (!) in Upper Egypt.
Among the Rwala the unit following the *ahl* in size is called
al. Among beduins the *hamula* is the unit of ownership of
wells, and also of land if it is their possession.[1] The *hamula*
generally moves together and camps together. This is also the
unit whose members vouch for one another in cases of blood
revenge. However, in some places this mutual responsibility
in murder cases has been limited and is effective only for males
whose consanguinity with murderer or victim is up to the fifth
degree. This principle is called *khums*.

(*c*) In some beduin tribes there is a unit intervening between
the *hamula* and the tribe, which usually includes foreign
elements and associated persons. This is sometimes a territorial
unit, particularly during later stages of settlement. It may be
termed a sub-tribe; its Arabic name is *rub'* in the Negev, *firqa*

jordan: A. Musil, *Manners and Customs of the Rwala Bedouins*, New York, 1928;
V. Müller, *En Syrie avec les Bédouins*, Paris, 1931; and Jaussen, *Moab*; for Southern
Iraq: Salim, *Chibayish*; for the Israeli Negev: E. Marx, 'Bedouin Society in the
Negev', *New Outlook*, Vol. II, Nos. 1 and 2, September (I) and October (II) 1958;
for Egypt: G. W. Murray, *Sons of Ishmael*, London, 1935; and Ammar, *Growing up
in an Egyptian Village*; and for Libya: E. E. Evans-Pritchard, *The Sanusi of Cyrenaica*,
Oxford, 1949.
[1] See for Upper Egypt Winkler, *Ägyptische Volkskunde*, p. 325; for Kurdish tribes,
Barth, p. 166; for Cyrenaica, Evans-Pritchard, *Sanusi*, p. 55.

in Syria; the Rwala call it *fariq* or *fariz*, Cyrenaicans *'a'ila*; in Southern Iraq it is the *hamula*, in Upper Egypt *hissa*. The head of such a unit usually bears an official title: *kabir rub'*, *sirkal hamula*; in Cyrenaica and Upper Egypt *shaikh*—the title normally reserved for the head of a tribe.

(*d*) The tribe of the Negev, Syria, and Iraq is usually known as the *'ashira*; but this unit, too, is termed *qabila* in Cyrenaica, Egypt, and Sudan.[1] While members of a single tribe do consider themselves to be related ('cousins'), the tribal unit is primarily *political*, including in its midst refugees, emigrants of other tribes, and persons under its protection. At times the whole tribe camps together during the summer (near a group of wells). Genuine beduins mark their camels with a tribal *wasm* (brand). The group is held together by common martial aims; as a unit, it has the protectorate of an area of settlements which pay it *khuwa*.

The tribe is headed by a *shaikh*. His position is generally hereditary (though not necessarily passing from father to son) within specific families. These families must be rich in order that they may bear the expenses of entertaining, which are contingent on a shaikh's status. The shaikh takes responsibility for decisions in matters of migration, war, settling of disputes, and so on. In such matters he is advised by a council of tribal elders (*majlis*), but its discussions and decisions are not formal, and even implementation depends on the shaikh's influence; he is no more than the first among equals. The shaikh represents the tribe in external contacts and collects government taxes from his people.

(*e*) An association of tribes is called *qabila* in the Negev, but it has been seen that in many regions this term is used for the tribe itself. The *qabila* is headed by a shaikh of one of the stronger tribes. He is titled *shaikh al-mashayikh*.

(*f*) Coalitions of *qabilas*, such as the Shammar or the 'Anaiza, formed under stress of inter-tribal war of the Arabian Peninsula desert; these, too, have blood relationships in beduin lore.

It must be stressed that this hierarchy, far from being rigid, is under continual modification; the complete set of units does

[1] For the Sudan see Trimingham, p. 26.

not exist in all tribes, and there are vast differences between the sizes of any two parallel units.

Beduins may also be classified according to two main factions, each tribe belonging to one or the other. The tribes of the Syrian Desert and the Fertile Crescent are divided between the Qais and the Yaman—descendants, as it were, of Northern and Southern Arabian tribes. (The tribes of Lower Egypt were divided, prior to their settlement, into the Sa'd and the Haram; the tribes of Upper Egypt belonged to the Sawami'a or the Wanatina.) In the Fertile Crescent these factions were meaningful among the settled populace too, even among non-Muslim sects. Again, each faction claims a single ancient father, of course. Apparently, the significance of the factions has decreased in the past generation.[1]

Among all beduin tribes of the Middle East which have been investigated there are continual permutations as individuals, families, and even whole *hamulas* are absorbed in a strong sub-tribe or tribe, or as such groups leave a weakening tribe. It is interesting that in such cases the absorbed element creates in its imagination, or is consciously deceived into believing in, a blood and family relationship with the unit which it joins, since any other connection is simply not feasible.

The scale of nobility of beduins is determined by the military strength of the various tribes. The tribes standing at the head of this scale are imagined to have a better known and longer genealogy (*asl*) than other tribes. For this reason, tribes of lower rank in the desert social scale try to find or invent relationships with stronger tribes or with tribes which are their protectors. (There is a special institution, a man known as the *jassas al-usul*, who concerns himself just with this.) However, the differences in social rank exist only between different tribes, while within any single one there is complete equality (so long as its habitat is the desert).

The social scale is headed by the large desert tribes—Rwala, Sba'a, Harb, 'Ataiba, Banu Khalid, Mutair, 'Amarat, Shammar, Wuld 'Ali. They are followed by tribes which are part of

[1] For the Syrian desert see Montagne, pp. 61–2; Patai, *Jordan*, pp. 38–40, 195. On Egypt see E. W. Lane, *The Manners and Customs of the Modern Egyptians*, London, 1944, p. 202; Murray, pp. 43–4; Mubarak, IX, 84–5; XIV, 54; XVII, 16–17. On the mainly Christian township of Ramallah in Palestine see Zarour, pp. 432–3.

the above groups, but which migrated to the environments of settlements—e.g., the Shammar of the Jazira. Lower on the social scale are tribes of sheep- and cattle-raisers; then farming tribes 'who have no lineage'. At a still lower level are insignificant tribes, such as the Shararat of Transjordan with their wretched tents, or the truly outcast tribes, such as the Slaib, who engage in hunting and serve as poets or jesters (their wives as prostitutes) among other tribes. At the very bottom of the social scale come blacksmiths and other craftsmen, black slaves, freedmen (who sometimes till the land at oases); but among beduins even such slaves are of higher rank than totally permanent settlers, as the former do have some lineage. (Beduins relate them back to Ham.)

The beduins of the Middle East are considered Muslims (apart from an insignificant number of Christian tribes). However, their *religion* is not the official and customary Muslim faith. They have practically no knowledge of the doctrines and ethics of their religion, and they do not observe (nor are they generally acquainted with) its edicts; they do not practise the rites of prayer, the fast of Ramadan, or pilgrimages to Mecca.[1] The beduin's belief in Allah is most primitive, depicted in the image of beduin society itself.[2] In extensive regions of the Arab East, and particularly in Sudan, Egypt, and Cyrenaica, saint worship is very common. Many strange superstitions abound. However, in these last two respects beduins are not basically different from fellahs of the same surroundings.

As in the spheres of faith and rite, so too in *law* and *judgement* the beduin is not bound by Islam. In various parts of the Muslim world the population retained its local unwritten customs (*'urf* or *'ada*) even after Islamisation. Beduins, too, have preserved tribal custom and law; they do not judge according to shari'a law, and their judges are not shar'i qadis.[3] In the Syrian Desert they are known as *'arifa* (plural:

---

[1] A realistic account of ignorance in matters of religion and neglect of religious precepts among the Ahl al-Hilla tribe of Upper Egypt before its settlement is found in Mubarak, XVII, 20–5. See also Jaussen, *Moab*, pp. 287–90.

[2] Murray, pp. 149–50, tells some instructive and amusing stories exemplifying the image of Allah, as the beduin sees him.

[3] Levy, pp. 242-3, 248-9. There are actually some tribes among whom the judge is called *qadi*, but this does not reflect his true function. See Jaussen, *Moab*, p. 182.

'awarif); the position is generally hereditary within certain families, usually passing from father to son, and there are special tribal judges for each branch of law: matters of blood vengeance (*'awarif ad-dam*), matters of honour, disputes over horses, etc. This traditional jurisdiction is more a matter of arbitration than of judgement, since the parties concerned are not compelled to act according to its decisions.

No distinction is drawn between criminal and civil law; in criminal cases too there is a damaged party who merits revenge or compensation. This is the first and main principle of beduin judgement. The second principle concerns mutual responsibility of a group; not the individual, but a well-defined group of relatives is required to pay or may be awarded compensation, for example.

3. CAUSES AND PROCESS OF SETTLEMENT

Beduin society as described here has been in a continual state of decline for the past 150 years, as nomads gradually become settled on the land. Censuses of nomads have never been taken, since their migratory habits and social structure more or less prohibit an exact count, but estimates clearly indicate that nomadism is on the decrease. In Egypt, for example, Cromer assessed the nomads at 250,000 in 1892; at the beginning of the twentieth century they were placed at 80,000–100,000; and censuses since 1927 estimate 30,000–50,000 tribesmen only.

This process of transition from nomadic to sedentary life is not new. Throughout the history of the Arabs there have been many cases in which beduins served as a force by whose aid new kingdoms were established or existing ones conquered, the beduins themselves thereby becoming permanent settlers. The process and its cyclic nature have been well analysed in the *Muqaddima* of Ibn Khaldun, Arab historian and sociologist of the fourteenth century. Droughts, or new forces which arose in the desert, have at times driven migratory tribes to the borders of settled regions, brought them into close contact with the local populace, and consequently have converted these desert migrants into settlers. Thus some of the Shammar tribe were ousted from Jabal Shammar of Arabia in the seventeenth and eighteenth centuries and became settled in the Jazira of Syria–

Iraq, partly because of the rise of the 'Anaiza tribe in the Arabian Peninsula. But never were there causes so strongly and so overwhelmingly in the direction of settlement as in modern times—since the nineteenth century and particularly in the twentieth.

These new causes will now be set forth:

(*a*) The first factor, which made its appearance in the nineteenth century in Egypt and the twentieth century in the Fertile Crescent countries, is the establishment of a *stable and orderly central government*. Being short of funds, the Government assumed the protection of agricultural settlements, including even those that bordered the desert, and prevented beduins from collecting the *khuwa* or from making their raids. Many of the tribes which moved along the edge of settled districts were in this way forced to surrender to the central authorities and eventually to settle, as a source of an important part of their livelihood was blocked. In certain places the authorities even made deliberate attempts to colonise tribesmen in military–agricultural settlements (the *Ikhwan* in Saudia). Even now, the Saudi Arabian Government makes various efforts to settle beduins, and tries to ease the process by supplying agricultural equipment, technical assistance, and credit on very easy terms.[1]

(*b*) Establishment of modern rule also involved *land registration* by modern methods; in Egypt this was accomplished at the beginning of the century, in the Fertile Crescent countries it began in the 1930s. Many areas which had previously been no-man's-land (*mawat*) became private property. This was a period in which agriculture passed from subsistence economy to cultivation of cash crops (cotton and sugar in Egypt, wheat and barley in Iraq, etc.). The beduin was attracted to the idea of registering land which had previously been his *dira*, in order that it might be his own property on which he could grow marketable crops and become wealthy.

(*c*) Within the past thirty years a further impulse to settle has been afforded by the influx of cars and planes to the Middle East. There was no longer a high value for horses, which had hitherto been sold to the authorities for military purposes, or for camels as a means of desert transportation. Then, too, the

[1] A. S. Helaissi, 'The Bedouins and Tribal Life in Saudi Arabia', *ISSB*, Vol. XI, No. 4, p. 536.

importance of the beduin as guide of desert caravans lessened; this had previously been an important source of income. A hard blow to the beduin guide was the laying of railroads across desert stretches, such as the line which crosses the Sinai desert, the lines connecting Northern Sudan with Egypt and the Red Sea, the railway between Syria and Iraq, and the Hijaz Railway. A similar effect was felt from the Suez Canal and the network of roads now crossing Saudi Arabia. There were no more payments for free and undisturbed passage of commercial caravans across the desert; this meant that a further source of income was forestalled, as such caravans were now no longer required.

(*d*) For the first time in history, overwhelming military supremacy passed into the hands of the central authorities. Previously, both parties had employed the same weapon—the rifle—and the same methods of transport—camel and horse. The beduin had often had the upper hand because of his greater mobility and because of the depth of the area from which he fought. Nowadays, the central authorities have armoured vehicles and bombs against the beduin's rifle.

(*e*) An important factor which handicapped beduins of the northern parts of the Arabian Peninsula and the Syrian Desert was the political adjustment on the division of the Ottoman Empire after the First World War, and particularly the establishment of frontiers between independent nations. These frontiers, and the treaties and agreements between the new nations, greatly limited the beduin's freedom of movement; the *dira* was curtailed and some of the tribes were even cut off from their traditional pasturelands.[1]

(*f*) A final factor which, over the past twenty years, has revolutionised the beduin way of life and caused a sudden transition to settled ways, is *oil*. The beduin of yesterday has now become the driller or machinist employed by the oil companies of Saudi Arabia, Kuwait, and the rest of the Oil States of the Arabian Peninsula.

During the Second World War many beduins worked as labourers with the armies stationed in Egypt, and they became

---

[1] For description and analysis of this problem, as well as a survey of the frontier arrangement of Northern Arabia in the 1920s, see A. Toynbee, *Survey of International Affairs 1925*, London, 1927, Vol. I, pp. 324–46.

accustomed to a relatively high cash wage. At the end of the war they had no desire to return to a nomadic life, and many are now wage-earning labourers in the cities and villages of Egypt. Beduins are also employed in the mines of the Sinai Peninsula. In Egypt, Arabia, and Israel, too, various observers have remarked that the beduins often adapt themselves to mechanised work better than the fellahs. Further, they prefer industrial work or even mechanised agriculture to farm labour, as the former do not bear the stigma attached to traditional farming. At the same time it has been noted that the sedentary farmers and farm labourers are more likely to seek work than are the nomads.[1]

The process of settlement of beduins involves fundamental changes in the typical aspects of their life discussed earlier. Naturally, it implies primarily a transition from rearing camels and sheep to crop cultivation. This transition has several stages. First, a beduin tribe or part of the tribe obtains land for supplementary earnings, over and above that afforded by its livestock. At this stage the land is often farmed by tenant fellahs or hired labour rather than by tribesmen themselves. Even beduins who farm their own land do so for only a short period of the year, continuing to migrate during the rest of the year. In successive stages they grow more and more dependent on farming; they become conscious of the need to remain by their fields to guard them; they realise that a sedentary life is more comfortable than nomadism, and so on. Eventually, the transition is completed. The change of occupation is accompanied by a corresponding modification of their home; the tent pitched on cultivated fields becomes more and more fixed, brick walls are set up around it, and eventually it is replaced by permanent housing.[2]

A tribe does not always remain settled for ever. In the past a weak rule often caused a return to nomadism, and even at the end of the nineteenth century war and lack of security led the

[1] Helaissi, ibid.; H. V. Muhsam, 'Sedentarization of the Bedouin in Israel', *ISSB*, Vol. XI, 1959, No. 4, p. 548; M. Awad, 'Settlement of Nomadic and Semi-Nomadic Tribal Groups in the Middle East', *International Labour Review* (*ILR*), January 1959, p. 34; F. C. Thomas, 'The Libyan Oil Worker', *MEJ*, Summer 1961, p. 269.

[2] Patai, *Jordan*, pp. 221–2, 226–7; Montagne, pp. 208, 215; Mubarak, XVII, 23, 33.

Huwaytat tribe to go back to complete nomadism after a trial period at agriculture. Only after the First World War did this tribe finally resettle.[1]

In short: the transition of the beduin to settled ways of life is not a one-stage revolution, but rather a gradual process. There are many tribes in Iraq and Syria which are still considered semi-nomads, such as the 'Uqaidat on the Euphrates and part of the Mawali and the Hadidiyin east of the Homs–Aleppo line. Other examples are the tribes of the Negev and many of the Transjordanian and Cyrenaican tribes. The range of their migration is very limited, and at times they have permanent housing (huts or even brick or clay buildings) at their summer location as well as their winter camps.

In certain parts of the Arab Middle East beduins have made a transition to the towns. Thus, for example, in Jordan, in the region of the oil industry, and in Cyrenaica, poor beduins who had camped near towns moved into them when new sources of livelihood appeared.[2] Incidentally, it is often the poor beduins who are the first to abandon desert life, together with the very wealthy beduins, shaikhs, and their families, while the 'middle classes' are generally the last to settle.[3]

There are also fundamental changes in *social organisation* accompanying settlement. The political and social importance of the tribe falls steadily until total disintegration. 'On settling, the tribe diminishes in size, and when the shaikh no longer controls its economic means, the tribe tends to split up into its hamulas.'[4] Writing of a tribe which settled in Southern Iraq in the first quarter of this century, Salim notes that the tribe no longer exists as a social or political unit, and the term 'ashira has become meaningless, particularly among the younger generation. Weulersse, speaking of the Syrian fellahs, notes that

[1] E. Epstein, 'The Nomad Problem in Transjordan', *Palestine and the Middle East*, 2 February 1937, p. 90.

[2] Ibid., p. 88; Evans-Pritchard, *Sanusi*, p. 43. For the Albu Muhammad tribe of Southern Iraq see F. Jamali, *The New Iraq—Its Problem of Bedouin Education*, New York, 1934, p. 132.

[3] Weulersse, *Paysans de Syrie*, pp. 304–5; Lipsky, p. 90.

[4] E. Marx, Part II, p. 30. Others claim, to the contrary, that on settlement the tribe grows as means of existence grow more plentiful. An example quoted is the Hadendowa in the Sudan (over 100,000 souls) and the Awlad 'Ali in Egypt, which is even larger. Part of the growth stems from the absorption of smaller tribal fractions—see Awad, p. 27.

the *'ashira* is no longer a social unit, except in regions in which the beduin spirit still prevails, e.g., in Saudi Arabia and Hauran, the Ma'mura, and the Jazira in Syria—and even here its importance is diminishing. (The 'tribe' still retains its meaning among some mountainous minority groups.[1])

A second characteristic of settlement is the increasing importance of religion in the life of the settlers. This has been recognised by authors describing nineteenth-century Egypt, and tribes of Jazira in Syria–Iraq in this century. There is more religious education, mosques are erected, Imams and other religious functionaries are consulted, there are pilgrimages to Mecca, prayers are observed in a more orthodox fashion, and so on.[2] The *Ikhwan* settlements of Saudi Arabia had a religious mission—to draw their members out of their primitive ignorance.

Settlement also meant an end to the special establishments of beduin jurisdiction. In early stages the arbitration systems of tribal society still remain, but the settling beduins have more and more recourse to the religious courts (for personal status) and to civil jurisdiction (for other cases).[3]

The most outstanding change accompanying settlement is the new economic, social, and political status of the *shaikh*. Among nearly all tribes which settled in the nineteenth and twentieth centuries the ex-shaikhs became large landowners, while tribal members were scattered among the fellahs (as among the Shammar, in the Jazira) or became tenants and labourers of the shaikhs (as in Southern Iraq).

By various means, large stretches of land came into the hands of shaikhs. In the Fertile Crescent, for example, their economic standing enabled shaikhs to register much of the tribal property in their names, and in Egypt the rulers granted them large stretches of uncultivated land in order to bring such land into agricultural use and to speed up colonisation of the tribes.[4] On

---

[1] Salim, pp. 133–5; Weulersse, p. 217.

[2] G. Baer, 'Some Aspects of Bedouin Sedentarization in 19th Century Egypt', *WI*, Vol. V, No. 1–2, pp. 95–6.

[3] Ammar, p. 60; Jamali, p. 73.

[4] For detailed description of this process, with bibliography, see Baer, *Some Aspects of Bedouin Sedentarization*, pp. 90–3. In addition to sources mentioned there, see Warriner, *Land and Poverty*, pp. 104–16; Epstein, pp. 89–90; Jaussen, *Moab*, pp. 136–7.

their part, the shaikhs were eager to become landowners as soon as agriculture changed from subsistence economy to production of marketable crops bringing in large profits (in nineteenth-century Egypt and twentieth-century Fertile Crescent countries).

Thus, settlement generally brought wealth to the shaikhs; many increased the number of their servants, built a castle or fortress, and even bought a car. Eventually, many shaikhs transferred to the towns, which became the centre of their economic and political activities. Here they have entered the high ranks of urban society by marriage connections, and have identified themselves with the vested interests of that society, while tribal connections have weakened completely. In early stages of settlement this has at times led to violent clashes between shaikhs and their tribes.[1]

4. *THE BEDUIN IN THE MODERN STATE*

Despite the growing settlement of the last generation, there is still a nomadic population in most of the Arab Middle Eastern countries, and there are still settled tribes which preserve their earlier traditions. Some of these traditions conflict sharply with the orderly administration of a modern state. A Government acting in accordance with modern principles of rule finds it difficult to put up with the *ghazw*. Another awkward question is whether and to what extent a Government can agree to tribesmen bearing arms. In some regions collection of taxes from beduins and definition of their land rights became difficult problems.

An attempt on the part of the 1934 Iraqi Government to impose conscription in tribal areas was one of the main causes of the 1937 tribal uprising against the Government.[2] Even in Egypt, beduins were exempted from military service according to the 1902 Law of Military Service, and an attempt to change the situation in 1926 aroused much opposition on the part of the tribes. The Conscription Law of 1947 no longer included a clause on beduin exemption, but in 1951, by a special law, the

[1] Mubarak, XIV, 38; XVII, 33; Montagne, pp. 199–200, 215–16; Jamali, pp. 72, 134; Baer, *loc. cit.*, pp. 93–5.
[2] M. Khadduri, *Independent Iraq*, London, 1951, pp. 62, 117–18.

Egyptian Government was again forced to release the inhabitants of its desert areas from their military obligations.[1]

Disputes between Iraq and Saudi Arabia, between the latter and Jordan, and between Syria and Iraq have been caused by beduin tribes on the two sides of the frontiers. There has been fundamental disagreement between the governments and the tribes on the question of blood revenge, or the custom of *fasl* among Iraqi tribes—that is, payment of women in compensation for murder or other damage.[2]

The last-mentioned problem, and altogether, the juxtaposition of tribal law and civil or religious law, has been solved in most of the states which were established after the First World War by means of special official tribal law courts. These courts are composed of shaikhs or beduin judges who conduct the trials in accordance with beduin practices, under governmental supervision. Meanwhile, the authorities have tried to abolish certain customs, such as blood-revenge, bestowal of women as compensation, etc. The Iraqi 'Tribal Criminal and Civil Disputes Regulation' of 1916 stipulated that a tribal *majlis* shall be set up to judge members by their customary code, but that the authorities are empowered to validate or nullify their decisions. The situation rested there, with only slight modifications, until the 1958 revolution. However, the authorities did not succeed in convincing tribal judges that *fasl* is not a suitable punishment for murder, or that the murder of a woman for moral misbehaviour should also be penalised by a death sentence; at any rate, in some respects, the beduin viewpoint remains victorious to this day. Similarly, in the Sudan legislation of the 1920s granted nomadic shaikhs juridical and administrative authority within the framework of State-established and State-controlled institutions. Theoretically, no such institutions were to be found in twentieth-century Egypt. In fact, however, there have been cases in which the *majlis 'urfi* of tribal heads was summoned to judge criminal cases under state supervision.[3]

---

[1] *OM*, VI (1926), pp. 496–7; and laws of 28 August 1947 and 30 September 1951.

[2] Salim, pp. 140–1, 145–6. The transfer of a woman as restitution for murder is also practised among Transjordanian tribes—see Jaussen, *Moab*, pp. 223–5.

[3] For Iraq see P. W. Ireland, *Iraq, A Study in Political Development*, London, 1937, pp. 85–7; for the Sudan—Macmichael, pp. 107–10; for Egypt—Sir Thomas Russell Pasha, *Egyptian Service 1902–1946*, London, 1949, pp. 68 ff.

In Palestine the British authorities set up a *majlis ad-dumum* ('blood council') in an attempt to settle old blood feuds, and in the 1920s, tribal law courts were established, appointments being made by the Government. Here too a district officer sat in the court of appeal, but the courts continued to judge by beduin practices. According to a law of 12 January 1936, tribal courts were established in Transjordan, composed of tribal judges ratified by the Emir. They pass judgement according to tribal customs; for example, in a murder case 'when the murderer is known' his relatives up to the fifth degree may also be tried. On the other hand, the system prohibited revenge and 'deals in which there was any trade of women'. The governor (the commander of the Arab Legion in the desert region) could appeal against any decision.[1]

A more radical attempt to reduce the legal autonomy of beduins was made in Syria in 1953. According to a regulation of 21 May 1953 on the status of tribes, murder was no longer to be tried by tribal law, but rather by the ordinary law, and the juridical authority of the 'tribal committee' of the Government was extended. In 1958 this law too was annulled, and by a regulation of 29 September 1958 the beduins are now liable to the same laws as other citizens.[2] In Iraq, after the revolution in 1958, tribal law was abolished and replaced by the ordinary legislation.[3] In Saudi Arabia the shari'a laws, which, at least in theory, are the laws of the State, apply to tribesmen also.

In the sphere of *administration* the Middle Eastern states were more rigorous in their attempts to adapt the beduin to the existing system of rule. In Egypt Muhammad 'Ali appointed beduin shaikhs to governmental posts in 1833. A similar effort of Midhat Pasha in Iraq, in about 1870, failed. However, under the modern administration, which was set up in Iraq after the First World War, shaikhs were granted official authority— a step which raised their standing and prestige. The same thing happened in some other countries in modern times.[4]

In Egypt, where the beduin problem was solved in the

---

[1] Text of the law in La Documentation Française, *Aperçu sur le problème du nomadisme au Moyen Orient*, No. 2.095, 3 November 1955, pp. 41–2.

[2] Ibid., pp. 37–9; *al-Ahram*, 29 September 1958.

[3] *OM*, 1958, p. 745.

[4] S. H. Longrigg, *Four Centuries of Modern Iraq*, Oxford, 1925, pp. 308–9; Jamali, p. 82; Ireland, pp. 94–5; Ja'far Khayyat, *al-Qarya al-'Iraqiya*, Beirut, 1950, pp. 44–5.

nineteenth century, a law of 1905 led to the complete amalgamation of tribes in the existing administrative system, by creating
official posts, not only at the rank of shaikh but also at lower
levels.[1] The Syrian law of 21 May 1953 tried to amend past
neglect in the same way: it raised the number of tribes, abolished the tribal status of 'semi-nomads', converting them into
ordinary citizens, simplified the legalities of transition from
migratory tribesmen to sedentary villagers, defined the 'region
of migration', limited the rights of tribes to bear arms, and
organised the appointment and dismissal of tribal chiefs and
mukhtars. It stipulated precisely that *ghazw* and forceful collection of *khuwa* are offences whose punishment is severe. Several
months previously, by a special regulation of 29 October 1952,
ownership of *mawat* land (land that the beduins had been
accustomed to treat as their own) was transferred to the State,
and beduin rights over some of the land they had previously
held were withdrawn. The regulation also repealed statutes of
the Mandatory period, according to which unregistered land
east of the 'desert line' had been explicitly excluded from state
control and handed over to the tribes.[2]

A further step towards adapting the beduins to a modern
state was made by granting them *political representation* in the
parliaments existing in some Arab countries. According to the
1947 Jordanian Election Law, the beduins received two seats
in parliament; their representatives are elected by two committees, each composed of ten shaikhs, representing the
northern and southern beduins respectively. A 1960 election
law raised the number to three.[3] In Syria the 1949 Election
Law stated that the 'special advisory committee of nomadic
beduins' shall elect six delegates to parliament from among the
literate members; there have been several changes since, none
of them fundamental, in the number of delegates and manner
of representation.[4] In Iraq tribes do not have proportional

---

[1] Text in Documentation Française, *Nomadisme*, pp. 45–6.

[2] Text in *MEJ*, Vol. 7, pp. 69–72. See also D. Warriner, *Land Reform and Development in the Middle East*, London, 1957, pp. 99–105. Apparently these regulations are
not actually put into effect—see *al-Ahram*, 19 April 1958.

[3] *Filastin*, 29 August 1961; *OM*, 1961, p. 600.

[4] H. M. Davis, *Constitutions, Electoral Laws, Treaties of States in the Near and Middle
East*, Durham, N.C., 1953, pp. 260, 434. Documentation Française, *Nomadisme*,
pp. 39, 43.

representation, but because of their great influence, shaikhs and tribal heads constituted a considerable proportion of the parliamentary representatives; by one estimation for the parliament elected in January of 1953, there were 66 shaikhs out of a total of 135 members.[1] In Saudi Arabia, until a few years ago, almost all the advisers of local emirs were shaikhs and tribal heads. However, the social and political trends of recent years, both in Saudi Arabia and in Iraq, have considerably weakened the political influence of tribal shaikhs.

B. THE FELLAH

1. *LAND AND LAND TENURE*

In most of the Arab countries of the Middle East some two-thirds of the population is rural.

Land is the main factor which determines the material and social life of the fellah. An outstanding feature of much of the Arab Middle East, however, is the fellah's detachment from the land, mainly because he is not its owner and also because of nomadic influences. This is particularly true of the plains of the Fertile Crescent, where the fellah is reputed for his contempt for land and agricultural work. It is also the main region of tenancy.

It was this region that Weulersse had in mind when he wrote:

Paradoxical, in our Western eyes even shocking, is the existence of a peasant population in the East which lacks all peasant atavism; here are people of the land who have no feeling for the land or respect for it, farmers who despise farming, tillers of the land who loathe the plough, villagers who disavow their village in order to remain faithful to their tribe. The peasant masses of the Middle East exist in a state of self-rejection. This is quite unique, an almost pathological situation among farmers in the whole world.[2]

In contrast, wherever the land is the property of small land-owners and nomadic influences are not great, the fellah's attachment to his land is greater. This is the case, for instance,

---

[1] *Hamizrah Hehadash*, IV, p. 193.
[2] Weulersse, *Paysans de Syrie*, p. 66.

in the orchard and garden area around Damascus, in the Lebanon, and in some other hilly regions of the Fertile Crescent.

According to Tannous, a deep attachment to the land is felt by the small-scale Lebanese farmer who has been a landowner for many generations.[1] In the hills of Lebanon land is a dearly loved family possession which is sold only under dire necessity and then, when possible, only to members of the family. Most authors describing Egyptian villages stress the strong ties of the fellah to his land and village, and Ayrout even claims that for an Egyptian fellah 'to desert the village means death'.[2]

At all events, land is of utmost importance in fashioning rural society, since *land tenure* is the basis of economic and social life of the villagers.

Until the start of the nineteenth century in Egypt, and until the middle of that century in the other Arab countries, land tenure took a form generally known as *Iltizam*, whereby tax-farming rights were granted to Mamluk soldiers, heads of prominent families, Beduin shaikhs, religious dignitaries, and so on. In return for a fixed payment to the State, each tax-farmer received a village or villages, the income from which was his for the extortion, as well as a private lot of land.

It would not be correct to call this system 'feudalism'. Except in the tribal regions, the tax-farmers were city dwellers, who were replaced from time to time and had no attachments to their estates. Their function was not to raise an army for the central authorities but only to pay over the taxes. There were, then, none of the formal ties of loyalty between tax-farmer and ruler. The basic reason for this system in Egypt, where it has existed since the sixteenth century, was the centralised nature of the Government and its importance for the economy and protection of the country. Only in those areas where the central authorities were not in complete control, such as the hilly

[1] A. I. Tannous, 'The Arab Village Community of the Middle East', *Annual Report of the Smithsonian Institution, 1943*, Washington, 1944, pp. 530–1. However, Tannous apparently tends to idealise the state of the fellah and to ignore the difference between the Lebanese farmer and the Arab fellah in general.

[2] For Lebanon see Touma, pp. 44, 150; Fuller, p. 6. For Egypt—H. H. Ayrout, *Fellahs*, Cairo, 1942, p. 108; and Ammar, pp. 21–2 and Chapter III. This does not mean that there is no emigration from Egyptian villages; on the contrary, emigration is on the rise in this generation. According to Berque, the number of emigrants from the village of Sirs al-Layan will soon equal the number of its present inhabitants (Berque, *Histoire sociale*, p. 23).

regions of Lebanon and the Kurdish hills, was there a state of landed and military feudalism, the feudal rule being transmitted as part of the inheritance within a certain family.

This system was abolished in Egypt by Muhammad 'Ali in 1812–14, and in the Ottoman Empire in the 1830s. The process was gradual, and in fact took several decades. The State took over ownership of the land, and taxes were collected directly from its tillers by officials, without the intervention of *multazims* (tax-farmers) or other persons having feudal rights.

The State, which owned most of the land, then began to transfer ownership rights to private individuals too. The process went through various stages and proceeded at different rates, more rapid in Egypt, slower and less complete in the countries of the Fertile Crescent. The State differentiated between *raqaba*—ownership of the land itself—and *tasarruf*—the right to use the land and enjoy its produce (*usufruct*). The *raqaba* of most land remained in the hands of the State, which could thus periodically redefine the rights of *tasarruf* owners: to what extent they could sell their rights, mortgage them, transmit them to heirs, and so on. The State, then, did not transfer full ownership of agricultural lands to private individuals; the land remained *miri* (from the word *amiriya*—of the state).

While *tasarruf* rights were strictly defined by the Ottoman Land Law of 1858, they were gradually extended in the Fertile Crescent, particularly by laws of 1913 and 1930–2 in Syria and Iraq, until they included the right to sell, mortgage, hand down to heirs (though not according to Muslim inheritance laws), and even to bequeath by will (except in Palestine), but not to endow freely as *waqf* (see below). Ownership rights of *miri* land, which even now constitutes the greater part of all agricultural land in the Fertile Crescent, are then largely similar to full ownership (*mulk*).

In Egypt there was at first only an extension of *tasarruf* rights over *miri* land (there called *kharajiya*, as against *'ushuriya*, land under full ownership), but it was very much more rapid, and at the same time the area of land held in full ownership increased. Moreover, at the end of the century the State, being in financial straits, was forced to grant full ownership rights (including *raqaba*) to such owners of *kharajiya* land as made advance payment of six years' taxes (the *muqabala* law of 1871); in the 1890s all differences between the two categories were abolished. Thus the twentieth century found the agricultural land of Egypt held with full ownership rights (*mulk*), and no *miri* land remains.

This is not the only difference between the Fertile Crescent and Egypt from the viewpoint of land tenure. After the abolition of *iltizam*, *tasarruf* rights were recorded in the two regions in the name of those possessing them. In Egypt registration was successful, while in the Fertile Crescent it failed completely, and to this day not all land is registered in the name of its owner.

The reasons for the failure were: (1) the administrative weakness of the Ottoman Empire; (2) the tribal, unsettled character of a considerable part of the population of the Fertile Crescent; (3) the practice, common in the Fertile Crescent, of holding lands collectively, in the name of the whole village (*musha'*), which prevented registration of individual ownership rights. For land-registration purposes, the *musha'* had to be divided up—a process known as *ifraz*. In fact, this is what was done in the Fertile Crescent countries, and in the 1930s registration started again. By the middle of the century, Transjordan had registered about two-thirds of all its land, Iraq about one-half, and Syria 45%, as compared with Egypt, all of whose land had been registered by the beginning of the century.

Registration was in terms of 'owners' and kinds of ownership. From what has been said, it is apparent that one kind of land exists in the Fertile Crescent countries but not in Egypt—that known as *miri*. The other categories are *mulk*,[1] *matruka* (public domain),[2] *mawat-mubah* (State domain), and *waqf*. The last two categories require further explanation.

Mawat-mubah is uncultivated land outside the settlement ('beyond the distance sound carries'), over which ownership rights may be acquired by the tiller. This regulation led to the

[1] *Mulk* land constituted no more than 0·3% of all land registered in Iraq up to 1951. Practically all agricultural land of Syria and Palestine is *miri*, houses and gardens alone being *mulk*. In Lebanon much agricultural land is *mulk*, i.e., held with full ownership rights.

[2] *Matruka* (public domain) accounted for the following percentages of all registered land at the middle of this century: Egypt (1949)—10·8%; Iraq (1951)—3·4%; Transjordan (1950)—1·5%.

appropriation of *mawat* land by influential notables, beduin shaikhs, and others; eventually the State found it necessary to claim full ownership over such land and unite it with other land under similar conditions of full State ownership. In Iraq a law to that effect was passed in 1938.[1] This problem of land tenure is particularly severe in Syria, and only in 1952 was the State granted full and indisputable ownership over such land. Legally speaking, the term *mawat* (or *mubah*) remains, but in practice it is nowadays called *amlak ad-daula* or *aradi al-hukuma* and in Iraq, *miri sirf*. The relative extent of *mawat* land is lower in Egypt (17% of all land in 1950) and higher in the Fertile Crescent: about 30% in Transjordan (1953), 40% in Syria (1952), and 60% in Iraq (1951). This is because there are more tillable areas in the Fertile Crescent, which are registered while not under cultivation and not privately owned.[2]

Waqf is a form of endowment unique to Islamic countries, but having elements in common with institutions which used to exist or still exist in other countries. When a certain piece of property is turned into waqf it may no longer be used in ordinary transactions. The income from waqf property is devoted to religious, cultural, or charitable purposes. A distinction is then made between waqf property ownership *per se*, which is not negotiable (its ultimate ownership being in fact somewhat ambiguous), and the right to income derived from it.

A person who turns his property into waqf decides who is to benefit from it as he sees fit (the settlement being recorded in the waqf document or *waqfiya*), on condition that the line of beneficiaries does not end. In order to fulfil this condition, the last in that line must be a religious or cultural institution or a charitable cause (the poor of a certain city, a particular mosque, etc.). The last beneficiary will, then, eventually receive the income from property turned waqf, though usually not at once. It is customary for the first beneficiaries to be the members of the founder's family, or some of them—for example, only the sons. This form of waqf is called *waqf ahli* (in the Fertile Crescent, *waqf dhurri*), as distinct from *waqf khairi*, the

[1] Salah ad-Din Nahi, *Muqaddima fi'l-iqta' wa-nizam al-aradi fi'l-'Iraq*, Baghdad, 1955, p. 17.
[2] For detailed treatment of this question see G. Baer, 'Land Tenure in the Hashemite Kingdom of Jordan', *Land Economics*, August 1957, p. 189.

income of which passes immediately to a religious, cultural, or philanthropic institution. Furthermore, the founder of a waqf must specify in the *waqfiya* who is to manage the property and supervise distribution of its income. The supervisor may be a centralised establishment (such as the Ministry of Waqfs, which was established in most of the countries concerned for running those properties which for any reason have no other supervisor) or a private individual, usually a respected public figure, a religious dignitary, or in many cases of *ahli waqf*, the head, in each generation, of the founder's family. Only property which is under the full ownership of the endower may be converted into waqf. Thus, in most of the countries of the Fertile Crescent (except Lebanon) the greater part of all agricultural land, being *miri*, could not be endowed, and thus most of the waqfs in these countries are urban properties.[1] This is not the case in Egypt, where by the middle of the century the area of agricultural waqf land reached 10% of all land (excluding State and public domain) and 7% of all registered land.

The main purposes of those who endowed their property as waqf were: (1) to strengthen the position and influence of their families and to maintain this position (for example, by turning the income of the waqf over to the family guest house); (2) to prevent the family from losing its land or property through sale or waste, and particularly to maintain large estates; (3) as a protection from confiscation or seizure of the land by the rulers. Indeed, the religious stamp of the institution of waqf has often helped a family to hold on to its property; (4) to bypass the Muslim inheritance laws, and particularly to disinherit daughters, who have rights to inherit according to these laws. This is done by an instruction in the waqf document stating that any daughter, or a married daughter, shall not have any part in the income from the waqf. This prevents loss of part of the property to the family which a daughter joins on marriage; (5) to avert the possibility of descendants sinking into debt. Many of those who have established waqfs in modern Egypt specified in the waqf document that a beneficiary who borrowed money thereby relinquished his rights to a part in the waqf income.

[1] In Iraq, *waqf* land constituted 1·2% of all registered agricultural land in 1951; in Transjordan the figure was 0·03% in 1950.

Waqf served an important cultural function by contributing the material basis for educational and scientific institutions at a time when there was no dependable governmental budget for such ends. In the twentieth century, however, waqf has lost any such significance, and its drawbacks are becoming increasingly evident; property is tied up in such a manner that it cannot be mortgaged or sold in part in order to finance its amelioration or development; large estates are maintained and concentrated in the hands of persons of high religious or political rank (King Faruq was in charge of about 120,000 feddan of waqf land in Egypt);[1] and finally, the administrators of waqfs have been notorious for the corruption and neglect which have spread among them, since the inception of the institution.

Distribution of Landed Property

The above discussion was devoted to the types of landowner-ship in terms of which the land was registered. Since this registration took place after the abolition of landholding by feudal lords of the various kinds, or *multazims*, it might be imagined that privately held land would be registered in the name of the person who cultivated it, and the result would be a more or less equitable distribution of landed property among the fellahs. In fact, this is not what happened. In most of the countries of the Middle East much of the land became con-centrated in the hands of a limited number of large landowners. How and when did this occur?

(1) One of the most important reasons in the Fertile Crescent was the actual registration of land. Various factors led the fellahs to register the land not in their own names, but rather in the name of a city notable or village authority. The factors were: (*a*) fear of taxation or conscription; (*b*) desire to prevent splitting of the *mushaʿ* (Article 8 of the Ottoman Land Law specifies that collective ownership is illegal); (*c*) for the sake of patronage land was registered in the name of a city notable in the hope that he would intercede with the authorities; (*d*) cheating and bribery by the notables, armed terrorising,

---

[1] *al-Ahram*, 11 August, 19 October 1952; 27 February, 5 August 1954.

and so on. The fellahs, in their ignorance and helplessness, dared not oppose.

(2) Seizure of *mawat* land, particularly in Syria.

These two factors operated chiefly in the Fertile Crescent countries.[1] Among causes equally relevant to Egypt, we may note:

(3) Seizure of the land of fellahs for payment of debts, incurred at exorbitant rates of interest. In particular, rich city merchants who bought the produce of the fellahs became land-owners; they then continued to lend money, using the profits to add to their estates. (In this way, for example, the merchants of Homs and Hama in Syria became large landowners.)

(4) The Sultan (in Egypt, the Viceroy—the Khedive) was at one and the same time owner of all State property and a private landowner. Hence he could confiscate State land as he saw fit and make it his own. This is how the ruling families became the largest landowners in these countries, until their land was transferred anew to the State (in 1879 in Egypt, 1908 in the Ottoman Empire). Nevertheless, the Muhammad 'Ali family of Egypt still remained the largest landowner.

(5) Not only did the Sultan and Khedive take over land for themselves but they also bestowed it on officials and other persons who served them.

(6) On settlement of beduin tribes, shaikhs became large landowners in Southern Iraq, in the Jazira and along the Euphrates in Syria, and in Central Egypt (Fayyum, Minya).

Some further factors operated mainly in Egypt:

(7) Transfer of uncultivated land to capitalists or to persons with economic and political power, for its reclamation. This is one of the main ways in which large estates were formed in nineteenth-century Egypt.

(8) Between 1880 and 1950 the State sold in Egypt approxim-ately $1\frac{1}{4}$ million feddan of land. The buyers were the new class of wealthy town-dwellers and village dignitaries, as well as foreigners and land companies established mainly by minority

---

[1] Details in Weulersse, pp. 95, 102, 115–17, 254–5; A. Latron, *La Vie rurale en Syrie et au Liban*, Beirut, 1936, pp. 213–15; A. Granott, *The Land System in Palestine*, London, 1952, pp. 50–2, 55, 74–5.

groups in Egypt (Jews, Christians, Italians, and others). These sales were the origin of many of the large estates existing in Egypt at the time of the agrarian reform.

This century has, then, seen larger and larger areas of land passing into the hands of large landowners in all the countries of the Arab Middle East. The new class of large landowners was composed of beduin shaikhs, heads of important families traditionally of leading rank in social and political affairs both in the cities and the villages, city merchants, the families of rulers and their officials, and in Egypt the founders of land companies also. Members of this new class were, on the whole, city-dwellers from the start, or eventually transferred to the cities. The large landowner took pains to avert resplitting of his estate or the sale of part of it by his descendants. Thus, 'presents' were made to one heir at the expense of the others; the estate was registered in the name of one of the sons during the lifetime of the father of the family (this was the custom in Transjordan, for example); and in Egypt estates were endowed as waqf. Intermarriage within the large landowner class also helped to keep estates together. This is not to imply that the new large estates formed in the nineteenth and twentieth centuries never broke up as a result of inheritance and sale, but at least all the efforts noted here had a conserving influence.

The case of small landowners was different. Their plots were split up and disintegrated. The process was particularly severe in Egypt, because of rapid population increase and because Muslim inheritance laws were applicable to Egyptian *mulk* property (in contrast to *miri* property of the Fertile Crescent, which was not transferred according to these laws). Thus, many Egyptian fellahs became the owners of minute land-holdings which were insufficient to support their family.

Furthermore, all over the Middle East there are small fellahs who have become landless, and as such now constitute a considerable segment of the rural population. Their number in Egypt is officially estimated at 1·5 millions (actually, far more), as against 2·7 million landowners (actually less); in Transjordan they constitute a third of the agricultural population, and in Iraq, according to official data, up to two-thirds. Loss of land was augmented during periods of crisis, such as those of 1907 and after 1929 in Egypt, when the small fellah lacked the means to pay his debts. Various State programmes—such as the attempt to sell land to the fellah on easy terms of payment, the setting up of institutions giving credit to the small fellah, and even the Five Feddan Law[1]—could not stem the process. The distribution of landed property at mid-century according to size is summarised in the following table. Data refer to countries of the Arab Middle East for which official figures have been published.[2]

Distribution of Landed Property in the Arab East at the Middle of the Twentieth Century

| Country | Year | % of total registered area in hands of | | |
		Small-scale owners	Medium-scale owners	Large-scale owners
Iraq	1951	15·7	17·2	67·1
Syria	1952	13·0	38·0	49·0
Egypt	1950	35·3	30·5	34·2
Transjordan	1950	36·3	49·5	14·2

Of course, this table does not reflect the considerable differences among various regions within the countries themselves. Generally speaking, the following regions may be singled out for small-scale landed property: most of the hilly parts of the Fertile Crescent (such as Northern Transjordan, Mount Lebanon, and Jabal ad-Druz), the orchard and garden regions near the towns (e.g., the Ghutah of Damascus), and in Egypt the densely populated provinces (such as Suhaj and Asyut in Upper Egypt and Minufiya and Giza in Lower Egypt). Regions of large estates are: the lowlands of Northern Syria (the districts of Homs, Hama, Salmiya, Ma'arrat an-Nu'man, Bab, Manbij), the lowlands of Lebanon ('Akkar in the north, al-Biqa' in the east and south), the environs of the cities of

[1] A law of 1912, which prohibited sequestration of the land and farm of a fellah for non-payment of debts, if his property was smaller than 5 feddans. See G. Baer, *A History of Landownership in Modern Egypt 1800–1950*, London, 1962, pp. 89–90.

[2] Egyptian and Jordanian data according to official statistical yearbooks. Data for Syria and Iraq according to IBRD, *The Economic Development of Syria*, pp. 354–5; IBRD, *The Economic Development of Iraq*, Baltimore, 1952, p. 142. For purposes of comparison, a small landowner is taken to be one who owns less than 100 dunums in Syria or Transjordan, less than 100 Iraqi dunums (250 metric dunums) in Iraq, or less than 5 feddans in Egypt. Large-scale owners are taken to own over 1,000 dunums, 1,000 Iraqi dunums, or 50 feddans, respectively.

'Amman and Jerusalem in Jordan, several tribal provinces of Southern Iraq (particularly Kut, 'Amara, and Muntafik), and in Egypt the development provinces in which individuals and companies have obtained large areas in the last fifty years (such as Buhaira, Aswan, Gharbiya, etc.).

It is to be noted that in certain parts of the Middle East in which water and irrigation supplies are limited there are clear-cut definitions and precise laws governing ownership rights of these sources, while ownership of the land *per se* is of secondary importance. This is the case, for example, in Southern Cyrenaica and in some districts of Syria.

Tenancy

Absentee ownership of land is common in the Middle East. The landlord lives in the city, while his property is tilled by a fellah who is himself landless.

Little has been published about the area of land leased to and cultivated by the fellah. It appears that in Jordan there is relatively little land that is not cultivated by its owner, for according to the 1953 census of agriculture 76·2% of the area of all holdings was the property of their holders. The picture is entirely different in Egypt, where the leased area was approximately 60% of all cultivated land at the middle of the century.[1] Nor did all the remaining 40% refer to holdings owned by small fellahs, for some of the large estates are cultivated 'directly' (*ala adh-dhimma*)—actually by hired labour. Examples are the property of the land companies during their amelioration, and some estates of Upper Egypt, where fellahs are employed as temporary workers in the densely populated regions. In Syria large estates are seldom farmed by hired labour.

Lease under terms of cash rentals is also very rare in Syria, while in Egypt this is nowadays one of the commonest arrangements in agricultural holdings. State domain, waqf land, tracts in the environments of the large cities, and some of the large- and medium-sized estates are usually let for cash rentals. At present sharecropping is on the decline in Egypt; the system,

[1] 1949—60·7%; 1954—57·0%. Sayyid Mar'i, *al-Islah az-zira'i fi misr*, Cairo, 1957, p. 230.

known as *muzara'a*, means lease of the land of an estate in exchange for part of the crops, or some other arrangement (such as cultivation of the estate for payment in kind, or lease of part of the land to the fellah, who farms it all—a system which was still common at the beginning of the century).[1]

On the other hand, sharecropping is very much in evidence in Syria and Iraq. In Syria it takes various forms, the most widespread being *muraba'a*, by which the fellah receives a quarter of the crops, the landlord supplying land, seeds, and farm animals. In orchard farms a system known as *mugharasa* exists, whereby ownership over different parts of the orchard is eventually divided between farmer and landlord. Most land in Iraq is let by the *muhassa* system, according to which the crops are divided among several factors, each person's share depending on the method of irrigation, the manner in which the land is owned, and the supply of equipment.[2] In some Middle Eastern countries there is evidently yet another system, whereby the fellahs, who are themselves small landowners, let their land to larger-scale landowners, not having the means to cultivate their own land. Syria is the scene of a new system— beduin shaikhs let their land to urban merchants, who own tractors and farm huge stretches of land in the Jazira with the aid of hired labour.[3]

In various parts of the Arab Middle East there are still traces of the *musha'* system. The lands of the whole village are divided up according to quality; every year or so they are distributed by lot among the families of the village, each family receiving one or more plots according to the number of its members (or the number of animals). Opinions on the origin of the system are divided. It was definitely the principal manner of landholding in Upper Egypt until the first half of the nineteenth century, and in the Fertile Crescent until the First World War. It predominated during the era of *iltizam*, when the village had to pay its taxes collectively to the tax-farmer and its inhabitants wanted to divide up the burden in a

---

[1] In various parts of Egypt a combination of these systems is applied. Inflation during the war was responsible for a temporary increase in *muzara'a* contracts.

[2] Khayyat, p. 22. Details in Sa'id Himadeh, *an-Nizam al-iqtisadi fi'l-'Iraq*, Beirut, 1938, pp. 147–51.

[3] Baer, *Land Tenure in Jordan*, pp. 192–3; Warriner, *Land Reform and Development*, pp. 89–93.

fair manner. The *musha'* began to disintegrate when differentiation within the village made its appearance, as a result of agricultural ties with the market, and when ownership rights were registered on an individual basis. The two developments are interconnected, and they made their appearance in Egypt some fifty years earlier than in the Fertile Crescent. Together with the disintegration of the *musha'*, some other functions of the village community were also abolished, such as collective responsibility for conscription to military service and to forced labour in public works.[1] In Egypt no traces of the *musha'* are left; in Syria it has remained chiefly in those villages in which the land was not registered in the names of its fellah cultivators, but rather in the name of a city notable, shaikh, or official-turned-landowner. Hence it is now to be found mainly in the regions of large estates. It should be clear that the *musha'* is not a form of land *ownership* (like *mulk* or *miri*—most *musha'* land being in fact *miri*), but rather a method of *holding* land.[2]

A matter that has scarcely been investigated is the *status of the large landowner in village society* in the present-day Arab Middle East. Undoubtedly it would be a mistake to call the land tenure of the Northern Arab States[3] 'feudal', since generally the large landowner no longer has sovereignty over the region of his estate in such matters as jurisdiction, maintenance of a private standing army, and the authority to impose taxes or to compel his serfs to do forced labour. Moreover, the farming economy in both Egypt and the Fertile Crescent is now largely individualistic and dependent on a capitalistic market. Nevertheless, there do remain some fragments of feudal rule from a social point of view. The 'Law of Farmers' Rights and Liabilities' passed in Iraq in 1933 more or less tied the fellah to a landowner's estate,[4] but in recent years the scope of the law has been greatly curtailed by economic processes, of which more will be said later. The rule of tribal shaikhs on their

---

[1] See G. Baer, 'The Dissolution of the Egyptian Village Community', *WI*, Vol. VI, No. 1–2, pp. 56–70.

[2] The best analysis of the *musha'* system is that in Weulersse, *Paysans de Syrie*, pp. 99–108.

[3] Information on land tenure in the Sudan and the Arabian Peninsula is so sparse that these countries have not been included in the discussion.

[4] *Qanun huquq wa-wajibat az-zura'*, No. 28 of 1933—Khayyat, p. 21; Himadeh, pp. 151, 197. The law was abrogated by the Iraqi land reform in 1958.

estates has been weakened by the disintegration of the tribe, although their influence in State affairs has, if anything, risen.

In the regions of tenancy and large estates in Syria the fellah is bound to perform personal services of various kinds on behalf of his landowner and to carry out forced labour, reminiscent of serfdom in the Middle Ages. In certain regions such services are rendered in exchange for the protection and hospitality which the fellah may claim from prominent urban families to whom the village belongs. Forms of rule having 'feudal' characteristics are common also in hilly regions where it is difficult to impose central rule, such as the Druze and 'Alawi mountains.[1]

In Egypt many arguments have been advanced to show that land reform purposed to 'abolish feudalism'; when a certain Egyptian economist was asked what he meant by a feudal estate he replied: 'It means that the landowner keeps a private army to defend his house and his person, and that armed men stand guard over the crops.'[2] During implementation of the reform there were also reports of large landowners who ruled over the villages neighbouring their estates in affairs of jurisdiction, education, and social life in general.[3] Since, however, no research on the subject is available, it is difficult to decide whether these descriptions are realistic or no more than propaganda for political ends. In all events, it is clearly true that in Egypt, as in Iraq, the power of large landowners was felt particularly by their influence on the central government, through their representatives in Parliament, their part in high officialdom, etc.

2. AGRARIAN REFORM

The system of land tenure in the Arab East was responsible for various aspects of life which were harmful from economic, social, and political points of view. In the first place, it impeded economic development in the following ways:

[1] See, for instance, Jaussen, *Naplouse*, pp. 26, 140; Weulersse, pp. 124–5; Boktor, p. 51.

[2] Quoted by Warriner, *Land Reform and Development*, p. 13.

[3] A notorious case was that of Prince Yusuf Kemal's estate at Nag' Hamadi in Upper Egypt—*al-Ahram*, 15 February 1953, 27 January 1954, 3 April 1955.

(*a*) Since the fellah does not own his holding and the landlord lives at a distance from his estate, the land has been neglected by both parties.

(*b*) The *muzara'a* system does not encourage the fellah to make efforts or to introduce improvements, as he enjoys only part of the fruits of his labours.

(*c*) Under the *musha'* system there is no incentive to invest for ameliorating land, which in any case passes sooner or later into the hands of others. The aim of a landholder under such conditions is to exploit the land to its utmost.

(*d*) The *waqf* system causes neglect of property.

(*e*) Because of fragmentation of landed property, many farms are too small for efficient exploitation to be worthwhile.

(*f*) The 'monopoly' of large landowners and their public and political power enable them to maintain rents at a high level or even to raise them, while keeping farm wages low. The resulting low incomes barely suffice for the basic minimal needs of most fellahs of the Arab countries. Two-thirds of all the population subsists at a very low standard of living, and hence is not a market for domestic industry.

(*g*) Because of high rents, the greater security of landed property as compared with other possessions, and the social and political status of landowners, capitalists preferred in the past and to a large degree still prefer to invest their capital in land (or other immovable property) rather than in industry or other productive enterprises. Those who do not extend their landed property tend to spend much of their agricultural profits on conspicuous consumption or on usury at high interest.

Land tenure has evidently had some severe social and political consequences too:

(*a*) The low income and low standard of living of the fellah, caused mainly by the land tenure, are responsible for a high incidence of disease, ignorance, and an inferior level of culture, and hinder the development of a modern state.

(*b*) Concentration of powerful economic forces in the hands of a narrow stratum of large-scale landowners gave them great political power also. This is the reason why advanced social and economic legislation has been frustrated and social development projects delayed or prevented. Outstanding in this respect was Iraq before the revolution, but the situation in Syria and Egypt before the revolution was not very different.

(*c*) By the middle of the twentieth century much tension had developed between fellah and landowner; in some Middle Eastern Arab countries this tension found expression in the form of rebellions and agrarian unrest. Social tension in the village, particularly intense in Egypt, led in scores of cases to the murder of landowners, their agents, their overseers and guards, or the '*umdas* (village shaikhs). Acts of a similar nature were frequent in the 'thirties after the crisis; following foreclosures of fellahs' land in the 'forties; and during breakdowns of supply, spread of epidemics, and a deepening of the scale of social differences after the war. In 1951 Egypt was the scene of several conflicts concerning rentals which led to clashes between fellahs and landowners.[1] In the same year there was friction between large landowners of the Homs and Hama districts of Syria and their fellahs, who refused to hand over the owner's share in the crops and drove them off the estates. In 1952 fellahs of the province of 'Amara in Iraq rebelled and refused to pay the shaikhs their share in the crops, and in 1954 fellahs staged demonstrations demanding equal shares of the crops for themselves and the estate owners.[2]

Despite social tension in the village, which has steadily grown since the Second World War, Egyptian political parties were unyielding in their objection to any reform in the distribution of landed property, or in the laws governing relations between fellah and landlord, up to the time of the military revolt and even afterwards. This attitude has its roots in the overwhelming influence that the large landowners had on every political party in Egypt. At that time a group of intellectuals demanded a mild agrarian reform, whereby existing estates would remain untouched and only the formation of new ones would be limited. A more extreme approach—to limit existing estates, to confiscate all land exceeding a certain area, and to distribute it among the fellahs—was voiced by a number of left-wing publicists only. On the other hand, there was some

[1] For the 1930s see Ayrout, *Fellahs*, p. 34; for the 1940s—'Aziz Khanqi, 'hawadith al-ightiyal fi'l-aryaf', *al-Ahram*, 23 October 1944; for the 1950s—Baer, *History of Landownership*, p. 221.

[2] Syrian and Iraqi Press as reported in *Hamizrah Hehadash*, III, pp. 59, 170–1; IV, p. 117; V, p. 211; *al-Ahram*, 10 February 1954.

disagreement among the Egyptian political parties on the subject of waqf. Some adhered to the conservative view, opposing any changes because of the religious nature of waqf. Others have demanded since the early 'twenties that changes in a modern spirit be instituted in the waqf laws, and there were even those who went so far as to demand abolition of *ahli* waqf.[1]

In Syria Akram Haurani's party was the principal claimant of agrarian reform, and in 1951 it supported the fellahs against the landowners. Its programme, after unification with the Ba'th party, included the demand 'to limit landed property in keeping with the extent to which the landowner is able to exploit it to the full, without exploiting anyone else...' (Article 30), but at later stages the party concentrated on its demand to improve the state of tenant and agricultural labourer.[2]

In Iraq, where the situation was perhaps more urgent, the demand for agrarian reform was less insistent than in Syria or Egypt. Towards the end of 1952 some parties (among them that of Nuri as-Sa'id) did include in their programme the slogan to limit landed property; however, this was apparently the result of fomentation among Iraqi fellahs and the reaction to Egyptian agrarian reform which had come into effect two months before. There are no signs that the proponents of reform tried to put their ideas into effect.

Of the three countries,[3] Iraq introduced the fewest agrarian amendments before the revolution of 1958. The only relevant legislation was the Law of Development of Miri Sirf Land of 1945 and its extension in 1951. This law called for the *distribution of state domain (miri sirf)* among the fellahs occupying it. Official figures on the territory divided up are very large, but actually a considerable part of the land was given over to shaikhs as the price for their concurrence with the law. In its very implementation, then, this law led to the establishment of new large estates. In Syria, too, a decree of 23 October 1952 stipulated that state domain be divided among the landless in

[1] Baer, *History of Landownership*, pp. 205–19.

[2] *Dustur hizb al-Ba'th al-'Arabi al-Ishtiraki* (n.p. or d., published in many editions); Warriner, *Land Reform and Development*, p. 109.

[3] In the rest of the Arab Middle East the only reforms carried out were land registration and division of the *musha'*.

holdings not exceeding 50 hectares in dry farming areas or 10 hectares in irrigated land.[1] In January 1953 provisions to implement the decree in the Jazira were made public, but the land was allotted mainly to beduin tribes, and no clear information on the results of the campaign is available.[2] The sale of public domain to small fellahs and the landless was also the avowed policy of all Egyptian governments up to the time of the revolution; in this way they hoped to avoid more drastic reform which might affect the estates of large landowners. The fellahs and landless peasants of Egypt did not benefit from these sales, since they usually did not have enough cash for the first payment, and thus could not compete in the public sales of state domain. The land was generally taken over by urban capitalists, who thereby amassed estates, or by existing landowners, who enlarged their properties.

The first country to institute *basic changes in the waqf system* was Syria. By Decree No. 16 of 16 May 1949 the establishment of new *dhurri* waqf or *mushtarak* (in part *dhurri* and in part *khairi*) was forbidden, and existing ones were abolished. By a second decree of 11 June 1949 the office of private administrator (*mutawalli*) of *khairiya waqfs* was abolished, and all such property was placed under the general Waqf Administration.[3] The Egyptian Government passed similar but more radical regulations after the revolution. According to a law of 14 September 1952, all waqf not endowed to charitable ends was abolished. Waqf property was distributed among the beneficiaries in the same proportions as its income had been divided. *Khairi* waqfs were not abolished, but according to a law of May 1953, private administrators of this type of waqf were instructed to hand their property over to the Ministry of Waqf, which was empowered to use the income as it saw fit (after ratification by the Supreme Waqf Council). A third law on waqf of July 1957 stated that agricultural waqf land is to be handed over to the Agrarian Reform Committee for distribution, and the sum received in exchange invested in development projects. These laws are being implemented, despite

---

[1] 1 hectare = 10 dunums = 2·4 feddans approx.

[2] Warriner, *Land Reform and Development*, pp. 159 ff. (Iraq) and 104 (Syria); IBRD, *The Economic Development of Syria*, p. 58.

[3] *OM* 1949, pp. 66–7.

certain difficulties encountered by the Egyptian Government.[1]

The Egyptian *Law of Agrarian Reform (al-islah al-zira'i)* of 9 September 1952[2] was the first law of its kind in any Arab country. The main clauses of the law may be summarised as follows:

(*a*) The maximal extent of landed property is limited to 200 feddan plus a further temporary allowance of at most 100 feddan for children. Exceptions are persons and companies engaged in amelioration of their land, industrial concerns which utilise the land for industrial products, and scientific concerns which utilise the land for industrial products, and scientific institutions, charitable societies, and *khairi* waqf.

(*b*) The area exceeding this limit will be confiscated within five years, the owners receiving as compensation a sum ten times the rent of the land (which is fixed at seven times the original tax). Payment is in the form of Government bonds at 3% interest, redeemable within thirty years. The bonds are non-negotiable, but are legal tender in payment for uncultivated land and land taxes.

(*c*) Expropriated land will be handed over to small fellahs, each receiving a small landholding of 2–5 feddan. The cost of the land will be the sum paid in compensation for its confiscation at an interest of 3% per annum plus 15% of the cost to cover expenses; equal yearly payments will be made over thirty years. The redistribution will be completed within five agricultural years.

(*d*) Those benefiting from the distribution, together with other landowners whose property does not exceed 5 feddan in area, will set up co-operative societies, whose concern it will be to grant credit to farmers, supply seeds and equipment, organise the application of efficient methods of cultivating the land, market the crops, and organise social services. These societies will act under the supervision of an official of the Ministry of Social Affairs.

[1] Details in G. Baer, 'Waqf Reform in Egypt', *St Antony's Papers*, Middle Eastern Affairs, Number One, London, 1958, pp. 71–6.
[2] Full text with all additions and amendments up to 1957 in Mar'i, *al-Islah az-zira'i*, pp. 313–36.

(*e*) It is forbidden to split agricultural land in any manner into units smaller than 5 feddan.

(*f*) It is forbidden to let agricultural land to anyone who does not himself till that land. The rental must not exceed seven times the original tax, or in cases of *muzara'a* it must not exceed half the crop after deduction of expenses. The period of lease is to be at least three years and the contract is to be in writing.

(*g*) The wages of an agricultural worker are to be re-evaluated yearly by a special committee. Agricultural workers may establish unions for protection of their rights.

The aims of the Egyptian agrarian reform may, then, be grouped in the following categories:

1. *Political Aims*. 'Abolition of agricultural feudalism (*iqta'*) in order to abolish political feudalism,'[1] i.e., cutting the ground from under the feet of Egypt's rulers by confiscating their estates and waqfs—the very basis of their rule.

2. *Social Aims*. Creation of a new state of social equilibrium and prevention of agrarian unrest by 'the establishment of a new class of small landowners';[2] raising the standard of living of the agricultural worker; and placing fellahs and agricultural workers under control of the State by means of the co-operatives and trade unions.

3. *Economic Aims*. Paving the way to industrialisation by diverting capital from the purchase of land towards investment in industry, and the formation of a domestic market by raising the standard of living of the village population.

Were these aims attained, or to what extent may they be expected to be realised in the near future?[3]

1. Of the 1,800 largest Egyptian landowners, nearly all areas of land beyond the 200-feddan allowance were confiscated over the five years immediately following agrarian reform. Furthermore, an order was issued (and carried out) in November 1953 for the expropriation of all property of the Muhammad 'Ali family, without exception and without compensation. This

---

[1] Binbashi (Lt.-Col.) Husain ash-Shafi'i in *al-Ahram*, 29 April 1953.
[2] Mar'i, *al-Islah az-zira'i*, pp. 33, 233, 227–8; and in *al-Ahram*, 4 September 1954.
[3] For detailed treatment of this question see G. Baer, 'An Appraisal of Egyptian Land Reform', *New Outlook*, October 1959, pp. 17–25.

step, and the appropriation of extensive areas of *khairi* waqf land from persons possessing powerful social and political influence, have completely overthrown the material basis of the political rule of that class.

2. From widespread evidence, it appears that the agrarian unrest which was prevalent before the revolution has quietened in recent years. However, agrarian reform cannot create the social equilibrium which was its intention, for five reasons:

(*a*) The confiscated and waqf lands have not yet been distributed in full; but even when they are, at some future date, they will account for only 10% of all the landless fellahs and owners of holdings smaller than 1 feddan. Thus, the reform cannot lead to the formation of a new class of small landowners, and it is even likely to arouse feelings of discrimination among those—the majority of fellahs—who do not receive any land at all.

(*b*) During the first years of the reform the clauses on lease were implemented and rents fell. However, there are clear signs that, at least since 1957, rents have been raised again in various regions and the part of the law dealing with their limitation is not being enforced. Nevertheless, in the final appraisal there has evidently been some fall in rentals, if not to the extent required by law.[1] There is little hope that the claim for land, which has its origin in the natural population increase, will lessen in the future, and hence there is no reason to believe that the clauses on rentals and lease can be enforced in the future.

(*c*) The minimal wage for agricultural labour, fixed as a consequence of the law, has not been enforced even by Government departments.[2] As to conditions of work of the agricultural labourer, what has been said on rent and lease are valid here too, except that supervision is perhaps even more difficult. Moreover, the reform itself caused a certain decrease in the employment of agricultural workers, since the new landowners

---

[1] *al-Ahram*, 7 August, 9 September 1957; 29 April 1958; *al-Gumhuriya*, 6 and 8 August 1958; Wheelock, *Nasser's New Egypt*, p. 91.

[2] This matter has been frequently discussed even in semi-official newspapers; see *al-Gumhuriya*, 8 and 9 August, 19 September 1958. In May 1962 a delegate told the Congress of the Popular Force that one of his fellow labourers earned 8 piastres a day (instead of the legal minimum of 18). In reply, 'Abd an-Nasir admitted that the law is not enforced. See *al-Ahram*, 29 May 1962.

themselves do jobs which had formerly been given over to temporary labourers.

(*d*) The clauses on the prohibition of splitting plots into units smaller than 5 feddan are not being executed.[1]

(*e*) The Government has indeed increased its supervision and control of fellahs and agricultural labourers by means of the co-operatives (under central government direction) and the agricultural labourers' federations (organised under the auspices of Army officers of the revolution); but simultaneously, because of the very existence of co-operatives and reform, the self-awareness of the fellah has grown and he has become less submissive.[2]

3. The main economic aim of the reform—paving the way to industrialisation—has not succeeded; it may still be fulfilled at some future time, if conditions are suitable. Capital which accumulated before the revolution and had been used by its owners for the purchase of land now goes towards construction and the purchase of urban immovable property. In the years 1954–6 the sum of private capital invested in industrial concerns was about 12 million Egyptian pounds, as against 100 million Egyptian pounds in immovable urban property. When the Egyptian Government tried to stem this tendency by limiting rents in new buildings also the former landowners began to hoard gold and to use their capital for speculation.[3] The main industrial investment of recent years has been governmental; as a result of the reform, the Government has the resources (e.g., the income from sale of waqf land and the property of the Muhammad 'Ali family) to divert capital to industry.

Evidently, the programme has a chance of succeeding only if general conditions in Egypt favour industrial development. The reform strove to create such conditions by raising the standard of living of the rural population. Undoubtedly, the income of those who benefited from the distribution of land has increased, since the yearly sum they now pay for their land is

[1] Mar'i, *al-Islah az-zira'i*, p. 183; *al-Ahram*, 2 July 1958.

[2] Sir Malcolm Darling, 'Land Reform in Italy and Egypt', *Yearbook of Agricultural Co-operation 1956*, Oxford, 1956, p. 21; Berque, *Les Arabes*, pp. 143, 145–6; *al-Ahram*, 5 and 11 February 1954; Mar'i, *al-Islah az-zira'i*, p. 112.

[3] *The Times*, 17 April 1957; Gharzuzi, *Thawrat al-islah*, pp. 47–8; Berque, *Les Arabes*, p. 126.

less than that which they formerly paid for its lease. The level of production in agriculture has not fallen, and in many cases has even risen, since the transfer from large ownership to small ownership was not accompanied by a corresponding change from large- to small-scale farming. (Many estates were leased in small units in the past too.) At times even the reverse is true—as a result of the establishment of co-operatives, land is now sometimes farmed in large units where in the past it had been let in small plots.

At any rate, future development largely depends on the income of the majority of the rural population—the 90% which will not benefit at all from the distribution of land—and on the rents they will have to pay and the wages they will earn. A recent advance is the law of July 1961, according to which the maximal extent of land a landowner is permitted to hold was lowered from 200 to 100 feddan.[1]

Following the Egyptian law of agrarian reform, a very similar law was enacted in the Syrian zone of the U.A.R. after the merger of Syria and Egypt in September 1958.[2] According to this law, a man may not hold more than 80 hectares of irrigated land or 300 hectares of dry farming areas, but he is permitted to pass on to his wife or sons a further 40 hectares of irrigated or 160 of dry farming land. The State will confiscate all land exceeding these limits within a period of five years. Companies of various kinds and co-operatives are not included under the law. Special committees will fix the rate of compensation, which will be paid in the form of bonds bearing an interest of 1·5%, redeemable within forty years, non-negotiable to foreigners. The land will be distributed among Syrian fellahs owning less than 8 hectares of irrigated land or 30 hectares of dry farming land, and their cost will equal the compensation sum with a yearly interest of 1·5% and 10% for expenses, paid in equal monthly instalments over forty years.

Implementation of the law is the responsibility of an independent body called the Institution of Agrarian Reform. Inherited land is not included under the maximal allotment, on condition that its recipient uses it; also, the owner of dry farming land may hold on to it if he afforests it or converts it

---

[1] *al-Ahram*, 26 July 1961; *OM*, 1961, p. 931.
[2] Details in *al-Ahram*, 28 September 1958.

into irrigated land. Those benefiting from the distribution, together with other small landowners having less than 8 hectares of irrigated land or 30 hectares of dry farming area, will establish co-operatives for granting credit, supplying seeds, fertilisers, farm animals and machines, applying efficient methods of cultivation, and marketing the crops. The co-operatives will operate under the supervision of the Institute for Agrarian Reform.

About three weeks before this law came into effect a second law was passed with the intention of regulating the relations between landowner and fellah in the Syrian zone.[1] It permitted the organisation of agricultural employers, farm labourers, and tenants in unions and federations, under State supervision. Contracts must be in writing and for periods not exceeding five years. The law prohibits agricultural work by children under the age of 12 years and sets down working conditions for young people of 12–18 years of age and for women. Special committees were to determine minimum wages. The law fixes the length of a working day, holidays, compensation, social insurance, etc. The right to organise employment offices was given to the workers' and employers' unions, to the Chambers of Agriculture, and to the municipalities. The law expressly prohibits employers from locking out and workers from striking. It fixes the exact percentages which sharecroppers are to receive. It specifies land to be allotted for the construction of housing projects for sharecroppers. According to the law, special arbitration committees are to be set up for settling differences between landowners and their labourers or sharecroppers.

After the military revolt at the end of September 1958 a law was passed in Iraq also, similar on general lines to those of Syria and Egypt.[2] The Iraqi law places the upper limit on landed property at 1,000 Iraqi dunums of irrigated land or 2,000 Iraqi dunums of dry farming land.[3] Societies and companies may retain a larger area of uncultivated land. All areas exceeding the set limit will be confiscated within five years, the rate of compensation being determined by committees chosen by authority of the Minister of Agriculture. The com-

[1] Details in *al-Ahram*, 7 September 1958.
[2] Text in *az-Zaman*, Baghdad, 3 October 1958.
[3] 1 Iraqi dunum = 2·5 metric dunum = 0·6 feddan approx.

pensation will be paid in Government bonds bearing 3% interest, redeemable within twenty years. The bonds are non-negotiable to foreigners. Confiscated land and state domain will be distributed among the fellahs, each receiving a landholding of 30–60 dunum of irrigated land or 60–120 dunum of dry farming area. The Government will set up an independent body for the implementation of this law. Those benefiting from it will be organised in co-operatives, which will be concerned with granting credit and supplying seeds, fertilisers, and machines. The law is specific in noting the relations between landowner and tenants or sharecroppers (including the share of each side in the crop) and forbids eviction of tenants or sharecroppers. Finally, the reform law specifies the rights of agricultural workers, including minimum wages and the right to establish trade unions.

It is evidently too early to assess the extent to which these agrarian laws have been put into effect in Syria and Iraq. Confiscation of the land and its redistribution among the fellahs is proceeding gradually. The process of confiscation is more difficult in Syria and Iraq than in Egypt, both because of the incomplete and inexact land registration in the former two countries and also because of the power of landowners, particularly in Southern Iraq. Indeed, they have actively sabotaged execution of the law.[1] On the other hand, in those two countries it is easier to satisfy the demands of the fellah for land, as large reserves of public domain are available. The two governments have expressly stated their intention to distribute public domain land.

However, the weakness of the central authorities in Iraq and Syria, compared with Egypt, was responsible for a more efficient show of opposition to the law on the part of estate owners; even more, it was the origin of more profound unrest among the fellahs during implementation of the law. In Iraq particularly, fellahs took the law into their own hands and redistributed land without waiting for action by the State. Many of the landowners fled from their estates and removed to the cities.[2]

[1] *az-Zaman*, 25 October 1958, 7 and 19 September 1959, 18 January 1960.
[2] *al-Ayyam* (Syria), 26–27 January 1960; *az-Zaman*, 20 October, 14 November 1958, 4 April, 13 and 17 May, 30 June, 21 September 1959; *The Economist*, London, 25 October 1958, 24 March 1962.

After separation from the U.A.R. Syria first introduced changes into the law in favour of landowners and later cancelled them. Considering the unstable situation in that country, it is still difficult to decide whether and to what extent the reform is being implemented.

3. *THE VILLAGE AND ITS INSTITUTIONS*

In external appearance and architectural structure the Middle Eastern village is fundamentally different from the European village. In the Middle East there are hardly any isolated farms, or farmhouses with their fields strung along the roadside or dispersed throughout the village territory. The Middle Eastern Arab village is a conglomeration of closely stacked primitive houses with almost no paths between them, and it is generally inaccessible by road.

The village way of life in the Arab Middle East has always been collective rather than individualistic. This has many reasons, which in themselves shed light on the main characteristics of Middle Eastern Arab village life.

(1) *Land Tenure.* Individual ownership by the farmer has never existed; the village, as a unit, was responsible for payment of taxes, and its land was farmed collectively (*musha'*). Large landowners preferred to keep their fellahs in a concentrated living area.

(2) *Security.* The fellahs have always been subject to the danger of *ghazw* by beduins; close neighbours were thus essential for protection from such attacks. On the other hand, there is little fortification, as the Middle Eastern village was never an organised and independent political unit. Only in a few mountainous areas were villages built in positions having a strategic advantage—generally to defend the independence or autonomy of some religious community (in Lebanon) or tribal group (Kurds), rather than the village unit *per se*.

(3) *Economic Factors.* Dispersed settlements would be impractical in many parts of the Fertile Crescent because of scarcity of water, and in Egypt because land is in short supply. Every handful of earth which could be exploited for agriculture had to be saved, and the Egyptian Government would periodically

162

reset the limits of the village proper, beyond which construction was forbidden.

Protection from flooding of the Nile also necessitated a centralised village, distant from its fields.

(4) *The Technical Factor.* In the Arab Middle East there has been very little development of wheeled transport (carts, etc.), and most of the village transport is done by animals. This is simultaneously the cause and the result of the fact that the network of intra-village paths, in so far as it exists at all, is neglected and tortuous, and roads are narrow and unpaved.

For security, Arab villages are preferably built on a rock or a hill (in Egypt, *kawm* [*kom*] or *tel*), or, for economic reasons, near a spring. However, many villages of the lowlands are situated arbitrarily, and their placement seems to have no rational purpose. Villages of various regions differ in building material; whatever is locally available, be it stone, clay, brick, wood, or reed, is used. Otherwise, however, villages exhibit much similarity. One may say that for a country such as Egypt with a single building material, 'there is nothing so like an Egyptian village as another Egyptian village'.[1]

Nevertheless, since the second half of the nineteenth century Egypt has had another special form of agricultural settlement —the *'izba* housing the tenants or workers of a large landowner on his estate. The *'izba* displays much more planning than the usual village, although its houses are not generally of superior quality.[2]

The monotonous appearance of the villages is heightened by the fact that there are few prominent buildings serving as communal institutions or social centres. Not every village has a mosque or school, and cafés are found only in the more highly developed villages, situated along the main roads and serving as stations for by-passers. The same is true of shops and bakeries; found only in the more progressive villages, they are establishments of the last generation. They are usually centralised around an open square and serve as a social meeting-place. In recent years clubs belonging to communal or political

---

[1] Ayrout, *Fellahs*, pp. 94–5.

[2] For detailed discussion of the *'izba* and other minor forms of settlement see Piot Bey, *Causerie ethnographique sur le fellah*, Cairo, 1900, p. 22; J. Besançon, *L'Homme et le Nil*, Paris, 1957, pp. 195–8.

groups have also made their appearance, but generally the village square alone functions as market-place and social centre. Women gather at the spring and the bakery, or the cemetery, where they come, usually on a special day, to mourn the dead.[1] They do not mingle with men and do not frequent men's meeting-places.

There are two further village institutions which function as social centres. One is the guest house, called *madafa* in Palestine, *madyafa* in Egypt, and *mudif* in Iraq. Sometimes, as in some parts of Egypt, the guest house is maintained by the *mukhtar* and is a State-authorised institution of the village. Sometimes it is kept by a *hamula* or by the whole village; notable families from among the large landowners may have their own guest house for the sake of social prestige. (In order to maintain such guest houses, special waqfs were established in the nineteenth and twentieth centuries in Egypt.) It is equipped with bedding and cooking utensils for guests, and is generally a meeting-place for men. A detailed and interesting description of the *mudif* is to be found in Salim's book on Chibayish. He notes that following disintegration of the tribe, many persons built *mudifs*, previously the privilege of tribal chiefs alone. A distinction is drawn between the *mudifs* of heads of *hamulas*, open all day, and smaller ones. The size of the *mudif* is a measure of its owner's social status. There are signs that the institution is declining, as a class of officials and merchants makes its appearance in the village; there is no longer time to spend long hours at the *mudif*. Ammar, too, speaking of Upper Egypt, observed that villagers are becoming less generous towards guests, for financial reasons.

A second institution, not in the village itself and usually shared by a number of villages, is the saint's grave, *wali*, pertaining to a local saint or famous Sufi shaikh, sometimes even to one of the prophets or some other renowned religious personage. The grave, generally domed, is known as *maqam*, *mazar*, or *ziyara*, i.e., a place of visits and prostration. The saint is given gift-offerings (for curing illness, for successful birth, etc.); prayers are offered up to him, and requests made of him. The *wali* or *ziyara* also has an important function in village

---

[1] The cemetery is also a principal meeting-place for urban women, as their husbands cannot forbid them to visit deceased relatives.

life as a meeting-place. Generally it is more important than the mosque or church, since folk religion, based on superstition, faith in saints, the evil eye, devils, witches, and so on, is more deeply imprinted on the soul of the villager than formal religion. Thus the festivals connected with saints take precedence in village life over the official Muslim and Christian holidays and many of them are common to Muslims and Christians.[1] These folk festivities are usually timed by the solar year, and are often combined with markets, competitions, amusements, etc. At times they are related to the saint's birthday, *mawlid*.

The most important position of the village is that of the *mukhtar*, or as he is called in Egypt, the *'umda*. In large Egyptian villages a number of 'shaikhs' are subject to the *'umda*. The *mukhtar* or shaikh is elected by village notables, but their choice is not final; they only offer his candidacy to the authorities, who themselves make the appointment. The whole matter involves quarrels and rivalry among various groups and parties. In pre-revolutionary Egypt appointment of the *'umda* was connected with the party system, and, on occasion, a change of government was the cause of bloodshed.[2]

The functions of the *mukhtar* and *'umda* are numerous and diverse. As the Government's representative in the village, he has many administrative duties: he registers and gives notification of births and deaths; he receives governmental announcements and passes them on to the villagers; he notifies the authorities of criminal occurrences; he hands over wanted persons to the police or Army, or attests that such persons are not to be found; he identifies villagers and signs documents, such as those dealing with landownership when the *musha'* is split; he makes the arrangements for division of water (in Syria);[3] he aids the Government in collecting taxes, and in

[1] See, for instance, Mubarak, XI, 70; Blackman, pp. 248, 258; and for the Lebanon, Fuller, *Buarij*, pp. 82–5.

[2] See, for instance, R. Chamberet, *Enquête sur la condition du fellah égyptien*, Paris, 1909, p. 43; Ayrout, *Fellahs*, pp. 42–3, 110; *al-Ahram*, 14 April 1955. For detailed discussion of the Egyptian *'umda*, his appointment, his functions, and his socio-economic and political position, see G. Baer, 'The Village Shaykh in Modern Egypt 1800–1950' in U. Heyd (ed.), *Studies in Islamic History and Civilization*, Jerusalem, 1961, pp. 121–53.

[3] On his functions in connection with *musha'* and division of water see Latron, *La Vie rurale en Syrie et au Liban*, pp. 158, 160–3, 227. For Egypt see also Berque, *Histoire sociale*, p. 55.

Egypt accompanies the village tax-collector (*sarraf*) on his rounds. In Egypt he is responsible for conscription of the villagers for Army service and forced labour (*sukhra*)—insect warfare in cotton-growing regions, fighting locusts, fortifying the dikes when there is danger of flooding. (Other forms of forced labour were abolished at the end of the nineteenth century.) The *mukhtar* is expected to safeguard the village and public security in its environs; for this, he has at his disposal *khafirs*, as they are called in Egypt (twenty to twenty-five in number at most). The *mukhtar* is expected to entertain important visitors to the village. In Palestine he would receive a salary from the authorities, depending on the scope of his activities, but in Syria, Lebanon, and Egypt his services are gratuitous. In Egypt part of the *'umda's* lands are exempt from taxes, and he himself from *sukhra* and Army service. Also, his standing enables him to profit from his post; for example, the fellahs may cultivate his land without recompense. The Syrian Law of Mukhtars of October 1952 forbade the *mukhtar* to receive any money from villagers.[1]

In many Egyptian villages the office of *'umda* is hereditary, and there are families which have retained the position since the nineteenth century. However, the status of the *'umda* in Egypt has declined steeply over this period. There were village shaikhs who owned 1,000 feddans of land in the nineteenth century, but none of the *'umdas* of today are considered to be large landowners. In the past Egyptian legislation fixed minimum landownership at 10 feddans for an *'umda* and 5 for a *shaikh*; however, it was not easy to implement the law, since persons otherwise suited to the position did not have even this amount of landed property, and some adopted various stratagems to circumvent the law.

Fragmentation of land and decreased wealth of *'umdas* has made it more difficult for them to practise the generous and gracious hospitality of the past; then, too, the new administration and modern police force have taken over many of the *'umdas'* traditional functions. Consequently, their social standing in the village has fallen. According to the new Egyptian 'Umda Law of April 1957, the Minister of the Interior can abolish the office entirely in villages which have a police

[1] *al-Hayat*, Beirut, 24 October 1952 (*Hamizrah Hehadash*, IV, 119).

station.[1] Similarly, the prestige of the *mukhtar* fell in Palestine and Israel following on the establishment of elected local councils. Strong central government and an orderly administration have weakened the position of *'umda* and *mukhtar* in most of the Arab countries; however, from time to time their power is temporarily restored—during periods of unrest and war.

Another significant reason for the loss of the *mukhtar's* prestige is the spread of newspapers and radio. As modern means of communication spread among the villagers, the *mukhtar* loses his role as their sole source of information, and his home is no longer so important as their meeting-place.[2]

Aside from *'umda*, *khafir*, and *sarraf*, certain other personages of Egyptian villages may be noted. Foremost among them is the *baqqal* or shopkeeper, generally a Greek, who sells groceries and other goods; sometimes, at the same time, he is the village moneylender, making loans at interest. A second important person is the *hallaq as-sihha* (or *mizayyin*), the barber, whose art is not limited to haircuts and shaves; he is also pharmacist, gives injections, does venesection (blood-letting), circumcises, is responsible for sanitation, and at times has other medical duties too, regardless of whether or not he has the qualifications. There are some villages, usually backward ones, in which the barber also deals in witchcraft. It should also be mentioned that in many villages there are one or more persons who amuse the villagers by storytelling. They generally practise some trade during the day.

Another important personage in the Arab village is the village teacher. There are two entirely different types of teacher: the shaikh of the *kuttab* (place of religious instruction) and the teacher of the modern (governmental) school which has been set up in most villages of the Arab East. The shaikh of the *kuttab* is the religious personage of the village, who also fulfils the function of *khatib* (preacher) and *imam* (leader in prayer) in the mosque. In many Middle Eastern villages the inhabitants pay him with agricultural crops or clothes, but some shaikhs are also supported by the Ministry of Waqf or some other

---

[1] *al-Ahram*, 12 May 1957. For the decline of the *'umda's* position see also *al-Gumhuriya*, 19 August 1958, and the very interesting report in the weekly *Akhir Sa'a* of 27 December 1961.

[2] Cf. D. Lerner and L. Pevsner, *The Passing of Traditional Society, Modernizing the Middle East*, Glencoe, Ill., 1958, p. 186 and *passim*.

governmental body. Villagers approach the shaikh of the *kuttab* with any problems of a religious nature, and he generally writes their letters and their charms against the evil eye. Among the ignorant villagers, his status is illustrious, as he represents religion in their eyes.

The teacher of the governmental school has acquired modern learning at a teachers' training college. His position in the village is largely dependent on his personality. Modern urban education tends to make him critical of the conservative village,[1] and his attempts at reform often encounter objective economic difficulties. His demand for regular attendance is in contradiction to the needs of agricultural work, and his pupils forget their lessons after they return to the fields. The teacher also tries to uproot superstition. All in all, his presence is a source of constant friction. Few teachers make the effort, tedious and stubborn as it is, to overcome these obstacles. The majority are contemptuous of the village and its people, and direct their efforts towards obtaining a post in the city. The teacher is not, then, popular with the villagers, although they treat him with the respect and distance that befits a representative of the city. Sometimes a teacher interferes with general village affairs, antagonises the village notables, and is even a rival of the local leaders.

4. *VILLAGE SOCIETY*

It was noted earlier that in the formation of the units of beduin society a single factor operates—consanguinity, real or imaginary. What are the factors that fashion the structure of fellah society, and to what extent is each factor significant?

Clearly, in fellah society too, a fundamental factor is the blood tie, i.e., family relationship or kinship. It was seen that the importance of the tribe lessens on settlement. Relationships based on a common ancestral father, who lived ten or more generations ago, and which include all members of a village or region, do still remain part of the fellah's heritage in most villages studied, but only as a myth which has no real bearing

[1] An illuminating example is Mahmut Makal's *A Village in Anatolia* (London, 1954). Makal, himself a village teacher, describes an Anatolian village, which is not very different in this respect from an Arab village.

on day-to-day life. However, a smaller unit based on family relationships is of foremost importance in village society also. For simplicity, this unit is here called a *hamula*, the term used in Palestine, though elsewhere other names are applied.[1]

The number of persons belonging to one hamula may vary greatly, even within a single village. In none of the villages studied had the common ancestral father of the hamula lived more than seven or less than three generations previous to the survey. The number of hamulas in a village depends on its size; sometimes the whole village is one hamula, while at the other extreme is a village such as Chibayish, for example, with a population of 9,768 in 1947, and 39 hamulas.[2]

What is the practical meaning of belonging to a hamula? Unlike the corresponding nomadic group, the village hamula has no collective ownership of land or wells. The predominant ownership unit in fellah society is the extended family, and in this respect, the hamula has no function (at any rate since the *musha'* was broken up). The functions of the hamula may be summarised as follows:

(*a*) Members of a single hamula generally live in a common quarter (*hara*). Thus the hamula is sometimes named after the area in which it is situated (the 'western', 'southern', etc.) rather than after the ancestral father or common place of origin; in other cases, quarters of the village are named after the hamula.

(*b*) There are villages in which members of one hamula have neighbouring fields.

(*c*) In many places the hamula has its own guest house, a single oven, and threshing floor. Among Egyptian villages the hamula has its own *dawar*, which is a meeting-place for its members as well as a hostel.

[1] Our discussion of the *hamula* is based mainly on the following works: for Palestine, Israel, and Jordan, *Survey of Social and Economic Conditions in Arab Villages 1944*; Rosenfeld, *Tayyiba*; Patai, *Jordan* and Y. Shimoni, '*Arvei Erets Yisrael*, Tel Aviv, 1947; for Lebanon, Tannous, *The Arab Village Community*; Gulick, *Social Structure and Culture Change*; Fuller, *Buarij*; and Touma, *Hadeth el-Jobbé*; for Iraq, Salim, *Chibayish*; and for Egypt, Ammar, *Growing Up in an Egyptian Village*; Blackman, *The Fellahin of Upper Egypt* (Upper Egypt); and Berque, *Histoire Sociale d'un village égyptien* and *Sur la structure sociale de quelques villages égyptiens* (Lower Egypt).

[2] Actually *fakhdhs*; in Chibayish, '*hamula*' is a larger unit.

(*d*) As among the beduins, so too Arab fellahs who are members of one hamula are mutually responsible in matters of blood revenge, they are collectively responsible for paying restitution or collectively have the right to receive such restitution in a case of murder.

(*e*) In villages of Muslims and most Christian sects marriage within the hamula is desirable. Thus, the bride price for a girl of the hamula is usually lower than the customary price paid for a 'foreign' girl. On the other hand, intra-hamula marriage is not agreeable to members of the Greek Orthodox community and other ancient Christian sects (except for the Copts); Gulick even considers this to be one of the most significant features of the hamula of Munsif. (Nevertheless, this is no law; intra-hamula marriages do occur even here.)

(*f*) Finally, the hamula is a unit providing its members with some degree of protection and security. In certain villages the youth are organised in gangs according to hamula. The hamula is also a social grouping for meetings of friends, parties, and festivities.

The head or heads of hamulas are neither elected nor appointed in any formal manner. They emerge spontaneously and naturally from among the elders of the hamula, heads of large families, and large landowners. Unlike beduin shaikhs, the heads of hamulas have no recognised official standing (unless they are themselves *mukhtars*, as is sometimes the case). Nevertheless, they are consulted in all the internal affairs of the hamula and take part in settling disputes and quarrels. In many villages a council composed of hamula heads is summoned, when necessary, to discuss village matters and to settle disputes. The decisions of such a council, while not actually binding from a legal viewpoint, are morally compelling.

In many places there is a traditional state of enmity between different hamulas of a single village which is periodically kindled by disputes over land, water, women, and legacies, appointment of the *mukhtar*, etc. Two hostile hamulas may request a third to act as mediator; the third hamula not infrequently quarrels with the aggrieved side. In order to protect themselves from hostile groups, several small hamulas sometimes attach themselves to a larger and more powerful one. Some have connections with city notables or urban families, as a result of their economic dependence on the land-owners or moneylenders. It is for this reason that the hamula also has its party-political ties. Villagers join a party (or other social group) only by virtue of their hamula membership. Thus, traditional parties were based not on individual member-ship, but rather on a standing committee of urban men of note who were influential with the village hamulas (and urban districts) and had their support. (In this matter, changes are appearing as the city develops, the traditional family structure weakens, and modern political groups arise.)

While blood relationship is the main factor shaping fellah society, it is not the only factor. Second in importance is the *religious* factor. The difference between fellah and beduin society in this respect is due to: (*a*) the religious homogeneity of the beduins, as compared with the diversity of religious sects dwelling together in fellah society; and (*b*) the greater import-ance of the formal aspects of religion and religious practices in daily life, which, as noted earlier, is characteristic of a sedentary way of life. It must again be emphasised, however, that villagers do not observe the rites of the formal Muslim religion with the orthodox townsman's zeal. The fellah's religion has far more elements of pre-Muslim folk religion, manifested as belief in saints, sacred trees, devils, ghosts, etc.

The importance of the religious community as a social unit in the Middle East was discussed in Chapter III; what was said there applies particularly to fellahs, since the influence formal religion has in forming beduin society is less marked, while in the town that influence is only one factor among many.

The influence of religion on Middle Eastern Arab village society is displayed in a number of ways:

(*a*) Communal and religious membership determines custom and law in various spheres of life, particularly personal status. It has been noted that all matters of personal status are under religious–communal jurisdiction; and in discussing the woman, communities, and land system, mention was made of the instructions of Islam and other religions—instructions which are a part of village society and which are implemented in the village by official representatives of the religions.

(*b*) In many Arab villages the Sufi orders form a frame of social life. They are widespread mainly in Egyptian villages (and even more in the Sudan), but they may also be found in the Fertile Crescent. The present importance of the orders is not well studied, and even less is known of their social functions.[1]

(*c*) In Islamic countries the religious community as a unit has political functions too. Any unit extending beyond village boundaries to which fellahs may belong will in general be a religious group.

(*d*) In villages of fellahs belonging to more than one community the communal group sometimes assumes the role of hamula, with all its functions.

(*e*) For the past few hundred years there has been no secular nobility in the Arab village;[2] the only nobility is one having a religious nature—the *sharifs* and *sayyids*, descendants of the prophet Muhammad. This class is at present in process of decline.[3]

It is, then, evident that the fellah's association with his religious community is still very close. Much less strong is his attachment to a *linguistic* group. There seem to be three reasons for this:

(1) By far the greater part of the fellah population is illiterate, and thus language as such has no cultural or historical value such as might form the foundation of national feeling.

(2) While non-Sunni-Muslim communities are scattered throughout the breadth of the Middle East, linguistic minority groups of villagers are found only on the fringes of the Arab countries, and only there does the rural populace have contact with them.[4] Other groups speaking non-Arab languages in the Middle East are townsfolk.

(3) Tradition of centuries based on the fundamental principles of Islam has emphasised religious ties and the unity of the religious community, while purporting to obscure linguistic

[1] Berque (*Histoire sociale*, p. 60) found that in Sirs al-Layan the political organisation of the Wafd Party was primarily based on the local Sufi order.

[2] Except for a few isolated areas where a local secular village aristocracy has been preserved.

[3] See Berque, *Histoire sociale*, pp. 61–2; Salim, pp. 150–4, 171.

[4] Weulersse, *Paysans de Syrie*, p. 73, has an instructive map showing contact of villagers with linguistic minorities in Northern Syria.

differences. The result has been a strong influence of religion and little of language.

We may next enquire into the role of the *territorial* factor in the fellah's life—i.e., how much is the Arab fellah of the Middle East attached to his village? Here, too, there are no absolute rules, just as no generalisations describe the fellah's attitude to his land. But in contrast to the sharp disagreement on the latter question, there is general unanimity on the subject of the fellah's ties to his village, among authors describing both Egyptian and Fertile Crescent villages. It is felt that territorial unity of the village is destroyed by commitments to the hamula and religious community. Speaking of the village of Kiman in Upper Egypt, Winkler claims that 'the family is the social unit; over it, the only meaningful unit is the community of believers, the Muslims . . .'.[1] Similarly, Weulersse writes that loyalty to the tribe implies rejection of the village, and at another point he notes that communal feeling undermines the territorial unity of the village. As a result, the fellahs have no spiritual links with their village, and 'le village ne forme pas un corps politique'.[2] 'Le village égyptien n'est pas une commune au sens civique du mot, pas un organisme, mais une masse . . .'.[3] Winkler adds that there is no co-operative spirit among the village youth, as in villages of other countries, and even more striking is the absence of organisations and associations on a village basis. ('Wir finden auch keinerlei organische Zusammengehörigkeit der Bauernschaft eines Dorfes.') Berque writes: 'à aucun moment de notre enquête, nous n'avons jusqu'ici trouvé la vie communale organisée. Pas même les rudiments municipaux . . .'.[4] Weulersse claims that his remarks apply especially to the villages of the Syrian lowlands; but in the hills too the fellah in his frequent wars has come to the defence of his tribe and religious sect rather than his village.

Nevertheless, there may be villages in the Arab Middle East which possess greater organic unity. In such cases it may always be asked whether the fellah's spiritual ties are really directed to his village, or is the village simply identical with a

---

[1] Winkler, *Bauern zwischen Wasser und Wüste*, pp. 136–7.
[2] Weulersse, pp. 66, 78, 240; Cf. Berque, *Les Arabes*, pp. 151–2.
[3] Ayrout, p. 111.
[4] Berque, *Structure sociale*, p. 214.

family unit (hamula) or religious sect[1] to which his true loyalties are directed. Also, there is evidence of a certain degree of solidarity among members of one village *vis-à-vis* other villages, landowners, or the State. This solidarity appears only on occasion, in the face of some external threat; it does not persist and does not assume organised form. The *mukhtar* represents the authorities in his dealings with his villagers rather than village interests in his contacts with the outside world. It is true that the village elders may sign and collectively present a petition (*mazbata*) concerning some or other village affair, but fellahs seldom take organised action for the sake of a common cause.

It should be noted that the Middle Eastern Arab village has no offices of local government, and recent efforts to establish such offices have encountered great difficulties—particularly internal discord. Among the 4,200 Egyptian villages counted in the 1947 census there were less than 100 village councils that had been set up in the thirty-year period preceding the count. Furthermore, such councils are headed by the *ma'mur*— the governmental official in charge of the district. By 1957, 138 village councils were in operation. Their main problem was lack of co-operation on the part of villagers, who were indifferent to the whole system. New regulations on the establishment of village councils were published in October 1958. They, too, stipulated that councils were to include representatives of the police and government, but that the majority of members were to be elected. A further reorganisation took place in 1960.[2]

Fellah society is only slightly influenced by *occupational* groups or division by *economic status*. In the traditional village there is almost no place for occupational specialisation and little scope for economic differentiation. Farming is practised for subsistence only, living standards are very low, and anything

---

[1] See, for example, Gulick, p. 177, who notes that in Munsif the three units— the territorial, kinship, and communal unit—are in fact completely identical (the village being a Greek Orthodox cluster in a wholly Maronite environment). The Muslim village of Buarij is most similar, in its Christian surrounding (Fuller, pp. 5-6, 79, 97-8).

[2] M. Z. 'Abd al-Qadir, 'Ikhtiyar al-'umad', *al-Ahram*, 9 April 1942; Dr M. 'A. al-'Arabi, 'al-Qarya al-misriya fi'l-'ahd al-jadid', *al-Ahram*, 4 December 1952; Gharzuzi, *Thawrat al-islah*, p. 124; *al-Ahram*, 6 October 1958; *MER*, 1960, p. 495.

the fellah produces over and above his bare minimal requirements is eaten up by taxes and other payments. As land has
never belonged to the fellah, there is not much differentiation
on the basis of small and large landowners, and the *musha'*
system has preserved equality among members of any one
village. Village trades are undeveloped; they are limited to
pottery-making, brick and basket making, and primitive weav-
ing. As connections with the outer world grow and villagers
begin to buy imported goods, village trades decline still further.[1]

The state of village society has altered somewhat in the last
generation, and in places even earlier. In all Middle Eastern
Arab countries land has become private property which may
be sold or mortgaged; in addition to the large estate-owners
there are now smaller-scale landowners. The farming economy
has become dependent on the market, and in consequence,
fellahs are liable to gain large profits or to lose heavily with
market fluctuations. Those who have become wealthy send
their sons away to study; a class of clerks and merchants has
appeared. Those lacking land or means frequently migrate to
the cities, and if they manage to save enough money from their
salaries they may return to the village and open a shop, for
example.

Of course, these changes vary largely from one region to
another. A most instructive comparison is afforded by juxta-
posing Ammar's picture of Silwa in Upper Egypt and Berque's
description of Sirs al-Layan in the Southern Delta. In backward
Silwa the fellahs are still apprehensive of leaving agriculture
for some other occupation, and there is little scope for specialisation, since each family supplies its own wants. Landless fellahs
are almost non-existent in this village; anyone who sells his
land is bound to leave eventually. Only two persons, neither
actually resident in the village, own 60 feddans of land each;
ten villagers have at least 5 feddans, while all the rest have
smaller plots. On the other hand, the fluctuations in the prices
of cotton, and the consequent periods of prosperity and
depression which came in successive waves, caused profound
social upheavals in Sirs al-Layan. New classes of rich and poor
came into being, as well as merchants, artisans, and even

[1] Cf. Blackman, Chapter IX; Adams, *Iraq's People and Resources*, p. 22; Fuller,
pp. 30-1, 94, etc.

professionals. In Munsif in Lebanon the number of persons engaged in urban occupations even exceeded the number of agricultural and other rural workers (while a hundred years previously, 'we were all fellahs').[1]

Even in Chibayish, in the marshlands of Southern Iraq, inhabited by beduin tribesmen at the beginning of this century, affiliation to the market has led to class differentiation and the formation of the following economic classes (according to Salim's classification): (1) the 'wealthy' (i.e., large-scale merchants, moneylenders, etc.); (2) landowners (mainly *sirkals*, heads of sub-tribes); (3) 'shop owners' (merchants of the village market); (4) artisans (boat-builders, constructors of hostels, blacksmiths, and weavers); (5) servants and guards (in the governmental offices of the village); (6) mat-makers and farmers, who still form the majority of the inhabitants of Chibayish.

The villager's loyalty towards the old social groups—the hamula and religious sect—has not disappeared, and generally has not been impaired, even among the villages which now have their new professional and economic classes. Berque mentions that in Sirs al-Layan the strong familial ties and the old social order remain untouched. Salim, describing in some detail the structure of the hamula, which continues to hold sway in Chibayish society, claims that villagers still regard new occupations with contempt. In his view, wealth in itself does not determine social standing, and fundamentally the old order remains pre-eminent.[2] Even in Munsif, the Lebanese village so greatly influenced by economic trends because of its ties with the town and with Western society (via inhabitants who emigrated to the United States and later returned to their village), Gulick reaches the following conclusions:

The truth, in the present writer's view, is that religion *retains* its potency in the political (i.e. group loyalty) sphere, both in Lebanon

[1] Gulick, pp. 56–9. There is, however, a distinct difference between Christian and Muslim villages in Lebanon, the latter preserving traditional occupations to a greater degree. See Fuller, p. 31.

[2] Salim, pp. 115–37, 172, 454, 458, 462. However, there are signs that in some villages economic wealth is beginning to determine the social status of villagers. This is Touma's impression (p. 92) in relation to Hadeth el-Jobbé. But this example is not to be interpreted too broadly, as indicating a fundamental and general change of values.

in general, and certainly without any question in Munsif.... Kinship: In the values surrounding kin groups, and by logical extension, the entire village group, *there have been almost no changes whatsoever.*[1]

Surveys of villages of quite diverse parts of the Arab Middle East seem, then, to show that even the professional and economic differentiation of the last generation have not basically modified the overwhelming importance of kinship and religion in Arab village society. It is too early to judge the extent of change that has occurred within the last few years, as a result of the profound social agitation of the early 1950s and agrarian reform, which has apparently aroused a certain degree of class consciousness among the fellahs, at least those of Egypt and Iraq.

C. THE CITY

1. *THE EXTENT OF URBAN POPULATION*

Since figures for the occupational structure of Middle Eastern countries are either non-existent or completely unreliable, the term 'urban population' will be used here for a population living in concentrations exceeding some given size. The pertinent question is what size? It is reasonable to choose quite a large population as the minimal group meriting the name *town* in Arab countries, since there are a number of settlements of considerable population which are mainly or totally agricultural, and which do not differ essentially from villages except that they are rather large. In the present volume a fairly arbitrary measure has been chosen: any settlement having a population of 25,000 or more is considered a city. However, not all the Arab countries have the necessary data for full comparisons of the extent of 'urban population' out of total population.

The two largest cities of the Middle East are in Egypt— Cairo and Alexandria—as are a further four cities each of more than 100,000 inhabitants. According to the 1947 census, the population of all towns of at least 25,000 persons was 4,965,976 —i.e., 26·1% of the total population. The larger cities, with a

[1] Gulick, pp. 154–5 (Gulick's italics).

population exceeding 40,000 persons, are listed in the following table:

Towns of Egypt with more than 40,000 Inhabitants

Town	Number of inhabitants in 1947
Cairo	2,065,113
Alexandria	953,259
Port Said	157,600
Tanta	129,372
al-Mahalla al-Kubra	110,765
Mansura	102,519
Suez	97,133
Asyut	88,730
Damanhur	84,352
Zaqaziq	82,912
Fayyum	71,752
Giza	66,156
Minya	65,528
Damietta	53,620
Isma'iliya	53,594
Bani Suaif	52,676
Suhaj	43,168
Qena	42,929
Shibin al-Kom	41,636

Detailed results of the 1960 census have not yet been published, but it may be expected that the urban population has risen to about 30% of the total population.

Until details of the Sudanese census are made available, there are only estimates of that country's urban population. The number of persons living in towns of over 25,000 has been assessed at less than half a million, i.e., less than 5% of the total population. About half of these townspeople live in the 'triple capital' of Khartoum, Khartoum North, and Omdurman. The rest of the towns, each with a population of some 30,000–50,000, are, in order of importance, Obeid, Wad Medani, Port Sudan, Kasala, and 'Atbara.

There are no details of the urban population of Libya. According to Lindberg, that group comprises about 235,000 persons, i.e., 20% of the total population. In fact, the only two towns are Tripoli (Tarablus), whose population was 185,517 in 1960,[1] and Benghazi (Bani-Ghazi).

For the towns of the Arabian Peninsula widely differing

[1] *OM*, 1961, p. 215.

population estimates have been published. Mecca's population has been given as being as low as 80,000, and as high as 200,000. Medina has from 30,000 to 50,000 inhabitants, Riyadh from 50,000 to 300,000, and Jedda from 30,000 to 250,000. The settlements of Saudi Arabia with populations of over 25,000 now certainly include Hofuf also. But even accepting the highest estimates, Saudi Arabia's urban population is not more than 10% of the total. In Yemen only San'a (50,000–80,000) and Hudaida (30,000–40,000) are to be included in the category of towns, and thus Yemenite townsmen are no more than 3% of the total population. The rest of the towns of the Arabian Peninsula whose population is by all estimates over 25,000 are Manama, the capital of Bahrain, with about 35% of the island's population, and al-Muharraq, the second town in size in the island; the city of Kuwait, with 60–75% of the population of the principality; and the town of Aden, which is practically identical, as regards population, with the colony.

The number of inhabitants of Iraq's towns, according to the 1957 population census, is summarised in the following table:

Towns of Iraq with more than 25,000 Inhabitants

Town	Number of inhabitants in 1957
Baghdad	784,763
Mosul	179,646
Basra	164,623
Kirkuk	120,593
Najaf	88,809
Karbala	60,804
Hilla	54,095
'Amara	53,311
Sulaimaniya	48,450
Nasiriya	39,060
Arbil	34,751
Diwaniya	33,204
Samawa	26,838
Kut	26,524
Tel-'Afar	25,543

Altogether 1,741,014, i.e., 26·6% of the total population.

In Syria and Lebanon the various sources of information on the number of town dwellers are contradictory to an astonishing degree. The official figures quoted in the following tables should be accepted with very great reservations.

The following table is taken from the official 1958 *Statistical Yearbook* for Syria:

Towns of Syria with more than 25,000 Inhabitants

Town	Number of inhabitants in 1958
Damascus	454,603
Aleppo	451,435
Homs	146,016
Hama	104,016
Latakia	58,948
Dair az-Zor	55,901
Duma	26,306

In all 1,297,227 (29·4% of the total population).

A still higher proportion of townsmen is found in Lebanon. Here, as in Syria, there seems to have been some confusion between towns and districts, or even provinces, and contradictions abound. The largest city is Beirut, with 400,000–450,000 inhabitants; next comes Tripoli, with 80,000 or possibly more, and Sidon, with 40,000 inhabitants. It is not clear whether Zahla has more than 25,000 inhabitants. At all events, the urban population of the Lebanon is certainly over one-third of the total population.

In Jordan the 1961 census is the source of the following table:[1]

Towns of Jordan with more than 25,000 Inhabitants

Town	Number of inhabitants in 1961
'Amman	244,599
Zarqa	91,295
Jerusalem	60,337
Nablus	45,658
Irbid	44,805
Hebron	37,911

The townsmen of Jordan thus constitute about 30% of all the populace.

Ranging the Arab countries of the Middle East according to the relative size of their urban population, we obtain the following table:[2]

[1] Figures according to the Director of the Jordanian Statistical Office, as published in *al-Manar* (Jordan) of 27 February 1962. See also *OM*, 1962, pp. 202–3.

[2] The Principalities of the Arabian peninsula have not been included. In some of them the inhabitants of one or two towns virtually constitute all the popula-

Country	% of Town-dwellers to general population (estimated)
Lebanon	35
Syria	30
Jordan	30
Egypt	30
Iraq	27
Libya	20
Saudi Arabia	10
Sudan	5
Yemen	3

It should be noted that the great majority of the urban population in the Arab world is concentrated in a very small number of large cities, while there are relatively few smaller provincial towns. In Lebanon, for example, almost 90% of the country's town-dwellers live in the two largest cities; in Syria this figure is 70%, in Egypt slightly over 60%, in Jordan 58%, and in Iraq 55%. In Sudan fully half of the urban population lives in the 'triple capital', and in Libya there are only two towns. It is interesting to note that, apart from these last two countries, there is a direct correlation between the percentage of town-dwellers in the general population and the proportion of town-dwellers living in the two largest cities; in other words, the overall percentage of urban dwellers in the general population depends to a large extent upon the development of the country's two largest cities.

2. URBANISATION

Many changes have taken place in the number of townsmen and their proportion to the total population during the last generation. In Egypt, for example, the population of the six largest cities constituted the following percentages of the total population in various years:

Year	%
1917	10·9
1937	14·1
1947	18·7

tion. For the same reason, Aden (Colony) was omitted. It must be emphasised that this table is the result of calculations based, in some cases, on estimates, and should thus be regarded as giving relative indications only.

These figures reflect the striking rise in urban population during the Second World War. During this period the total population increased by approximately 20%, while the number of inhabitants of towns rose by 49%; the population of Cairo rose by 60%, of Isma'iliya by 89%, and of Suez by 116%. A comparison of the number of urban residents in Iraq according to the 1947 and 1957 censuses reveals that Kirkuk has grown by 76·5%, Baghdad by 68%, and Basra by 62·5%. During the 1930s 'Amman, capital city of Jordan, had a population of about 30,000; now it is at least eight times as great. Manama in Bahrain grew by 43% between 1941 and 1950. It is possible that the pace of urbanisation in various cities and towns was even more rapid than in the examples given, but the lack of censuses in most of the Arab countries makes it difficult to obtain reliable estimates of this trend.

What are the causes of this urbanisation process which characterises much of the Arab East, and why has it become so much more rapid within the last generation?

(1) The most important reason is the *economic and social conditions which impel fellahs and tribesmen to leave their agricultural areas*. This factor operates mainly in two regions, in each of which it appears in a different form. In Egypt the fellahs were driven to the cities by the rapid natural increase of the population, which outpaced the increase of farmland, by the great density, and by the consequent fragmentation of farmland in various provinces. This propulsion was felt mainly in certain provinces of Upper Egypt, but it was also in evidence in the densely populated region of the Nile Delta; the principal object was Cairo, but Alexandria, Port Said, and Suez also absorbed these new town-dwellers. In Iraq, on the other hand, the drift to the towns had its roots in the system of land tenure which gave control of the land to the shaikhs, led to the disintegration of the tribal framework, and turned the tribesmen into tenants suffering from the exploitation and oppression of the owners of the new large estates. The movement was intensified in the 1950s, when attempts were made to legalise this situation. The chief sources of migration were the 'Amara and Muntafik (Nasiriya) provinces, from which fellahs and tribesmen moved to Baghdad and Basra.

According to the Iraqi population census of 1947, 'Amara liwa (Province) alone had supplied almost one-quarter of all the Iraqis who were then living outside their liwa of birth. Of all the people born in this liwa, over one-quarter were living outside it. Of the emigrants of 'Amara, 80% lived in the liwa of Baghdad and Basra, particularly in the *'asima*, the shanty town near Baghdad. According to a 1957 survey of this settlement, almost 90% of the inhabitants were formerly landless fellahs. Many, on being asked the reason for their transfer, answered that they had been oppressed by the 'shaikh' or had had quarrels with him.[1]

When conditions outside the town are the main stimulus to urbanisation, as was the case in certain parts of Egypt and Iraq, the process is usually accompanied by the creation of a layer of permanently unemployed persons, who engage in petty trade, begging, etc.

(2) In certain Arab countries it was the *economic development* of the towns that attracted the rural population (or completed the propulsion described above). It should be stressed that this economic development was not always industrial. True, there are cities in the Middle East whose growth has been due to industrial development; for example, al-Mahalla al-Kubra in the Nile Delta grew from a small town of 30,000 inhabitants at the turn of the century to an industrial town with a population of over 80,000 in the late 1930s, as a result of the establishment of the 'Misr' textile plant. The industrial boom in Aleppo in Syria, just after the Second World War, attracted thousands of villagers, sometimes more than could be absorbed by the still young industry. The growth of the oil industry, too, has led to the rise of various towns, such as Kirkuk in Iraq, whose population has increased almost threefold since 1941.

The development of the oil industry in Libya has led, in recent years, to a large-scale abandonment of the land in all regions and a sudden growth of the cities of Tripoli and Benghazi. The oil industry also encourages urbanisation in an indirect way, as the following description (of Libya) shows:

For most of the rural population, their first contact with the oil industry is when an exploration party moves into the district and hires some labor from the village. The farmer who has only a few

[1] Phillips, *Rural-to-Urban Migration in Iraq*, pp. 409, 413.

animals may entrust them to his brother or near kinsman and go to work. But after a while he usually quits the job; or the party moves to another district and he is laid off. He returns to his village but rarely does he go back to farming, especially if his land has not been worked during his absence. Instead of embarking on the major task of repairing the irrigation channels, rebuilding fences, and breaking up the soil, he waits for a while and then looks for another job. If another oil party comes into the area, he may be in luck; if not, he may consider going to Tripoli or Benghazi to obtain work.[1]

But in many places urbanisation was sparked by economic developments in other fields. The growth of Qamishli was caused by the expansion of agriculture in the Jazira region during the last ten years, while the growth of Latakia followed the construction of its new harbour. 'Atbara in the Sudan, formerly a small village, became a town of 40,000 inhabitants after it was chosen as the focal point of the Sudanese railroad system. The development of maritime communications has led to the expansion of several coastal towns; these towns, as well as some internal commercial centres, attracted new inhabitants because of the trade expansion which followed the strengthening of the link between agriculture and the urban market. Indeed, in Syria economic development in these fields has had a greater influence on the drift towards urbanisation than industrialisation, which put many artisans and craftsmen out of work.

(3) In the remarkable growth of the Arab East's urban centres in recent years, *political factors* played no mean part. The division of the Ottoman Empire, and the creation of a number of separate states which later became independent, brought in its wake the establishment of new centres of government, with all that this entailed: a considerable increase in the number of people employed in Government departments, among them the constantly increasing members of the bureaucracy, and the creation of new employment openings in building, transport, and other services, such as restaurants, laundries, and so on. There is no doubt that this is one of the main reasons for the growth of all the capital cities, and to a lesser extent of other towns. The weight of this factor is particularly noticeable in Riyadh in Saudi Arabia (which already has a population of

[1] Thomas, *The Libyan Oil Worker*, pp. 264–5.

300,000, according to the latest estimates) and in 'Amman, since the establishment of the Hashemite Kingdom of Jordan and the annexation of Arab Palestine; it was strengthened by another political factor—the presence of the Palestinian Arab refugee, who hoped to find employment in the capital.

Another political factor of importance spurred the process of urbanisation in the Middle East during the Second World War. The presence of the Allied forces in the area, particularly in the towns and their immediate vicinity, attracted thousands of villagers to the towns, where they worked as labourers in auxiliary services. After the war, when these armies were evacuated, not all the villagers returned to their former rural occupations; they had tasted city life and grown accustomed to incomes larger than they had obtained on their farms.

(4) Finally, there are the *social and cultural changes* which brought about or speeded up urbanisation. Through closer links between agriculture and the market, improvement of communications, and a general attraction towards the city and its institutions which followed the introduction of modern administration, the rural population came into more intimate and frequent contact with the cities. Many of the villagers who saw the difference in standards of living between the village and the town, and the different opportunities they offered for social and cultural advancement, were drawn towards the towns. In periods of agricultural prosperity fellahs who became wealthy often flocked to the cities, where they spent their profits —often on conspicuous consumption, and particularly on building.

The development of education was especially important. Only in the city was it possible to obtain any education other than the most elementary. As a result, in the last generation there has been a considerable drift of the children of well-to-do fellahs to educational institutions in the cities, where those who could eventually remained.

Sociologists who have studied the problems of urbanisation in the modern world believe that Egypt suffers from 'over-urbanisation', in other words, that the urban population has reached a higher percentage of the total than in certain Western countries with a higher level of industrial development. The reason for this is that urbanisation has been caused not only by the cities' economic development but also by the drifting in of surplus population from the villages.[1] The result is the creation of a broad layer of unemployed and unproductive persons in the cities and towns of Egypt. There is no doubt that this thesis contains more than a grain of truth; but it is not the whole truth. First, it was seen that in a country such as Syria the percentage of the urban population exceeds that of Egypt, despite the fact that in Syria there is no surplus rural population drifting away from the villages and the country is less industrialised than Egypt. Second, urbanisation in the Middle East and the West cannot be adequately compared on the basis of the relation between the percentage of the urban population and the index of development of urban industry and economy. The reason for this is that in the Arab East industrial plants are entirely concentrated in the large cities, mainly in the two largest cities; there are hardly any industrial establishments in the rural areas. Further, in the Arab states of the Middle East the city is the sole centre of all economic, administrative, and cultural institutions and activities, apart from agriculture. Thus the 'surplus rural population' is not the sole cause of the relatively high proportion of town-dwellers in the Arab countries. It seems therefore that the term 'over-urbanisation' is misleading, especially as a smaller degree of urbanisation would not have offered any solution to their social problems.

The process of urbanisation in the Arab states of the Middle East is accompanied by several demographic phenomena. As a rule, the first to migrate to the towns are the men, who attempt to find temporary or permanent employment, while the women and children remain in the village. As a result, during the initial stage of urbanisation the percentage of males in the large cities usually exceeds the percentage of males in the general population. In Iraq, for example, the percentage of males in the total population, according to the 1957 census, was 49·8%, while in Baghdad the percentage was 53%. In provinces that were sources of emigration the percentages were much lower: Nasiriya (Muntafik), 46·2%; Kut, 47·2%; Diwaniya, 48·5%; and 'Amara, 49·0%.

[1] See K. Davis and H. H. Golden, 'Urbanization and Development of Pre-Industrial Areas', *EDCC*, Vol. III, No. 1, October 1954, pp. 16–20.

A similar trend may be observed in Egypt. Whereas the proportion of males in the population of Cairo was 50·8% by the 1947 census, and that of Alexandria was 50·5%, the male proportion in the rural provinces closest to these towns, Minufiya and Buhaira, was only 48·7% and 48·0% respectively. The percentage of males was particularly high in the Canal Zone and in the town of Suez (52·3% and 52·7% respectively); the lowest percentage, by contrast, was recorded in Aswan Province—46·4%—from which there was a large emigration. A survey carried out in Khartoum recently arrived at similar conclusions.[1]

In addition, it is natural that the villagers who move to the towns should mostly be young people of working age. In 1947, people between the ages of 10 and 39 made up 47·5% of the population of Baghdad, but only 37·1% of the general population of all districts in Baghdad Province apart from the Baghdad district. In Egypt the 15–19 age group constituted from 25 to 27% of the population in Suez, Port Said, Alexandria, and Cairo in 1937 (the highest figure being 27·0% for Cairo), but in the densely populated areas of Upper Egypt it was only 22·1% in Asyut and 21·9% in Girga.

The *Sa'idis*, inhabitants of Upper Egypt, are particularly frequently found among the emigrants to large Egyptian cities, where they commonly work as pedlars and servants. A phenomenon worth mentioning is the fact that emigrants of a certain province tend to concentrate in one city. According to the 1937 population census, which contained revealing information on the immigration of peasants from the four most remote provinces of Upper Egypt (Asyut, Girga, Qena, and Aswan), 42·1% of the new town-dwellers who settled in Cairo came from Asyut, 37·5% of those going to Alexandria came from Girga, and 44·4% of those settling in Suez came from Qena. There are no comparable figures for other Arab countries, but similar trends have been reported in relation to the urbanisation process elsewhere. Members of certain tribes showed a tendency to drift to Khartoum in the Sudan, for example. The majority of immigrants to Baghdad came from the province of 'Amara, and most of those reaching Basra were from Muntafik

[1] Saad ed-Din Fawzi, *The Labour Movement in the Sudan 1946–1955*, London, 1957, p. 11.

and Diwaniya. In all these instances the immigrants from a common area or background tend to settle in the same suburbs; for example, in the *'asima* of Baghdad, houses were frequently grouped according to tribe.[1]

Urbanisation is not a factor affecting the growth of all the towns in the Arab East. On the contrary, some towns are declining in population and importance at the expense of other expanding towns. The rise of Baghdad attracted capital and labour from Mosul, and led to the loss of the important position it had occupied under Ottoman rule. Similarly, in Egypt the towns of Aswan, Rashid (Rosetta), and Fayyum increased less between 1937 and 1947 than did the total population.

During the first stages of urbanisation the move to the cities is not a permanent step. Many fellahs come to the cities in order to earn money for a definite purpose (to buy land, build a home, get married, and so on), returning to their villages once this purpose has been accomplished. But over a period of time more and more fellahs settle in the towns. Some of these have found permanent work (or chances of permanent work) which offers a better income than farming; others have acquired a trade or profession which can be practised only in the city (Government officials, etc.). Others find that their economic situation in the villages is so desperate that they are ready to settle in the towns even without any permanent employment, and to work at whatever job they can find (such as petty trade). Many of the fellahs who come to save a sum of money for a definite purpose or because they are attracted by temporary work (in Army camps during the Second World War, the building of houses and industrial plants, etc.) become accustomed to the city way of life, its entertainments and its public and political activity. As a result, it is difficult, if not impossible, to persuade them to return to their homes, and attempts to return them by force have met with strong opposition.[2]

[1] Adams, *Iraq's People and Resources*, pp. 57, 59; Phillips, pp. 411, 413.

[2] In connection with the agrarian reform in Iraq (October 1958), the Government launched a propaganda drive whose object was to persuade the inhabitants of the slums and shanties of Baghdad to return to their villages (e.g., Radio Baghdad on 25 October 1958).

3. DISTRICTS AND QUARTERS OF THE TOWN, AND URBAN INSTITUTIONS

In contrast to the relatively uniform structure of the Middle Eastern Arab village, there are great differences between one Arab city and another, in terms of both *external structure* and *division into regions*. The reasons for this are clear: there are no great dissimilarities between villages of many hundreds of years' standing and villages built only within the last generation, while in the cities old districts are entirely different from modern ones built under European influence. The same is true in the sphere of economics: over the centuries no significant economic and class differences have arisen among inhabitants of a village, or between villages, and even now the variations that do exist are slight. In the town class and economic differentiation has progressed rapidly. Thus, there is much scope for comparison of cities or quarters of a given city. While any two villages have similar economic functions, there is a world of difference between ports and cities of the interior, between industrial centres and holy cities, between commercial towns and major capitals where the administration is concentrated. It is then not easy to pick out such characteristics as are both general and specific to the cities of the Arab East, particularly since research on the modern Middle Eastern city is a neglected field.[1] Here, some attempt will be made to depict the typical kinds of districts and the typical institutions of the Middle Eastern Arab city.

Frequently, the 'old city' is still the nucleus. The boundaries of most old cities are quite distinct; the whole district is nearly

[1] The following monographs on modern Arab towns of the Middle East have been published: J. A. Jaussen, *Naplouse et son district*, Paris, 1927; J. Sauvaget and J. Weulersse, *Damas et la Syrie Sud*, Damascus, 1936; J. Sauvaget, *Alep*, Paris, 1941; S. Chehabe ed-Dine, *Géographie humaine de Beyrouth*, Beirut, 1960; M. Clergé, *Le Caire—Étude de géographie urbaine et d'histoire économique*, Cairo, 1934; and G. Hamdan, 'The Growth and Functional Structure of Khartoum', *GR*, January 1960. In addition, we have used the detailed descriptions of Syrian and Lebanese towns in Thoumin, *Géographie humaine de la Syrie Centrale*, and of Jordanian towns in Patai, *Jordan*. However, these sources and studies do not provide enough material for the classification of Middle Eastern Arab cities into their various types; this will be possible only after the publication of a large number of additional monographs and studies on Arab towns, particularly the smaller ones.

always walled in, although the wall may not be complete. In many cities houses themselves form a sort of wall, and the smaller roads do not have an exit to the new city, the only outlets being the main streets, each leading to a city gate. Even these main streets are very narrow, but are arranged in a more or less regular manner, with interconnecting winding lanes and blind alleys leading up to the inner houses of the old city. Curves in these alleys were often put in on purpose, for defence, and at

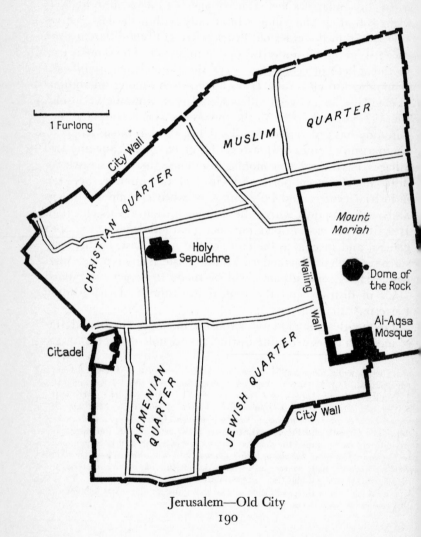

Jerusalem—Old City

times a passage may have been blocked by a house built across it, so that the lane may be more impenetrable. Many of these lanes, and also the main roads of the old city, are covered by arches. Multiplication of the population and lack of space has, over the generations, led to a spread of houses towards the street. Upper stories in particular were extended, so that in many places the whole street became covered. The density of building reaches a peak in the old city, but the population density is less striking, because houses are not usually many stories high and the ground floor frequently serves as shop or workshop.

The two most prominent buildings of many old cities are the great mosque and the ancient citadel, the latter to be found at the edge of the old city (in Cairo), on an ancient tel (as in Aleppo), on a hill, or at the summit of the hill on which the city is built (as in Tripoli and 'Amman).

Over the centuries and until the second half of the nineteenth century the old city was gradually joined by an accruement of districts of various kinds, here termed 'old districts'. The roads and alleys of such districts form a maze as jumbled as that of the old city, if not more so. These parts are inhabited by beduins, farmers, pilgrims, merchants, etc.; each new-comer built a house wherever he found space, with no sense of order or method. Here, too, roads and lanes are narrow and twisting (except for the main throughways), but since the area was never circumscribed by a wall, it was seldom that upper stories overhang the road. Examples of old districts are Maidan in Damascus and ad-Darb al-Ahmar in Cairo.

Old districts, and even more so, the old city, are divided into quarters (*harat*; sing., *hara*). In the old city they are fairly secluded from one another. The number of entrances to the quarter is small, and each has a gate which may be shut, and sometimes is, even in these days. The quarter was an inde-pendent unit until recently (and in some cities it still is), with its own *mukhtar* (*shaikh al-hara*), religious functionary, night-watchman, etc. In some Arab cities the quarter still retains its importance in a political sense, a *hara* often being affiliated to a certain political party. In the not so distant past there used to be disputes and sometimes actual fights between groups of youths belonging to different parts of the city.[1]

In many cities there used to be much segregation of religious sects by quarter, and in some parts this remains the case. Thus, for example, there is a Jewish quarter in Damascus and Beirut, a Samaritan quarter in Nablus; the al-Azbakiya quarter of Cairo was known as the Coptic quarter. Perhaps even more commonly, members of a single linguistic or national group live together in a quarter. In Damascus there is a quarter known as *al-Akrad* (the Kurds), and in Baghdad, too, quite considerable numbers of Kurds tend to have settled in special quarters of the old city. Shabsugh is a quarter of Circassians in 'Amman; in Khartoum there are special quarters of Italians, Greeks, and Egyptian Copts; tribal immigrants from French Sudan have settled in the slums of the southern part of Khartoum, with complete separation of tribes one from another; special districts of Armenians are found in Beirut, Aleppo, and several other cities.

In time, communal isolation gives way to a process of integration. Sometimes, as in Beirut, this is part of the trend to segregate residential districts on the basis of social strata. The well-to-do of all communities move to modern districts, while the Armenians in their slums have been joined by poor Shi'is and Kurds who only recently came to the city. Whereas in the days of Muhammad 'Ali, travellers still reported that the Copts of Cairo had their own quarter, it appears that at the end of the nineteenth century they outnumbered Muslims in less than five *shiyakhat* (sub-quarters) out of almost 200; and even in the few parts where Copts were in the majority there was a strong element of other communities.

The third type of town sector is the modern district—i.e., any district built in the twentieth century, and especially since the First World War, under European influences and with the planning of European authorities. The streets of a modern district are straight and regular; they cross at right angles or are arranged in star formation. The wealthy native-born live in the modern districts, as well as foreigners with their institu-

[1] For Cairo see Mubarak, II, 84; for Damascus, Berque, *Les Arabes*, p. 18 (also pp. 225–6 on the social and political importance of the *hara* in some towns even today).

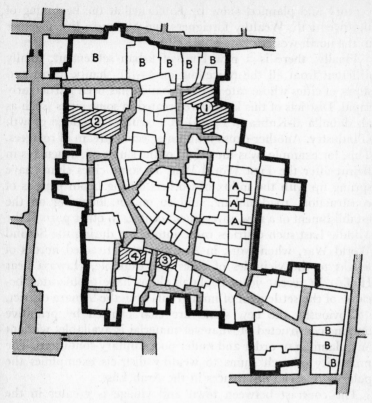

Typical Quarter of Damascus

A. Inner House; B. Houses the walls of which form the boundary of the quarter; 1. Bathhouse; 2. Khan; 3. Mosque; 4. Shops, coffeehouse.

tions (hospitals, schools, consulates). The houses are therefore larger and more impressive here, and generally also lighter; even in the nineteenth century, a whitewashed house was a status symbol of wealth, and of present-day Khartoum it has been said that 'the higher the socio-economic status, the brighter and lighter the wash tint of the residence'.[1]

Modern districts include, for example, Jisr and Shuhada in Damascus, Garden City and Heliopolis in Cairo. Another example is Khartoum, which was destroyed in the nineteenth

[1] Hamdan, p. 40. (For nineteenth-century Egypt see Mubarak, *passim*.)

century and planned anew by Kitchener at the beginning of the twentieth. Wealthy foreigners and Sudanese live together in the north-western part of the city.

Finally, there is a new kind of urban settlement, totally different from all the preceding ones—the shanty towns and slums of cities whose rate of urbanisation has been particularly rapid. Districts of this kind were created in some cities (such as al-Mahalla al-Kubra in Egypt) as a result of a sudden growth of industry. Another cause is an unexpected stream of refugees. This, for example, was the origin of the slums of Armenians in Beirut after the First World War. In some cities slums have sprung up with the influx of workers during boom periods of construction, road-making, and so on, or following on the establishment of a new government centre. In other parts of the Middle East such districts came into being during the Second World War, when work in Army camps attracted hordes of fellahs to the vicinities of cities (for example, Hawasa near Haifa). In recent years Baghdad slums have proliferated because of the settlement of immigrants from the 'Amara district.

Obviously, the new slums are characterised by primitive housing constructed of whatever material is available, without any planning or order and under poor sanitary conditions. The proximity of such slums to wealthy districts exemplifies the polarity of social differences in the Arab East.

The contrast between town and village is greater in the Middle East than in Europe.[1] The Arab city is not only a centre of industry, commerce, and finance but also of administration and jurisdiction, of religion and culture. Activity in all these spheres is concentrated in the city, to the almost complete exclusion of the village. Thus, all institutions connected with industry, commerce, administration, religion, and culture are to be found in the cities. This situation has not altered despite developments of the last generation. Rather, the contrast has if anything become still sharper. All the institutions newly introduced in the process of westernisation, such as modern factories, hospitals, libraries, places of amusement, and

---

[1] The historical background of this contrast is dealt with by H. A. R. Gibb and H. Bowen in their *Islamic Society and the West*, Part I, London, 1950, p. 276. The contrast is sometimes the origin of deep hatred between villager and townsman; see Khalid, *Min huna nabda'*, pp. 73-4.

so on, became a part of the cities and especially of a few large cities.

Furthermore, the gap in social development between village and town has grown within the last generation, because means of modern communication are almost all concentrated in the city. Even in a country such as Lebanon, with its relatively well-developed villages, Beirut and Tripoli together have more than 70% of all cinema seats, and Beirut alone more than 60% of all radios. All Egyptian daily newspapers are published in five main cities, more than half of them in Cairo. Cairo accounts for about half of all Egypt's radios, and Alexandria has more radios than all Lower Egypt.[1]

The main typical institutions of the Arab city are:

(1) *The Market (suq).* The market or bazaar is sometimes considered to be the secular Middle Eastern institution *par excellence*. It is a centre where all commercial transactions take place. The market deals in all kinds of traditional goods required by the local population, and the workshops producing most of these goods are situated there. Each branch of merchandise or craft has its own street or area: coppersmiths (*suq an-nahhasin*), druggists (*suq al-'attarin*), etc. In Damascus, for instance, there are streets named Suq as-Suf (Wool Market), Suq al-Harir (Silk Market), etc. While the traditional market does sell European commodities (clothing material, cigarette lighters, and so on), the shops containing expensive European and American manufactured products (such as automobiles, refrigerators, radios, and so on) are generally situated outside the market, in modern districts. The market itself is in the old city, often near the citadel. It is arched in by overhanging houses on either side of the street, or is covered by some material. Shops face the street, without door or windows, and are closed only by shutters. Streets are narrow and winding, and inaccessible to vehicles. This type of construction, and the location of the market within the walls of the old city, were dictated by the needs of defence in case of raids from outside. Weekly or seasonal fairs for the nearby farmers are held in an open space or square, generally outside the city. The market is usually near the main mosque of the city, and fellahs take

[1] Lerner and Pevsner, *The Passing of Traditional Society*, pp. 191–2, 253.

the opportunity provided by their weekly visit to the city on Friday to combine business and prayer.

A typical commercial structure in the Arab town is the *khan* (in Egypt, the *wakala*): this is a large square building with an enclosed courtyard; on the ground floor are shops facing the courtyard, which serves as a warehouse. The upper stories are living quarters for merchants (commercial travellers or permanent inhabitants) or they are again used as warehouses. The *khan* has only one entrance, which is closed at night. With the development of modern forms of storage and lodgings, the *khan* is in a state of rapid decline.

(2) *The Mosque.* Muslims are obliged to take part in Friday noon prayers, *salat al-jum'a*, in a mosque. Usually small mosques are scattered throughout the city, and they are the more numerous the older the quarter. However, in order to unite the members of various Arab tribes, large central mosques—*masjid jami'* or simply *jami'*—were built in most cities even during the period of the Arabian kingdom and the Islamic Caliphate. In some cities, such as Damascus and Jerusalem, there is one main *jami'*, in others (Cairo, for example) there are several. The mosque is not only a place for prayer, reading from the Koran, and sermons; it also has extensive social functions. In the past it was the place of judgement, and even now many mosques contain religious law courts. In some cities the mosque is a centre of learning and education, with its attached *madrasa* (high school). The mosque also has great importance as a political centre; public meetings are held here for leaders to voice announcements of a political nature. Such meetings take place in the large court (*sahn*) by the mosque.

(3) In the past the *baths* (*hammam*) served as a place of meeting for public affairs. Over the years it has been replaced by the *café*, which is a club-house where men meet for talk, political discussions (political parties and associations often hold their meetings there), and for entertainment; the café is the home of the story-teller, the *hakawati*, and the stage for the *karagöz*, shadow play, and so on. In this last capacity, however, the café has recently been replaced by the cinema, which more and more is superseding traditional forms of entertainment.

(4) Naturally, the city also has government institutions

(central and municipal), some housed in old buildings outside but in the vicinity of the old city, and some in more modern buildings, in the new districts built by Mandatory governments or by the independent states. New districts also house hospitals, high schools, and colleges, also mainly built within the last generation, as well as banks and modern business buildings, which again are a relatively new phenomenon.

(5) Finally, there are the modern factories of the last few years. These were built in the large cities, often in special districts (such as Shubra al-Khaima in Cairo, Karmuz in Alexandria, etc.).

4. *URBAN SOCIETY*

The literature on the towns of the Arab East is almost entirely concerned with the history, geography, and economy of these cities. No survey of the social structure of any city has been carried out, and there has not even been much research on special groups of the urban population. It is thus impossible to summarise results of research in the present discussion, which will be limited to trends of development only.

The discussion of urban society is divided into two parts: (*a*) a summary of the main trends differentiating modern Arab urban society from village and beduin society, in terms of subjects discussed in the first two chapters of this book (demography, the woman, and the family, together with certain associated questions); and (*b*) an analysis of the differences between town and village in terms of factors forming the social units (kinship, religion, language, territorial ties, occupation, and class).

It was noted that urbanisation implies two main differences between the composition of the rural and urban populations: the percentage of men, and of persons of working age, is higher in the city than in the village; and the age groupings in the city are likely to develop towards a composition that is less 'young' than in the village, as a result of a more rapid fall of the birth rate and death rate in the city. However, even in the few Middle Eastern countries that have issued more or less exact statistical data, no research projects have ever been directed towards an analysis of the direct influence of these

o

factors on urban age groupings during the process of urbanisation.

For the same reason, it is difficult to compare natural increase in town and village. Clearly, health standards are rising more rapidly in the city, because there are more doctors and health services there (even though conditions may actually be worse in the slums). On the other hand, the city has more suitable conditions for a lowered birth rate: the young child does not participate in the family livelihood as does the village child, and furthermore, the expenses of raising children are greater in the city because of higher standards of living and because of more prolonged attendance at school. With the extension of education in the city, there is a rise in the age of marriage and fewer children are wanted, in order that each may be given a better education and may rise in the social scale. For all these reasons there is a greater tendency towards birth control in the city than among village families.

However, there is as yet no material evidence which might indicate which of the two processes—towards a lower death rate or a lower birth rate—is more rapid, and it is thus impossible to say with any degree of certainty where the natural increase is at present greater, and where the rise in the natural increase is greater, in Middle Eastern cities or villages. Official statistics published in the Arab countries are not very helpful. From statistics on the registration of births and deaths in Egypt one gets the impression that rates of birth, death, and natural increases are greater in Cairo and Alexandria than in the rest of the country; but this is due to the more exact *registration* in these two cities. Dr Marzouk, noting this fact, tried to analyse the situation on the basis of the 1947 census. His conclusions were that the number of children who died per married woman was lower in Cairo and Alexandria than in other parts of the country; also, the average number of children who lived per married woman was smaller in these cities than in other regions, particularly rural parts.[1]

[1] G. A. Marzouk, 'Fertility of the Urban and Rural Population in Egypt', *L'Égypte contemporaine*, January 1957, pp. 28, 32–4. Saaty's assertion ('The Middle Classes in Egypt', *L'Égypte contemporaine*, April 1957, p. 54) that the average urban family is larger than the average village one because of a lower rate of infant mortality, appears to be unproven, to say the least. On the other hand, Chehabe ed-Dine makes use of figures apparently indicating a higher death rate for Beirut

The differences between urban woman and fellah or beduin woman are most striking. Polygamy is more common in the village and desert than in the city, divorce less so. The urban woman participates less in economic affairs than her village and beduin counterparts, who are often compelled to carry out hard labour. In quite a few cities women are still veiled, while village and beduin women generally expose their faces. For these two reasons the urban woman is more secluded from the men's world. On the other hand, recently, education of women has spread more in the city than in the village; women have even reached the universities and assumed professional status. Urban women were the first to start participating in politics. In short, the city has both the more secluded woman and the more progressive woman who has taken great steps towards emancipation.

This progress of the urban woman is due also to changes that have occurred in urban family structure—changes which surpassed those of the village. It has been seen that the appearance of new sources of livelihood in the city, enabling young persons to break their ties with the father of the family, was one of the main reasons why patriarchal family life has lost its hold and the extended family has split into smaller units. Both processes were stronger in the town than in the village. Furthermore, the practice of endogamy is apparently disappearing in the city, while in the village, and particularly among the beduins, it has been maintained; however, there is no evidence available from actual research for confirmation of this impression.

Fragmentation of the urban extended family does not automatically nullify the family tie as a factor determining the structure of urban society. In discussing the division of the city into districts and quarters, it was seen that the familial tie often united members of a certain quarter. Indeed, in towns which developed from large villages, and particularly in old towns which have preserved their traditional character, the hamula is still the unit of social organisation among part of its inhabitants. This also explains the nature of social power in such towns: power is in the hands of large, wealthy, and prominent families

than for village regions of Lebanon. In fact, the difference is small, and quite explicable in terms of the more precise registration in the cities. (Chehabe ed-Dine, pp. 212-13.)

(hamulas).[1] Some such small towns with a structure largely based on the hamula, which have been described in the literature, are Irbid, as-Salt, and Ramallah in Jordan.[2]

Nevertheless, social organisation based on families is weakening in the city, and in some parts is actually disappearing, for a variety of reasons; one is differentiation, which has slowly insinuated itself into the family, splitting it into its rich and its poor, and also into various economic and professional groups of unequal social and civic status. Urbanisation also challenges the old organisation by family; immigrants usually do not come to the city as complete hamulas. Loyalty to the hamula is being replaced by other loyalties and new frameworks, economic and political. The larger and more modern the city, and the more outsiders it assimilates, the weaker the organisation of its inhabitants by hamula. Another important factor is the establishment of various associations and clubs (*nadi*; plural, *andiya*) in most cities of the Arab Middle East since the start of this century; the clubs, frequented by hundreds and thousands, are dissolving organisation by hamula, although it is much rarer that they affect the religious or communal sect.

The declining importance of the hamula in forming the structure of urban society is generally accompanied by a corresponding trend in the *religious and communal tie*. True, there are more religious communities concentrated in the city. Members of various Christian denominations and Jews are exclusively town-dwellers, while extensive rural areas are homogeneous in communal structure. The meeting-ground of communities in the city is liable to strengthen the sense of community membership among townsmen. Moreover, only in the city have associations and organisations been founded on a communal basis; they also help to consolidate the community as a social and political unit. For example, there are community philanthropic associations in scores of Arab Middle Eastern towns; youth movements, women's organisations of Muslims, Copts, Maronites, etc.; semi-military organisations, such as the *Kata'ib*,

---

[1] Cf. Shimoni, Chapter 11; Jaussen, *Naplouse*, pp. 138–9 (who noted the declining social influence of large and prominent families of Nablus even in the 1920s). On Damascus see also Berque, *Les Arabes*, pp. 16–17.

[2] Patai, *Jordan*, pp. 273–6; Zarour, pp. 432–3. The characteristics of hamula organisation were considered earlier, in the section on village society; in so far as it is preserved the city hamula does not differ from the rural one.

Najjada, and even parties, as the Muslim Brotherhood. Such organisations are formed in the city partly because it is the centre and main sphere of activity of religious functionaries. Obviously, this is true mainly of certain small towns of special religious character, such as Hebron or Najaf and Karbala—the holy cities of the Shi'a in Southern Iraq. But in all the towns the political clash with Christian European powers, and a reaction to the influx of Western culture and civilisation have led in the most recent years to an intensified consciousness of belonging to the Muslim community, all over the Middle East, and especially in the cities.

On the other hand, in some respects city life engenders a weakening of religious and communal ties. First, there is again the disintegration of the extended family and hamula organisation. In the Middle East a person does not belong to some community as an individual but as a member of his family and hamula; loss of identification with the kinship group is, then, liable to lead to a similar break with the religious community. In the city religious faith and observance of religious precepts are on the decline—as a result of the gradual development of rationalistic attitudes, the spread of education, and contact with the West. These processes do not proceed at an equal rate among all urban classes. As in the case of the emancipation of women, here, too, it has been observed that the upper classes are quicker to cast off their faith than the middle classes.

The authors of a book on modernisation in the Middle East found that among those questioned, villagers attended the mosque much more frequently than townsmen, both in Egypt and in Jordan. When asked what was their favourite radio programme, 89% of Egyptian villagers and 71% of Jordanian villagers mentioned readings from the Koran, while in Egypt this was the answer of only 64% of labourers, 38% of clerks, and 28% of professionals; among those questioned in Jordan, it was the favourite programme of 14% of all entrepreneurs and 4% of the city *élite*.[1]

It was stressed in Chapter III that when the religious way of life loses its attraction there is not an immediate change in

---

[1] Lerner and Pevsner, pp. 230, 234, 317, 330. However, at least with regard to attendance at prayers in the mosque, these conclusions require further investigation. Cf. Fuller, *Buarij*, p. 81.

the Middle Eastern individual's feelings for his religious community as a group possessing certain social and political functions. However, indifference to religion must eventually lead to a growing degree of indifference towards the religious community as a social grouping. Moreover, in the last generation the city even more than the village has witnessed a decline in the importance of the Sufi orders. In connection with village society it was mentioned that these frequently constitute the framework of social life; decline of the orders means that one of the important social functions of religion has been lost. Finally, religious and communal ties in the city have been weakened at the expense of other ties, developing from within the city and establishing new social units, such as language, local attachments, occupation, and class.

Each of these factors, and its influence on the structure of the urban social structure, will now be considered.

The *linguistic factor* has grown to a prominent position in urban society for the same reasons that it remained insignificant in the village. The Arab rural populace encounters linguistic minorities only at the fringe of the Arab countries,[1] while the Arab urban populace is almost daily in contact with persons speaking foreign languages, such as the Turks, Armenians, Persians and Europeans. The linguistic groups often live together in their own special districts, and this, of course, strengthens their group-identification. Feelings are further nurtured by education—reading and writing in the national language and understanding its cultural heritage. In this sphere the city is naturally ahead of the village. Kurdish national consciousness, for example, had its first impetus in cities in which a Kurdish educated class arose and the Kurdish language and literary heritage were recognised. Linguistic group-consciousness is fostered often in order to bridge the differences between members of different communities or regions. It is also strengthened by interaction with a foreign rule and European culture. In the last generation all these factors together have helped to make the urban populace aware of itself as an Arab people whose common denominator is the Arabic language.

Loyalty to the Arab people comes into conflict with other loyalties, based on kinship, religious community, socio-

[1] Except for the Sudan.

economic status, and even geographical–territorial ties (such as Egyptian nationalism, Iraqi nationalism, etc.). On the other hand, there has been little conflict with loyalty based on *local ties*—local patriotism of members of a certain city. It is indeed true that politics have sometimes kindled enmity between cities, such as that between Damascus and Aleppo, or between certain Iraqi cities, but this was never based on civic awareness of townsmen, but, rather, usually involved the vested interests of a very limited group of upper-class people only.

The Arab city, like the village, was never an 'organism' but only a conglomeration, and even today it has few institutions of self-rule. The Arab town of the Middle Ages was without independent or autonomous municipal institutions. Since then, the inhabitants have had some share in their city's management, and in most Middle Eastern Arab cities there is a *baladiya* (municipality). But even now, central authorities have a firm hand on these bodies; in Egypt they are composed of representatives elected and appointed by the authorities, but are headed by a delegate of the *mudir* (governor of the province) or the *ma'mur* (governor of the district). According to the new 1960 law of local government, the authorities appoint the head of the local council and also have a major influence in choice of the council's members.[1] In Iraq heads of municipalities are appointed by the Minister of the Interior. In Saudi Arabia, too, most of the members of the municipalities are appointed. In this connection it is noteworthy that the lack of solidarity among townsmen is due mainly to the lack of a well-developed middle class (see also Chapter V). As a result, in contradistinction to Europe, the Middle East has witnessed the growth of ties of a linguistic–national nature long before the growth of local ties. 'C'est un paradoxe de l'Orient que, contrairement a l'histoire européenne, l'entité nationale y précède l'entité communale.'[2]

Differentiation by occupation, almost non-existent in the village, has a highly consequential place in the social structure of the city. Chapter V is devoted to the significance of occupational division and the economic status of various groups in the Arab city, from the viewpoint of urban social structure and changes in the social stratification of the Middle East.

[1] *MER*, 1960, p. 495.   [2] Berque, *Les Arabes*, p. 152.

V

STRATIFICATION

Analysis of the class stratification of Arab society in the Middle East is hampered by the almost complete absence of research material in this field. There has not been a single attempt to investigate the stratification of a sector of Arab society using criteria such as power, status, or prestige. Even on more concrete criteria, such as wealth or economic function, there is only a very limited extent of information, since not one of the Arab countries has actually issued statistics on income. Statistics on distribution by occupation exist for Egypt alone, and even here they leave much to be desired. The following discussions can, then, only suggest general ideas which some future research may complement by filling in the details or correct on the basis of new material and new conclusions.

Because of insufficient data, it is unwarranted to attempt to divide Arab society into a large number of well-defined classes. A more practical and realistic method, and that adopted here, is to analyse the special characteristics of economic and occupational groups within each of three main classes—upper, middle, and lower.

The 'upper class' is taken to include groups in whose hands abundant possessions or great wealth are concentrated, the social power groups in most Arab villages and towns; these groups also held political sway until recent years (whenever foreigners were not in control). Apart from large landowners and merchants, this class includes entrepreneurs and industrialists who have close ties to the former two groups (indeed, they are generally identical), and thus are not to be included among the 'middle classes', as is the practice in the West.

In the 'lower class' we include persons without property who are wage-earning labourers, or who are engaged in undefined work, as well as fellahs whose small landed property is in-sufficient for upkeep of the family, and who are therefore compelled to lease land from larger estate-owners or to work for a wage, while also farming their own plots. This class does not include persons whose earnings are gained from work involving any degree of education, since the differences in standard of living, way of life, social standing, and power between clerk and physical labourer are so much greater in the Middle East than in the West. Furthermore, the bureau-cracy is mainly of higher-class origin.

The 'middle class', embracing all groups not belonging to either of the other two classes, is very heterogeneous and diversified, including fellahs of limited means, professionals, small merchants, and army officers, among others. The middle class has remnants of a traditional society in the process of disintegration and new developing branches. Despite its variegation, the class is still much smaller than its counterpart in the West. True, as it is difficult to pinpoint the class in any precise fashion, its size cannot be determined accurately either; there are enormous discrepancies between the results of two recent attempts in this direction. Two authors tried to work out the number of gainfully occupied persons who may be said to belong to the urban middle class of Egypt, the only country which has issued any statistical information.[1] One arrived at the figure of 112,900 and the other at 499,164. Even assuming that the higher figure is an underestimate of the actual number of gainfully employed members of the middle class, it is still true that the middle class is relatively much smaller in Egypt than in the West. In all other Middle Eastern countries, except for Lebanon and possibly Syria, the urban middle class constitutes an even smaller percentage of the total population than in Egypt. The result is a great polarity of class stratification and marked class differences.

It is still more difficult to define the *rural* middle class and to estimate its scope. Here, statistics (again, for Egypt alone) are likely to be even more misleading. Indeed, the authors quoted earlier arrived at the figures of 620,395 and 134,562, respectively, for the rural gainfully employed members of the middle class.

[1] Saaty, p. 57; Berger, *The Middl Classes*, pp. 63–4.

At any rate, it is clear that because of the existence of large-scale landed property, the middle class is relatively limited in the village, particularly in countries such as Iraq with its almost total absence of middle-sized estates. Nevertheless, there is no doubt that the middle class is steadily gaining ground in the Arab world, and its first intimations have been heard even from countries such as Saudi Arabia.

Before discussing the various strata and classes in any detail, two remarks are pertinent. Differentiation between groups does not signify that each occupies a well-defined and clearly distinguishable position. On the contrary, a basic characteristic of Middle Eastern society is the personal or familial identity of landowners and big businessmen, or even industrialists, and the ties between landowners and a large proportion of the educated classes and the bureaucracy. Furthermore, strata are not rigid, and it is common to find transitions from one to another and from class to class. This phenomenon of great social mobility is connected with the fact that Islam and Middle Eastern society in general has no exclusive nobility or aristocracy preserving marriage ties within its own close circle. Also quite foreign to Islam is the system of castes, prevalent in much of Asia. Hence also the cultural differences between classes are slight, and, for example, there are no class dialects such as are found in other countries.

This mobility has increased in the last generation as a result of urbanisation, economic development, and spread of education, and as a result of the political upheavals which terminated the privileged political and social position of foreigners and local landowners. Abolition of the special status of these groups had its greatest impact on urban society. To take one example, the boundaries between the living-quarters of this former *élite* and those of other groups have blurred. The following statement, written of Khartoum, is more or less valid for other cities: 'With the recently increasing social and political mobility, class segregation has become much less rigid than it was a few decades ago, when residential zoning was avowedly on a class and race basis.'[1]

[1] Hamdan, p. 33.

A. UPPER CLASSES

The large landowners of the Middle East are generally town-dwellers, although their income derives from agriculture. This is no novelty peculiar to the twentieth century: throughout the history of the Arabs, the group which ruled the village generally lived in the city rather than on a rural estate. The class has undergone changes in keeping with political permutations, but its members have remained mostly in the cities. This is also one of the reasons why a real landed aristocracy has never been formed in the Middle East.[1] There are a few exceptions to this rule: for instance, some prominent families of certain minority groups living in mountainous regions which were autonomous during the period of the Ottoman Empire.

The large landowners of today are a new class, formed, as noted in the discussion of land tenure, in the nineteenth and twentieth centuries. Its manner of formation, discussed earlier, explains the urban nature of this class. Every one of the large landowners whose property was confiscated in Egypt (up to the end of 1955) lived in Cairo or Alexandria or both cities. (Occasionally, the city residence was additional to one on the estate or in a nearby provincial town.) In other Middle Eastern countries the situation is similar. The urban location of this class is due not only to the fact that many rich and prominent people of the city became landowners within the last hundred years; also beduin shaikhs and village notables who became landowners transferred to the cities in search of new fields of economic activity. Furthermore, cities were the centres of administrative and political influence, and when the Arab states won independence cities became the seats of parliaments in which these landowners acted as delegates.

Large landowners and their families fulfilled functions of primary importance in civic and national public life, and in many places their position has remained unaltered to this day. They themselves, their sons who studied law, or members of other prominent families related to them by marriage, had strong representation in the Government, the high bureaucracy,

---

[1] Arab names have no titles denoting nobility, like the French *de* or the German *von*.

parliaments, municipalities, various committees, and all political parties (except those formed recently after the Western pattern). An investigation of the sources of income of Syrian Members of Parliament in 1937 disclosed that among those from whom details were elicited (60 out of 85 members), at least 20 were landowners. (Possibly a further 9 lawyers and 2 other persons, previously Ottoman officials, should be added to the list.) Similarly, an Egyptian newspaper found that among the 319 Egyptian Members of Parliament elected at the beginning of 1950, 115 owned land amounting to more than 100 feddans each, 45 owning at least 500 feddans of land. In the Lebanese Parliament of the early 1950s there were 21 landowners out of 44 delegates.[1] Even the Egyptian women's movement was headed by a member of the Sha'rawi family (one of the largest landowners of Egypt). In Egypt the rule of this layer took the form of high legislative and executive authority granted to the king, the largest of landowners. However, political rule by landowners has now been abolished in some of the more important Arab countries by the revolutions of recent years. As agrarian reform proceeds, the economic and social standing of landowners is also undermined.

As mentioned earlier, the group of large landowners is not exclusive or clear-cut. On the contrary, it is interwoven with the group of large-scale merchants, real-estate owners, contractors, and even industrialists.[2] At times landowners or members of their families have participated in all branches of urban activity. An outstanding example of this is Egypt in 1929–35, when an agricultural crisis and protective tariffs led many landowners (e.g., the Badrawi-'Ashur, Sultan, and Wisa families) to invest their capital in industry.[3] Similar examples may be found in Syria (the Mudarris family of Aleppo, for instance). On the other hand, there are large-scale merchants and contractors who have invested their profits in land, and some have become landowners by accumulating capital from moneylending or other means (the Ahmad 'Abbud family; cotton merchants such as Amin Yihya, Muhammad al-

[1] *OM*, 1937, pp. 471–95; *Images* (illustrated weekly), 28 January 1950; Lerner and Pevsner, p. 454.

[2] Many examples for Egypt are given in Baer, *History of Landownership*, pp. 140–2.

[3] A. A. I. Gritly, 'The Structure of Modern Industry in Egypt', *L'Égypte contemporaine*, November–December 1947, p. 376.

Maghazi, al-Wakil, and others; merchants of Homs and Hama; and so on). The amalgamation of merchants and landowners is one of the principal reasons why there is no sharp contrast in the Middle East between the urban bourgeoisie and the landed aristocracy, while that contrast is an essential feature of the history of some European countries at the dawn of the modern era.

A second group of the upper class, having strong ties with the large landowners, is that of large-scale merchants. Commerce, unlike agriculture, has always been an esteemed activity among Arabs. However, with the spread and development of trade with Europe, important positions in large-scale commerce were taken over by Europeans, and later by members of minority groups. The commercial activities of large-scale Muslim Arab merchants, which also spread in all countries of the Middle East, were concerned chiefly with internal trade, and dealings in agricultural produce rather than industrial goods. These merchants have always engaged in moneylending and banking as well as commerce.

Over the last generation, the wealthy mercantile class has been the major source of a third group—the entrepreneur class of contractors and industrialists.[1] This group is still small, chiefly for the same reasons that held back development of industry in the Middle East: backwardness and a low standard of living in the village, and hence a limited domestic market for the young industry; lack of independent growth of the city, which was ruled by the same group as the village; retarded spread of education, and in particular, the low standard of technical skills; and finally, since the nineteenth century, obstruction of industrial advance because of trade relations with Europe, or even sometimes, because of the deliberate policy of European powers which were not interested in the growth of local industry. Possibly in the past the Islamic tradition of fatalism, prohibition of usury (*riba*) and risk (*maysir*) may also have obstructed the development of an entrepreneur class. However, even in the Middle Ages, Muslims used to circumvent these interdictions, and nowadays their influence is negligible.

[1] For detailed discussion see C. Issawi, 'The Entrepreneur Class', in S. N. Fisher (ed.), *Social Forces in the Middle East*, New York, 1955.

Local industrialists derive their capital primarily from large-scale commerce, and to a lesser extent from the profits of large landownership. On the other hand, the new stratum was only to a small extent drawn from the group of artisans (its source in some European countries); the latter group lost its wealth as a result of the import of European goods, which outsold local produce. Furthermore, the class of artisans and medium-scale industrialists is altogether limited in the Middle East. More will be said of the structural polarity of Arab industry in the discussion of the working class.

Many of the new entrepreneurs were originally members of minority groups—Armenians and Arab Christians, Jews, Greeks, and other European minorities. But Islam does not preclude capitalistic or industrial enterprise; in Syria, for example, the majority of industrialists are Muslims, and so, too, in present-day Egypt and Iraq. Investment in Lebanese local industry was provided by merchants whose capital had been formed by brokerage, merchants dealing in inter-Arab trade, and financiers, as well as merchants who emigrated to America and Africa and amassed their capital there. Most Syrian industrialists were merchants (importers, representatives of foreign firms, etc., such as the owners of the *al-Khumasiya* firm, the Sahnawi group of Damascus, Hariri, and Shabarik of Aleppo). The new Syrian entrepreneurs, leasing land in Jazira from beduin shaikhs and cultivating it as large-scale capitalistic farms with mechanised agricultural equipment, were also formerly merchants (e.g., the Mamarbachi, Asfar, and Najjar families).

The Egyptian entrepreneur class too, is mainly of mercantile origin, but it is more variegated than its counterpart in other Arab countries. There are large landowners, contractor engineers such as 'Abbud, professionals such as 'Afifi, and others. Many have continued to engage in their original occupations in addition to their activities in industry. This may explain one characteristic of the Middle Eastern upper class which has already been mentioned: the absence of internal economic and political conflict. As an example, we may consider the professional organisations within the class. In the cities of Lebanon there are combined chambers of commerce and industry; in Egypt (1958) these organisations were separate, but of the six executive officers of the Egyptian chamber of commerce in Alexandria, three were at the same time presidents of industrial organisations. In Syria there are separate chambers of commerce (formed before the First World War in Damascus and Aleppo) and industry (all formed within the past two decades). In Iraq and the Sudan there are no chambers of industry.[1]

Some claim that entrepreneurship in the Middle East is at the same stage of development as in the era of commercial capitalism in Europe, with all that that implies—absence of rational business practices, operation without visible records, direct management by the owner, etc. An outstanding characteristic of entrepreneurship in the Middle East is the persistence of the family firm. The social status of merchants is at least as estimable as that of industrial entrepreneurs, and generally it is regarded even more highly.[2]

Close ties are not limited to industrialists–entrepreneurs and large-scale merchants. Many persons of the upper class still prefer to invest their capital in immovables rather than in industry; industrialists, for their part, tend to invest in land, partly because of the social prestige which landownership implies. This is one reason for the common vested interests of industrialists and landowners. A further reason concerns the newly emergent working class, engaged in a fierce struggle against industrialists. This, and the general social tension in the city, has checked the industrialists from open conflict with the rule of landowners. Thus, there was no Middle Eastern party representing industrialists which called for agrarian reform, for instance; in all traditional parties landowners and industrialists have gone hand in hand.

Even after the rule of landowners was abolished, following the military revolts in many Arab countries, private enterprise was not impelled towards a fresh spurt of industrial development. For various reasons the new régimes replaced private enterprise by government-sponsored enterprise, and even suppressed the efforts of private industrialists. Some of their

---

[1] *The Middle East 1958*, Europa Publications, London, 1958, pp. 127, 196, 283, 332, 363.
[2] A. J. Meyer, *Middle East Capitalism*, Cambridge, Mass., 1959, pp. 34-9; cf. Berque, *Les Arabes*, pp. 106, 109.

reasons were the need for rapid development with the aid of loans and grants from abroad; disbelief in the capacity of private enterprise to turn to industrial development (capitalists displayed a trend towards investing in urban immovables or hoarding gold rather than investing in industry); a desire, in Egypt, to get rid of members of foreign minorities in high economic positions; fear of the creation of a new socio-political power which would not yield to the central rule; and the need and desire to carry out a social policy for the benefit of the lower classes without obstruction. In 1961 a series of laws was passed in Egypt whose object it was to restrict private enterprise and to place a large number of industrial concerns in government hands.

Consequently, in several Arab countries, especially in Egypt, a new type of entrepreneur-bureaucrat has appeared: 'L'entrepreneur du moment, c'est l'activité bureaucratique.'[1] Examples are the officials in charge of management of the Suez Canal when it was put into operation after nationalisation. Obviously, it is too early to assess the character of this new group.

B. MIDDLE CLASSES

The middle classes in the Arab countries have not consolidated like the upper class, and they contain many highly diverse elements. It is the middle class which in fact bears the greatest burden of public activities in the city—religious and secular, social and political. This class has been the main source of active party members. (One of the outstanding expressions of the political struggle in these countries was the closing of shops and workshops, and demonstrations by students.) Although the middle class has also produced its spokesmen, organisers, and even leaders, the main leadership has generally remained, until recently, in the hands of the upper class. Up to a few years ago the middle classes, unlike the upper class, played no independent role in social and political life.

As a non-employing class, the middle class in the Arab world has little economic power, and has been, as a class, rather distant from the fount of all power in that area, the government. The other major component of the middle class, the civil servants, are of course

[1] Berque, *Les Arabes*, p. 118.

closer to the seat of power, but are a rather pliant instrument in the hands of the real holders of political and economic power.[1]

Recently there have been changes, but it is still difficult to evaluate their character. At any rate, in some Arab states groups such as the army officers have emerged and come out openly against the formerly dominant upper class.

Of course, all this applies to the urban middle classes. The rural middle class is very small, and its members are scattered among thousands of villages, so that it lacks any power or activity as a group. It has indeed provided a good many of the political and spiritual leaders of the modern Arab states, particularly Egypt (Muhammad 'Abduh, Sa'd Zaghlul, 'Abd an-Nasir, and others). However, as a class, it has not participated in public affairs like the urban middle classes and has not actively contributed as they have to the changes of recent years.

The largest group among the urban middle classes is probably that of artisans and small tradesmen. This group, whose contact with Western influences and culture is slight, has suffered from the infiltration of Western merchandise. Outstanding in this respect is Syria, which before the First World War was an important centre of traditional handicraft. The number of persons employed in the traditional crafts changed as follows (according to a survey by the Mandatory Government in 1937):[2]

	1913	1937
Damascus	39,511	25,404
Aleppo	44,889	38,005
Homs	19,530	6,500
Hama	6,743	1,915
Total	110,673	71,824

The same survey indicates that, over a certain period, modern industries did not develop at a rate comparable to the decline of the traditional handicrafts, and thus could not absorb those workers who lost their jobs. Traditional small-scale commerce has also suffered as a result of competition with modern shops, which have increased in number as consumer tastes change. In various parts of the Arab East, particularly in Egypt, the appearance of department stores has seriously harmed the

[1] Berger, *The Middle Class*, p. 66.   [2] Grunwald, p. 244.

traditional sector of small tradesmen. (Most of the owners of the modern shops were foreigners or members of minority groups.) As a result, artisans and small tradesmen in various parts of the Arab world have become vociferous in their opposition to and hatred of foreigners and Westernisation in general.

It should be noted that a decline in the absolute number of the artisan and tradesman group has not occurred in all parts of the Middle East. The trend towards urbanisation over the past generation, and in particular the growth of new governmental and military centres, has created favourable conditions for increased numbers of shops, laundries, barbers, and other services required by the new government officials, labourers in the building trade, and in transport, etc. Despite the lack of reliable statistics, it seems unlikely that in the long run this class has suffered a numerical decline. On the other hand, social consolidation and organisation of the class have clearly been harmed as a result of the economic developments and Westernisation of the last few generations. As late as the end of the nineteenth century, artisans and tradesmen were organised in corporations, each headed by a shaikh. They afforded their members considerable social security, and fulfilled other important functions in social and economic spheres. At the end of the nineteenth and the beginning of the twentieth centuries the corporations disappeared, and they are no longer to be found in the cities of the Arab East.[1] They have not been replaced, however, by new social bodies, and the group of artisans and small tradesmen is now amorphous, lacking any organised form.

Besides artisans and tradesmen, the middle classes are largely composed of various groups whose occupations demand some degree of education, i.e., religious functionaries, the bureaucracy, professionals, and the educated class in general. Among these groups there is much differentiation, between *muftis* and local *imams*, for example, or between the high officialdom and small clerks. A small but important sector of this group definitely belong to the upper class by origin, income, influence, and

---

[1] Remnants of craft guilds are to be found in Yemen (Fayein, p. 102), and in Qatar among artisans and merchants of the lower classes, who keep up the traditional rites (oral information).

attitudes; another larger part is proletarian in social standing. However, the majority undoubtedly lies between these two groups—that is, in the middle classes.

The group having the longest tradition is that of religious functionaries. In theory there is in Islam no clergy who might claim to intervene between man and God. However, as Islam assumed more rigid forms, a group of persons commanding social and religious authority and prestige similar in kind to that of the Christian clergy came into being. They are collectively known as the *'ulama*—versed in law and theology and their interpretation. The group is composed of the following professions: *qadi* (judge); *mufti* (who expands on questions of law); teachers at all levels, from shaikh of the *kuttab* to professor at religious seminaries; the *imam* (leader in public worship); *khatib* (deliverer of the sermon in public worship); and *wa'iz* (preacher). The group also includes other employees of religious institutions whose work does not require religious training, such as the position of the *mu'adhdhin* (who summons the believers to prayer) and a long list of officials and servants of the mosque. Also to be counted in the group are the heads of the *sharifs* (descendants of the family of the Prophet) and of the orders, which over the years have been joined by orthodox men of religion.

The gamut of religious functionaries is, then, most diverse. In Muslim history this class has been subject to many vicissitudes, and its state has differed from country to country. In general, however, it may be said that until the nineteenth century the class was one of the important elements of the old social structure of the Arab world. With the establishment of modern systems of rule in the Middle East its influence and power have dropped; none the less, it has maintained considerable authority among Muslims, as its members still pass judgement in all questions of personal status and related matters, such as inheritances, wills, etc. It is recognised as a body defending the interests of the Muslim masses. Religious functionaries are in direct contact with almost every individual of the urban (and rural) Muslim population, via the *imams*, *khatibs*, and shaikhs of the *kuttab*. An institution which helped them to retain their influence was the waqf, the income of which was an important source of revenue to charitable causes and religious or educational establishments, and which were in many cases managed by religious functionaries. In some countries the Sufi orders channelled contact and influence of the religious establishment to extensive sectors of the population, particularly to small-scale craftsmen and merchants. In the last generation, with the decline of the orders, a new form of middle-class organisation under religious direction has appeared—clubs and associations of Muslims with philanthropic, social, and political aims.

As against these factors, which tend to preserve the influence of the religious group, there are many developments of the nineteenth and twentieth centuries whose effect has been to weaken their position. First, their economic position has declined: previous to modern development many religious functionaries amassed capital as *multazims*. However, after tax-farming had been abolished few religious functionaries continued to be large landowners. Furthermore, the institution which provided them with their most important source of income, the waqf, has considerably changed. The number of waqfs which were established in favour of religious bodies is small, and the supervision of religious functionaries was restricted when the management of waqfs was taken over by the State.

The social standing of the religious group has also been greatly affected. Earlier, it was mentioned that the standing of *sharifs* and *sayyids* has declined; so has the social importance of the orders. It is still too soon to assess the social function of religious clubs and political parties as substitutes for the orders, but there are indications that the importance of these organisations is less now than it was ten or fifteen years ago. The spread of education and literacy meant an end to the monopoly of religion in that sphere. The establishment of a secular school system also had much the same influence. Finally, there are some indications that religious functionaries are about to lose their juridical monopoly in matters of personal status also. Obviously the future position of religious functionaries depends more than anything else on the future of religion as an element of Arab society.

The rate at which religious functionaries are losing their hold varies, of course, from country to country; Egypt and Syria, in the throes of Westernisation, differ from conservative Saudi Arabia and Yemen. But it is not only the degree of Westernisation that counts. In Lebanon, for example, the influence of religious functionaries has been preserved more than might be expected of a country which is perhaps more Westernised than any other in the Arab East. The decisive factor here is Lebanon's unique political structure with strong communal representation. The standing of the religious establishment depends on other factors too, such as the deeply rooted tradition of the orders in the Sudan and Cyrenaica, or the strong representation of the Shi'a in Iraq, particularly its southern regions (the position of the Shi'i *mujtahid* being much stronger than that of the Sunni *'alim*).

It was mentioned earlier that, until recently, middle classes had no independent function in the Arab East, but were dependent on the upper class and supported that class. This is certainly true of the religious functionaries.[1] While their support seems to have been shaken somewhat since the Second World War, it is not they but rather the secular educated groups and the army-officer group which have challenged the old social order.

The group of religious functionaries is one of the oldest social groupings in the Arab city; the secular educated class is a young group, about a century old, which arose with the great extension of secular learning and its institutions. Most of the 'educated' are officials, and especially government employees, and this is a profession highly esteemed among the Arabs. Actually, Berger, in his investigations of the high officialdom of Egypt, reached the conclusion that officials among themselves do not regard their profession so highly; but to the public, their prestige is as great as it ever was.[2] Other signs, too, indicate that much of the urban population regards the bureaucrat's position as superior and that education of sons has this occupation as its object. The sons of many upper-class families are engaged in clerical work, since family means are not sufficient to provide for all its members; also, it is hoped that the family may thus manage to gain influence among the public and with

[1] See Issawi, *Egypt at Mid-Century*, pp. 259–60, 264.
[2] M. Berger, *Bureaucracy and Society in Modern Egypt*, Princeton, 1957, pp. 94–5 and Chapter 4.

the authorities. Seventy per cent of all officials included in Berger's survey had private resources; nearly all derived some income from possessions to supplement their salary; and a large percentage of them were of landowning families.[1] Also among the middle classes, rural and urban, officialdom is a coveted occupation, freeing men from physical labour and raising them to a higher social rank.

The enormous expansion of the bureaucracy began mainly after the establishment of independent governments. According to a former Iraqi Minister of Finance, 'Ali Mumtaz ad-Daftari, the index of the number of officials in government departments (based on 100 in 1936) was 130 in 1940, 159 in 1944, and 218 in 1947.[2] According to a civil service commission in Egypt, the number of governmental posts rose by 61% between the years 1940-1 and 1954-5, reaching 381,615. The number of posts requiring at least a primary education rose, in the same period, from 47,480 to 170,345—i.e., more than two and a half times. According to another survey of the Egyptian civil service, the percentage of the total population engaged as governmental employees was higher there than in Britain; expenditure on bureaucracy, expressed in terms of the percentage of the total budget, was again higher than in Britain, and has risen in recent years, reaching 46% in 1952-3.[3]

Until the achievement of independence there was much competition for these positions between local candidates and foreigners. Even after the establishment of independent governments in some Arab countries the struggle persisted between Muslim candidates and members of the minorities (Copts, Armenians, and Syrians in Egypt, Christians in Syria), who held many posts by virtue of their high level of education. This is one of the causes of the nationalistic resentment common among both the educated classes and those whose ambition it is to place their sons in clerical posts.

A group somewhat similar to the bureaucracy in character and occupation is that of teachers. This has never been so well regarded a profession as the clerical. Many teachers are of middle-class origin, whereas more officials derive from the

---

[1] Berger, *Bureaucracy*, pp. 45, 107.
[2] *az-Zaman*, 3 May 1949.
[3] Berger, *Bureaucracy*, pp. 82-3.

upper class. With the spread of education, the number of teachers has risen greatly: in Egypt, for example, there was a more than twofold rise from 1913–14 to 1942–3 (to almost 50,000), and in the ten succeeding years (to 1952) the number of teachers increased to 64,000. In Iraq the number of teachers at government schools rose almost tenfold between 1920 and 1941, in the following ten-year period it again doubled, reaching 10,000 in 1951, and in 1960 it amounted to 24,367.[1]

The origin of many professionals, such as doctors, engineers, etc., is the upper class. The number of doctors and engineers is as yet small in relation to needs, but the number of lawyers is very great. Many families of the upper class sent their sons to study law in order that they would later be able to protect family business affairs and would enter the political arena as family representatives. The increase of professionals in Egypt is well illustrated by the following table:[2]

	1937	1947
Doctors and Dentists	3,700	6,300
Pharmacists	1,200	1,600
Engineers	8,400	15,800
Writers and journalists	1,200	8,200

The last figure again indicates the definitive trend towards political activity.

Despite a notable increase in the number of positions filled by officials, teachers, agronomists, and lawyers, there is, of course, a limit to the capacity for absorbing these groups—a limit set by the general standard of living and by government budgets. Thus, in some Arab countries the spread of education, particularly higher education, has surpassed the potentialities for absorbing professionals. Development of industry has been limited, and even where there was a lack of engineers, supervisors, and technicians, the educated classes were not prepared to take up those professions and saw no future in them. Among the educated of the Middle East, and particularly in Egypt, there is thus a problem of unemployment.[3] The problem is

[1] Matthews and Akrawi, pp. 37, 140; Cohen, p. 189; *Directory of the Republic of Iraq*, 1960, p. 487.

[2] Makarius, p. 31.

[3] The problem of thousands of unemployed among graduates of agricultural schools was one of the concerns of the land reform committee. See, for instance, *al-Ahram*, 15 January 1955; cf. also Lerner and Pevsner, pp. 237–8, 276.

especially serious because of the contemptuous attitude to manual labour which prevails among most educated persons in the Arab world. For a long time it was customary in Iraq to send orphans (who have always been allotted the more despicable jobs) to the Kulliyat al-Handasa (Engineering College).[1]

There are other reasons, deriving from the present social structure of the Middle East, which underlie the frustration which is so typical of the contemporary Arab intellectual. Education and contact with the outer world have given him personal ambitions directed towards raising his standard of living, and idealistic ambitions to help his country towards rapid modernisation. But he is conscious of the enormous disparity between himself and the masses, which prevents any real mode of communication with most of his fellow countrymen. Furthermore, the existing social and economic structure prevents him from fulfilling either his personal or his national and social aspirations.[2]

In the face of the general social tension prevailing in the city there was much bitterness among intellectuals regarding the existing state of affairs, and this is undoubtedly one of the reasons for the lively political activity of students in the Arab countries. Another reason is that the universities and secondary schools are among the most important concentrations of large numbers of people (another such concentration being the factories), and for intellectual youth there is hardly any social activity other than politics. For example, it may be remembered that in the Sudan a congress of college graduates has been the nucleus for the formation of political parties in the past twenty years. When the army officers revolted against the old order they found that much of the educated class was their willing ally.

The last group to be included in the middle classes, small in scale but important in its function in Middle Eastern society, now as in the past, is the group of army officers. Throughout the modern history of the Middle East (since the nineteenth century), army officers have periodically seized power over the country in order to introduce fundamental social reform: 'Urabi in Egypt in 1881; the Young Turks in 1908; in Iraq

---

[1] Berque, *Les Arabes*, p. 92.
[2] Cf. Lerner and Pevsner, pp. 92–3, 236–7, 277–9.

between 1936 and 1941 and again in 1958; in Syria in 1949 and following years; and in Egypt in 1952.

What is the reason for the instability of army officers' loyalty to the ruling classes? Unlike most Western countries in the various stages of modern development, the Middle East has an army-officer group characterised by the following qualities:

(*a*) Their origin is generally middle class rather than upper class (except for the highest ranks, where appointments were made on the basis of proximity to the ruling *élite*, e.g., Isma'il Shirin, Faruq's brother-in-law, in pre-revolutionary Egypt, or General Taha al-Hashimi of Iraq). Many officers are members of the educated classes who despaired of a professional career. (Naguib, for example, studied law, and there are many other instances of lawyers and teachers.)

(*b*) In some Arab countries the religious or ethnic community of army officers was also different from that of the ruling classes. The clash between Arab officers and the Turkish–Circassian ruling elements was part of the background of the 'Arabi rebellion of 1881; Bakr Sidqi, who headed the Iraq revolt of 1936, was of Kurdish descent; the Syrian Army of the 1940s, which was the heritage of French rule, had especially strong minority-group representation (Kurds, Circassians, 'Alawis); and even in the Egyptian revolution of 1952 the contrast between the insurrecting officer group of Arab origin and Muhammad 'Ali's family, of Turkish descent, was given great publicity.[1]

(*c*) In the Middle East and other Eastern countries young army officers were the pioneers of Westernisation and social reform. The Army was the first body to be modelled on the Western pattern; it was an agent for the dissemination of Western influences, including concepts of social reform. Moreover, the blemishes of the old social order are openly reflected in army life. The ignorant and sick fellah is an inefficient soldier; retarded industry greatly harms the Army's capacity for technical performance; and the corruption affects fighting ability. The Army learnt of these consequences of the old social order from its experience in the Arab–Israeli war.

[1] See G. Baer, 'Egyptian Attitudes towards Land Reform', in W. Z. Laqueur (ed.), *The Middle East in Transition*, London, 1958, pp. 95–7.

These characteristics of the new army-officer group in the Middle East go far to explain why it has assumed political rule with the object of bringing about social reform. There are, however, other reasons. Since the urban middle class was formerly always a small group, and remains fairly small even today, it has not constituted a broad foundation on which some form of democracy could develop, as in the West. Even those members of the class who earnestly strove for reform had no power to carry it through. Therefore the parliamentary system was applied in a way that actually left all the power in the hands of the upper class. At the same time, social differences grew greater; corruption spread; the helplessness of the upper class was disclosed in foreign affairs, both military (the Arab–Israel War) and diplomatic (relations between Egypt and Britain); and the internal rule of the class was undermined by increasing social and political tension (in Egypt, Black Saturday in January 1952, and the November demonstrations of Syria in 1948, during which the Army was summoned to save the old order). The Army's confidence in and loyalty to the upper class faltered and gave way. However, there was no other social body—group or class—with the power to change the state of affairs. The Army would thus assume power in order to carry out reform on its own and to maintain that social equilibrium which is in the interests of the middle class.

The Army, however, was unable to build up rapidly a broad intermediate stratum which would be capable of preserving equilibrium and maintaining the reform imposed, under conditions of democratic rule. Hence it was always compelled to institute military dictatorship, without wide public backing.

C. LOWER CLASSES AND LABOUR

The lower classes form the majority of the population of the Arab East. From the viewpoint of standard of living, it would be suitable to include much of the beduin population in their ranks, but because of its single economic function, beduin society cannot be split into classes. Even recalling that at its lowest rung, the social scale of beduins includes artisans and black slaves, these two groups together do not make up any significant proportion of beduin society.

In this connection, it must be stressed that in the Arabian Peninsula slavery still exists. True, it was abolished by law in the colony of Aden long ago, in Bahrain (1937), Kuwait (1947), and Qatar (1952), but for all that, slaves are still to be found, especially among household servants, in the Aden Protectorate, Trucial Oman (which has prohibited traffic in slaves), Yemen, and most of all in Saudi Arabia. Here the rulers prohibited the import of slaves in 1936, but they continue to ignore that regulation.[1] According to various witnesses, slave traffic is mainly from Africa, and there are some private markets. The offspring of slaves and Negro couples also contribute to the slave class. Sometimes freeborn Negroes, who are found in large numbers throughout Saudi Arabia and are generally regarded as of inferior social standing, sell their children into slavery because of financial straits. The impression is that economic prosperity and the high incomes of the upper classes of Saudi Arabia have resulted in an increased demand for slaves in the last generation and have preserved the institution of slavery. Slaves and slave girls are employed primarily for household labour. A few are bodyguards of personages in high administrative positions, and these slaves, like those of important shaikhs, sometimes gain considerable power for themselves. Slaves are not employed in agriculture (except for isolated cases in the large estates of Hijaz).[2] Use of slaves in the Army and bureaucracy, formerly very common all over the Middle East, ceased in the nineteenth century.

The largest group of the lower classes is made up of landless fellahs and fellahs whose plots are insufficient for their livelihood. Since large landowners are generally town-dwellers, and few middle-class folk live in the villages, it is obvious that an exceedingly high proportion of the rural population must be considered lower class. However, as we have noted, village class stratification according to occupation or economic standing is a recent phenomenon and one limited to certain areas; even where some differentiation has set in, the traditional social structure has usually remained intact.

From the viewpoint of income, some of the groups treated as

[1] Sir Reader Bullard (ed.), *The Middle East, A Political and Economic Survey*, third edition, London, 1958, pp. 74–5.
[2] Lipsky, pp. 29–30, 67–8, 175–7, 210. For the Yemen see Fayein, pp. 163–4.

middle class should really be included among the urban lower classes. However, since there is no information on the income of these classes, the division was of necessity based only on occupation and economic function. By these criteria, the urban lower classes may be divided into two main groups: (*a*) those lacking any fixed and definite livelihood; and (*b*) the class of urban wage-earners. The boundary between the two groups is by no means clear-cut.

The sector of those lacking a fixed and definite livelihood has reached quite a size in some cities of the Arab East. It came into being as a result of urbanisation, which is more rapid at times than the growth of potential sources of employment in the city. This group also contains persons of other class origin (such as artisans) who lost their livelihood. While the group is most extensive in all Middle Eastern cities, Baghdad being a typical example, it is particularly large in the two great cities of Egypt, Cairo and Alexandria. Some of its characteristics—impermanence of work; the search for jobs wherever they may be found, even if they involve crime (theft, robbery, smuggling, etc.); and the low level of education (most members are illiterate)— have made this group a convenient tool in the hands of powerful personages in the small towns or in town quarters of the cities, and of those who have political ambitions, particularly when the object of their attack is minority groups, foreigners, and their shops and stores. This lower-class sector, lacking as it does any opinion on public affairs and any concern over its leaders' objects, is easily incited when there is some profit to be gained on the side.

The urban wage-earner class is a recent development, from the second quarter of the twentieth century only, in most Arab countries. Its precise dimensions are difficult to assess, because what data there are relate to all persons engaged in a certain occupation, both self-employed and wage-earners (population censuses) or cover only industrial workers (industrial censuses). The various attempts in the early 1950s to compute the number of Egyptian workers, on the basis of incomplete and inaccurate statistics, put the figure between 900,000 and 1,100,000 engaged in industry, construction, mining, transport, and communications, out of a total gainfully employed force of 7 to 8 millions. While these "workers" also include self-employed, there can be no doubt that the overwhelming majority were wage-earners. According to Husain ash-Shafi'i, Minister of Social Affairs, there were 725,000 workers in industry and construction in Egypt at the end of 1957.[1] Data for the Sudan are also incomplete. To the 25,000 persons employed in industry and crafts (including self-employed), most of the 25,000 railroad workers should be added, as well as an unknown number of other transport workers and mining and construction workers.[2]

In the Arabian Peninsula the only available figures are for workers employed by the oil companies; these workers, however, make up the bulk of the urban wage-earning class in these countries. Aramco employs 20,000, two-thirds of whom are Saudis; the Bahrain Petroleum Co. about 8,500, 6,000 of whom are Bahrainis; the Kuwait Oil Co. about 8,000, of whom 5,000 are Arabs; and several hundred persons are employed in Qatar and the Kuwait Neutral Zone.[3] In the refineries of Aden there are 1,700 workers, and many others are employed at the port. The 1956 industrial census of Bahrain found a total of 29,596 persons engaged in industry, construction, mining, commerce, transport, and services, of whom 12,203 were foreigners.[4]

The number of workers employed in industry and crafts in Iraq is estimated at 75,000 (among them 30,000 small craftsmen) and in transport, 45,000.[5] These figures apparently do not include construction workers, whose number has grown in recent years. Even without their contribution, a comparison of Iraq and Egypt indicates that in the former country there are relatively more workers in commerce and fewer in industry and communications. Indeed, without doubt the working class is greater, even relatively speaking, in Egypt than in Iraq.

According to official figures, Syria had 91,167 workers in 1953, including more than 8,000 in communications, 6,000 in oil installations, and 4,000 in building; some claim, however,

[1] *al-Gumhuriya*, 14 February 1958.

[2] Fawzi, *The Labour Movement in the Sudan*, pp. 9, 36.

[3] D. Finnie, 'Recruitment and Training of Labour—The Middle East Oil Industry', *MEJ*, Spring 1958, pp. 127–37.

[4] W. A. Beling, 'Recent Developments in Labor Relations in Bahrayn', *MEJ*, Spring 1959, p. 158.

[5] IBRD, *The Economic Development of Iraq*, pp. 2, 129, 149; United Nations, *Economic Developments in the Middle East 1945–1954*, New York, 1955, p. 99.

that the figures are incomplete.[1] On the basis of several sources, Grunwald tenders the following estimate of industrial workers in Lebanon: '25,000 employed in "modern" industries, 25,000 in the "traditional" industries, either on a permanent or seasonal basis, and an unknown number in the oil industry.'[2] If building and communications workers were added, Lebanon would have, relatively, a sizeable labour class. No reliable figures are available for Jordan and Libya; the number of labourers in the oil industry of Libya was 6,300 in 1960.[3]

It would thus appear that, in most of the Arab countries of the Middle East, the urban working class is larger than might be expected, considering how limited has been the development of private domestic industry. This is because workers are largely concentrated in transport (railways, railway workshops, ports, shipyards, etc.) and other public services (electricity, water supply) and oil installations—in other words, in enterprises established by foreign capital or by the Government. Railway and port workers in Basra, for instance, form a considerable part of the working class of Southern Iraq; oil-company workers and their dependants make up a third of the population of Kirkuk; in many other oil centres they form an even higher percentage. (In Saudi Arabia workers of the oil companies constitute 40% of all industrial workers.) Of the 40,000 inhabitants of 'Atbara in Sudan, 90% are railway workers and their families.[4] Similar trends are evident in Egypt and Syria, countries with some degree of private domestic industry.

These factors, which have contributed to the formation of a working class in the Arab East, also explain, at least partially, another characteristic of that class. Industry in the Middle East is composed of a large number of very small enterprises and a limited number of very large ones which employ thousands of workers; the medium-sized plant is rather rare. The largest employer in Sudan, the railway, has more workers than have several hundred small enterprises combined. It is learned of Bahrain in 1956 that 96.6% of all concerns engaged 0–10

[1] Y. Hadas, 'Hapo'el hasuri', *Hamizrah Hehadash*, VII, p. 102.

[2] Grunwald, p. 254.

[3] Thomas, p. 266.

[4] International Labour Organisation (ILO), *Social Conditions in the Petroleum Industry*, Geneva, 1950, pp. 10–11; G. Lenczowski, *Oil and State in the Middle East*, New York, 1960, p. 254; Fawzi, *The Labour Movement in the Sudan*, p. 36.

labourers, accounting for 32·9% of the labour force, while at the other extreme of the scale were 0·5% of all concerns, each of which engaged over 200 workers, accounting for a further 46·9% of the labour force. According to the 1954 survey of industry in Baghdad, one-third of all workers were employed in enterprises of more than 500 workers, and another third in enterprises of less than nine workers. The three largest concerns together employed 20% of all workers. In the 1940s 93% of all enterprises in Egypt employed less than five workers, and the remaining 7% accounted for 72% of all workers. The two largest textile factories (*Misr* in al-Mahalla al-Kubra, and *Filature Nationale* in Alexandria) employed over 30% of all textile workers.[1]

Two additional factors influenced the uneven growth of the working class: (1) the late development of Arab industry. In order to meet the competition of advanced Western industry, it has tried to rationalise procedures by the establishment of large enterprises; and (2) the lack of capital and industrial credit, and a limited domestic market. These factors hindered or prevented entrepreneurs from setting up competing establishments; as the market grew, existing undertakings expanded.

A third characteristic of the working class in the Arab East is that it is largely concentrated in a few cities, usually no more than two—the capital and one other city (in some countries the port city). Seventy per cent of the industrial workers of Iraq are centred in Baghdad, and the overwhelming majority of transport workers are to be found in Baghdad and Basra. In Syria most urban workers are in Damascus and Aleppo, although Latakia's share has apparently grown in recent years. Beirut and Tripoli in Lebanon occupy a similar position. Various censuses conducted in Egypt have shown that over 50% of all workers were employed in plants located in Cairo and Alexandria.[2]

Authors have put forward three explanations for this fact, in the case of Egypt (and they are largely true of the other countries as well): (1) industry was not dependent on sources of

[1] Fawzi, ibid., pp. 9, 36, 94; Beling, p. 159; UN, *Economic Developments 1945–54*, p. 99; Gritly, pp. 488–98.
[2] UN, ibid.; IBRD, *Economic Development of Syria*, pp. 357–67; Gritly, pp. 469–76; UN, *The Development of Manufacturing Industry in Egypt, Israel, and Turkey*, New York, 1958, p. 59.

raw materials and was built up near the centres of consumption. A large percentage of all the population, and especially of its urban sector, are to be found in the two main cities, and the purchasing power of that group is proportionally still higher; (2) the major cities are provided with more adequate transport networks, water supply, and gas and electricity facilities than other cities, and they are centres of skilled labour and possess repair and maintenance shops: (3) these cities were the seats of foreign capitalists and entrepreneurs from minority groups who pioneered the development of industry.

The working class in the Arab countries is young both in its own existence and in the age of its members. This is related in part to the generally low age-composition of the population in Arab countries; in part to the fact that villagers who come to the city to earn their living are young (and this factor tends to be self-sustaining, because village emigration still continues and older workers are constantly being replaced by new-comers); and finally, to the high percentage of child labour in Arab industry, because of defective labour legislation, poor implementation of the law, and weak trade unions. Industrial censuses conducted in Egypt and Iraq in the 1940s showed that children constituted 8% of all industrial workers, and the same percentage appeared in the 1937 census of modern industries in Syria and Lebanon. These censuses did not include small work-shops, in which the percentage of child labour is much higher, as indicated also by the data on traditional industries of Syria and Lebanon in 1937 (13%). Some evidence seems to suggest that the percentage was actually still higher. In 1955–6 child labour in the Sudan made up more than 20% of the total labour force. There are indications, however, that child labour is on the decline.[1]

A further characteristic of the Arab working class is the relatively high proportion of unskilled workers, a characteristic of countries whose industries are young. As a consequence, until recently, and in many areas even at present, foreigners and various minority groups have provided the skilled and manager-ial man-power, though this may be the result of other factors as

---

[1] ILO, Regional Conference for the Near and Middle East 1951, *Manpower Problems*, Geneva, 1951, p. 17; Grunwald, p. 246; Issawi, *Egypt at Mid-Century*, p. 172; Fawzi, *Manpower Distribution in the Sudan*, p. 27.

well: the contempt for manual labour and the inferior social status associated with it have led Arabs with any degree of education to aspire to an official or administrative position. A second reason for the preponderance of Arab unskilled labourers is that workers recently arrived from the villages and desert find it strange to conceive that the individual should strive to gain greater responsibility and rise above his fellow men. In their view, authority does not stem from skill, experience, and achievement, but from lineage and wealth. Finally, foreign firms, particularly the oil companies, have frequently followed a policy of employing foreigners in all grades above that of unskilled worker, in order to maintain full control over operations. These practices created wide gaps between the wages of unskilled workers and those of skilled workers and managers; as a result, the latter identified themselves with the employers rather than with the workers. There is an even greater gap between the incomes of worker and official; this is one of the reasons for the outstanding disparity between workers and members of the middle class in the Middle East—a disparity both social and economic in nature.[1]

Since the Arab working class is such a recent development, many of the early industrial workers were either villagers or members of tribes, and represented the first generation of workers in their families. A survey conducted in 1954 among port workers of Port Sudan showed that the fathers of only 11% were also port workers, while the fathers of 83% were engaged in agriculture or raised livestock. The percentage of workers of tribal or rural origin in Cairo, Alexandria, Aleppo, Beirut, and similar cities is probably lower. Many of the workers still maintain close ties with their villages, as is seen by the organisations on a tribal or village basis at places of work (investigated in Port Sudan, Aramco, and the 'Misr' works of al-Mahalla al-Kubra).[2] Workers regard their employment in the city as temporary, and plan to return to their previous way of life as soon as they have earned a certain sum of money. Indeed, work in the city is frequently of very short duration,

---

[1] Fawzi, *Labour Movement*, p. 10; Hadas, pp. 102–3; Issawi, *Egypt at Mid-Century*, p. 172; Finnie, *passim*; Thomas, pp. 272–3; Makarius, p. 36.

[2] Fawzi, *Labour Movement*, pp. 10–11, 36–7, 101; T. B. Stauffer, 'The Industrial Worker', in S. N. Fisher (ed.), *Social Forces in the Middle East*, pp. 89–92.

and many enterprises have a rapid turnover in their labour force. In Syrian textile mills absenteeism in summer months has reached 15%. In the I.P.C. and A.I.O.C. oil companies, the turnover during the Second World War was 21%, and in Aramco, at certain later periods, it was even greater, especially when expansion was under way. Naturally, the largest turnover of all was registered during periods of oil exploration, when the teams were mobile. One Egyptian economist reported an average annual turnover of 50–100%, and in the textile mills of al-Mahalla al-Kubra it was once 300%. One of the consequences of a high turnover is that a large proportion of the workers remains in low-wage brackets. This lack of permanence also stems in part from the seasonal character of the industries, particularly those based on agricultural raw materials.[1]

There are, however, certain indications pointing in the direction of greater stability of the labour class. As workers acquire a skill, they work more regularly, and more of them tend to remain on a permanent basis. The establishment of housing for workers also reduces the incidence of turnover. The Misr concern claimed that by building a 'workers' city' it succeeded in reducing the percentage of workers who left their jobs from 35% in 1946 to 5% in 1949. Nevertheless, the prevailing lack of stability prevents the consolidation of Arab workers as a movement.

The characteristics of the Arab working class, as noted above, go far to explain the size, structure, and nature of the trade-union movement (*niqabat al-'ummal*) in Arab countries. Reliable data on trade unions are available for only a few of the countries. Over 900 trade unions, with a total membership of over 250,000, were registered in Egypt in the middle 1950s, but many of these unions existed on paper only, and the actual number of organised workers was estimated at less than 150,000. Since then, that number has undoubtedly risen, but the periodically published figures should be treated with some caution, as there is a great difference between paper unions and actual ones. At the end of 1956 there were 150 trade unions in the Sudan, whose members numbered at least 100,000; however,

---

[1] A. A. Allouni, 'The Labour Movement in Syria', *MEJ*, Winter 1959, p. 71; Lenczowski, pp. 296–7; Thomas, p. 270; Stauffer, p. 89; Issawi, *Egypt at Mid-Century*, pp. 165–6; ILO, *Manpower Problems*, pp. 14–15.

these figures also included organisations of clerks and employers. After the military revolt of late 1958 the activity of Sudanese workers' unions was outlawed. In February 1960, a new law on trade unions and labour disputes placed even greater restrictions on workers than the former legislation. Unions hitherto existing were dispersed, and the establishment of new unions was the subject of bitter conflict.[1]

Unions are also found in some countries of the Arabian Peninsula. In Aden there were 11,500 organised workers in 1957, and the Bahrain Federation of Labour claimed that its membership was 6,000 in 1956; but the federation was dissolved at the end of that year. In Saudi Arabia workers are forbidden to organise in trade unions.[2]

In Iraq there were quite a number of trade unions in the 1940s, but most were later outlawed, and the legal movement was very limited before the revolution. In January 1959, after the revolution, workers were again permitted to organise, and in late 1959 a General Federation of Iraqi Labour Unions was established. In Syria official figures mention 256 trade unions in 1956, with a membership of 32,943. Jordan had approximately 11,800 organised workers in 1957. The number of Lebanese unions was thirty-five to forty in the middle 1950s, and by their own estimation they had approximately 60,000 members. Thus, of all Arab countries, Lebanon and Sudan have the greatest percentage of organised labour. In 1956 an inter-Arab federation of trade unions (the 'International Confederation of Arab Labour Unions') was established; it is mainly concerned with politics, and the scope of its activities depends largely on the political relations among the Arab countries.[3]

In terms of membership and geographical distribution, the trade unions naturally reflect the characteristics of the Arab working class, even to an exaggerated extent. Of the 146,000 Egyptian workers organised in 488 unions in 1951, 86,000 (59%) belonged to the 255 unions (52%) of Cairo and Alexandria. In 1958 the provinces of Damascus and Aleppo claimed 53·5% of all Syrian trade unions and 67·5% of their total membership.[4]

[1] *MER*, 1960, pp. 411–12.
[2] *ME Aff*, March 1960, p. 89; Beling, pp. 161–3.
[3] For details see Lenczowski, pp. 281 ff.; Wheelock, pp. 266–8.
[4] Issawi, *Egypt at Mid-Century*, p. 174; Europa Publications, *The Middle East 1958*, p. 363.

The Arab trade-union movement consists of a few large unions and a very great number of small ones. According to official 1951 Egyptian figures, of 491 unions with a total membership of 149,424, twelve had 55,730 members and 392 (with less than 300 members each) had only 46,946 members. In 1947 about 30,000 workers were organised in the two unions at al-Mahalla al-Kubra and *Filature Nationale*, compared with 16,460 organised in 82 individual unions in the field of transport. In the Sudan one union (railroad workers), out of a total of 41, encompassed 45·7% of all organised workers in 1951, and even after the establishment of several dozen trade unions in subsequent years, this union with its 25,000 members, or a quarter of the total number organised, remained unrivalled in terms of size.

The large number of small trade unions may be explained by the manner in which Arab trade unions were organised. Each union included at first only the workers of a particular plant. This form of organisation prevails in the Sudan and Aden, and formerly in Egypt also. In Egypt, however, particularly in recent years, the trade unions in specific economic branches formed national organisations, while in a few cases the trade unions in a particular provincial town formed a general organisation. At the end of 1956 the General Federation of Egyptian Workers (*Ittihad 'Ummal Misr*), which included the most important trade unions and labour associations in the country, was formed. In June 1959 trade unions were organised in the two regions of the U.A.R. with the object of establishing a common organisation, divided into branches by trade; in practice, the scheme encountered some difficulties, and it was still incomplete at the time of the U.A.R. split. In the Sudan a general labour federation was established in 1949. Syria has many trade unions, each covering workers in a single trade or occupation in a given city; these in turn are associated with any one of three organisations, distinguishable from one another by the political leanings of their leadership and by geographical concentration. In Lebanon the differences among the four trade-union associations are also based on political orientation.

Wide fluctuations in size and composition of membership characterize the trade unions in the Arab countries. The chief reason for this is the instability of the working class itself. The organising of labourers who come to the city for short periods presents serious difficulties. But even the unions which are composed of permanent workers lack stability. In practice, only a small nucleus of active workers maintains contact with the union, and then only when a burning issue faces the movement. Even those workers who are registered in a trade union as permanent members do not pay regular dues, and their interest is largely determined by the immediate union benefits. Ordinarily, when no strike or negotiations for better conditions are taking place, they are apathetic towards the union.

The unions' poor financial situation and limited funds contribute further to the apathy, as well as being one of its results. Wages in Arab countries are low, many unions are small and fragmented, and they have no sources of revenue other than membership dues. They hesitate to press workers for back dues lest they lose them altogether. One trade-union leader declared in the 1940s that 'the financial reserves of the most successful trade unions in Egypt do not exceed fifty pounds'.[1] Consequently, the services which the unions can provide, such as assistance during a strike and in times of sickness, or legal and medical help, are limited. Funds are often so scanty as to prevent organising activity or the efficient administration of the union itself. Badaoui has noted that many unions in Egypt did not have their own quarters and held meetings at the president's home or in a café. The staffs of most of them consisted of volunteers who engaged in union activity after working-hours. At the beginning of 1946, when the trade-union association in Lebanon had tens of thousands of members, no more than three or four union officials were paid. The secretaries of the unions, including the secretary of the 4,000-member railway workers' union, served as volunteers during the evening hours. This situation prevailed in the trade unions of all the Arab countries during the 1940s and 1950s.[2] It should be noted that the larger and well-established unions naturally fare much better, and that financial support by various political elements has sometimes provided staff and facilities.

---

[1] *al-Ba'th* (Cairo), 1 February 1946.
[2] Z. Badaoui, *Les Problèmes du travail et les organisations ouvrières en Égypte*, Alexandria, 1948, pp. 118–22; A. Cohen, *Tenu'ath hapo'alim ha'aravith*, Tel-Aviv, 1947, p. 78. See also Hadas, p. 106; Fawzi, *Labour Movement*, pp. 99–100.

The poverty and ignorance of the majority of workers, as well as their indifference, explain the character of the labour-movement leadership and its attitude to union members. As a rule, the lower echelons of union officials come from the ranks of the workers (skilled workers or those with some education); the top leadership, which has contacts with the authorities, organises labour associations and acts as liaison between the trade unions and political groups, comes from the intelligentsia —teachers, officials, and other educated persons connected with political movement. Lawyers have played a particularly significant part in the Egyptian trade-union movement. Aware of their own limitations and inexperience, workers not infrequently entrusted the protection of their interests to lawyers, who saw in this labour activity a source of income as well as a stepping-stone to a political career, or a means of strengthening their standing in the local or national political arena. Lawyers played a prominent part in trade-union activity in the 1920s and 1930s, and even more so in the early 1940s, when the Wafd attempted to organise the trade-union movement on a large scale, on the basis of 'leagues' and 'fronts'. One of the leaders of the Egyptian trade-union movement, Sawi Ahmad Sawi, is a lawyer by education. A member of the royal household, Prince 'Abbas Halim, headed the Egyptian trade-union movement for about twenty years. Similarly, some Lebanese trade unions were directed in the 1950s by politicians and powerful notables, such as Khalid al-Khuri, son of the Lebanese president at that time, and Henry Pharaon, a rich business man of Beirut. In some instances, however, workers themselves have risen to positions of leadership (e.g., Muhammad Yusuf al-Mudarrik in Egypt in the 1940s and Subhi al-Khatib in Syria).

The social and educational gulf that exists between the leadership and the workers does not, naturally, provide a basis on which union democracy and workers' participation in the management of union affairs can develop. Trade unions in the various Arab countries have not lived up to their democratic constitutions. The provision calling for periodic general meetings has been completely overlooked, and all union affairs have been conducted by the leadership. Many trade unions are, in fact, under the control of employers. In Egypt this practice seems to be declining as a result of the strong links that have developed between the union leadership and the ruling army-officer group, which has imposed stringent controls on trade unions. In contrast to company-sponsored unions in Egypt, the prevalent form of labour organisation in Syria and Lebanon was a joint body of employers and workers (e.g., the transport association in Lebanon).

In spite of strong outside influences on the trade unions, the workers of the Arab East have for many years been waging a continuous struggle for their demands. In Egypt the first wave of strikes broke out immediately after the First World War (1919) in protest against the privations suffered during the war and as part of the national struggle against the British authorities (the workers' demands being in part social, in part political). Following a long period of quiet, a new wave of strikes broke out in the early 1930s in the wake of the world-wide depression. After smaller waves in 1936 and 1938, the Second World War brought full employment and an emergency régime, and there were no strikes.

But at the end of the war the rise in the cost of living, coupled with lay-offs and unemployment, led to a new period of unrest. This was also in part due to the gathering political campaign of those years. The outcome was a series of strikes greater than any previous one and lasting three years, centred first in Cairo's industrial suburb, Shubra al-Khaima, and then spreading to other points, such as al-Mahalla al-Kubra (in September 1947). The Arab–Israel war, the resulting emergency régime, and the introduction of compulsory arbitration brought another pause which lasted until 1950. But the refusal of employers to abide by the Wafd administration's cost-of-living allowance law triggered a wave of strikes which aimed at forcing employers to carry out the provisions of the law. The closing down of many enterprises in 1951–2 because of export difficulties following on the Korean War, and the ensuing unemployment, contributed further to labour unrest. During this period the authors of a book on modernisation in the Middle East who were in contact with Egyptian workers reached the conclusion that these workers have developed a very strong class-consciousness.[1] The height of the crisis was the strike of Kafr ad-Dawar

[1] Lerner and Pevsner, pp. 229, 232–3, 260–1.

workers and the sympathetic strike of the Muharram Bey workers in Alexandria, in August 1952. The revolutionary régime has so far been generally successful in maintaining 'industrial peace' in Egypt, through improving the lot of the workers, instituting a complex machinery for compulsory arbitration, exerting influence on labour leaders, and through sheer Army and police power.

The trade-union struggle in the Sudan reached its high point in 1947–8, when the railway workers declared two long strikes. Improvements in working conditions and unionisation ushered in a two-year period of peace, which came to an end in 1950, when there was a rise in the cost of living. A number of general strikes were at their most severe in 1952. In Saudi Arabia there was a large-scale strike at the Aramco concern in October 1953, and in consequence, working conditions were considerably improved; labour disputes continued until strikes were prohibited by a royal decree of 11 June 1956. In Bahrain, too, many strikes, some forming part of the national movement, broke out in the 1950s; in Aden waves of strikes swept the country in 1959 and 1960; in Iraq the oil industry workers' struggle reached a climax in July 1946 with large-scale strikes involving demonstrations, and again in December 1953.

In Syria the first wave of strikes swept the country in 1936–7 as the result of a decline in the value of the franc and rising prices. A second wave after the Second World War (1946–9) may be traced to inflation, to the adverse effects of the resumption of imports on the young Syrian industry, and to governmental instability. (There was a wave of strikes in Lebanon at the same time.) The military régimes attempted to improve labour conditions and suppress strikes, and it was not until the overthrow of Shishakli that another series of strikes erupted, three in number, each comprising some 20,000 workers, in 1954–6. A fresh wave of strikes hit Lebanon in 1960.

Several major features have characterised the labour struggle in the Arab world. Many strikes have broken out spontaneously, without prior organisation of any kind; the workers themselves walked out when conditions became intolerable. This lack of organisation has often led to inconsistency in policy and to the early termination of the strike if it did not immediately attain its objectives. The trade unions' weakness prevented a united, co-ordinated campaign. The numerous walk-outs which occurred in Egypt in 1950 all revolved around one basic demand—implementation of the cost-of-living allowance Bill—but they were entirely unco-ordinated. Even between two such closely associated groups as the port workers of Alexandria and Port Said, there was no co-operation.[1] However, the struggles were very intense. The living standard of the Arab worker is so low that any further deterioration as a result of increased living costs hits his essential needs, his very subsistence, and impels him to put up a desperate fight. But the bitterness of the struggle also stems from its form. Since the unskilled workers faced the unrelenting pressure of the rural and urban unemployed, who threatened to undermine the effectiveness of the strike, they frequently resorted to the sitdown strike. Employers' attempts to dislodge them from the factories, with the help of the police or armed forces, resulted in pitched battles and many casualties (mainly in Egypt, but also in Syria and other Middle Eastern countries).

The labour struggle was no doubt one of the factors chiefly responsible for the extensive labour legislation in the Middle Eastern countries which have a working class. The principal laws were enacted during periods in which agitation by the labour movement was strong. In Egypt two statutes (child and female labour, and working hours) were adopted in 1933 and 1936. The Wafd government promulgated several laws in the early 1940s, an arbitration law in 1948 following the wave of strikes in that year, and a whole series of laws in 1950 (sickness funds, accidents, social security, and collective agreements). In 1952 the revolutionary régime introduced a new set of labour laws (the individual labour contract, trade-union organisation, and an amendment to the arbitration law).

The principal labour legislation in the Sudan (trade unions, labour contracts and working conditions, arbitration, and health and accident compensation) were enacted in 1948 following on the first wave of strikes.[2] In pre-revolutionary Iraq there had been no new legislation since the 1939 law concerning safety and hygiene in factories, and the 1942

---

[1] *al-Ahram*, 6 and 14 April 1950.
[2] For detailed analysis see Fawzi, *Labour Movement*, Chapter 7.

amendment to the 1936 labour law regulating working conditions, child labour, compensation, arbitration, and unionisation. After the revolution a new general law and various
regulations on labour came into effect in 1958 and 1959. They
deal with employment, trade unions, accident and illness
insurance, compensation, and housing.[1] In Syria and Lebanon
labour legislation was first introduced at the beginning of the
Second World War; in both countries the main law—which
covered working conditions (wages, hours, days off, holidays),
work by women and children, arbitration, trade-union
organisation, and other provisions—was enacted in 1946. The
'Labour and Workman Regulations' of Saudi Arabia were
enacted on 10 October 1947, and those of Bahrain on 1 January
1958. Labour legislation in Aden, including compulsory
arbitration, was violently attacked by a congress of trade
unions of the colony in August 1960.[2] On 5 April 1959 the
U.A.R. issued a general labour law for Egypt and Syria. The
law includes clauses on labour exchange, employment of the
disabled and foreigners, apprenticeship, individual and collective labour contracts, working hours, employment of women
and children, work in mines and quarries, wages, trade unions,
and arbitration.[3]

While there are serious gaps in the laws themselves in some
countries, the main problem is that many of the provisions of
existing laws are not implemented. The reasons for this are not
far to seek; ineffectual control over the many small dispersed
plants; the influence of employers on the bureaucracy and on
the Government itself; the weak status of the workers and the
trade unions. The laws are, of course, most effectively implemented in the large plants, in the big cities, where strong unions
exist, and in those countries where the régime is genuinely
interested in carrying out the laws.

The lack of worker representation in the legislative bodies
of the Arab countries may be another reason for the inadequate
labour legislation and the poor implementation of the labour
laws. Various attempts by workers' representatives to win a seat

[1] Details in the *Directory of the Republic of Iraq*, 1960, pp. 572–3.
[2] *al-Ahram*, 7–10 August 1960; *The Times*, 16 and 19 August 1960.
[3] Law No. 91 of 1959, French translation of full text in *Cahiers de l'Orient contemporain*, XL, pp. 287–322.

in the Egyptian Parliament ended in failure. Thus, in the January 1945 elections there were seven candidates supported by the trade unions and the Egyptian Labour Party which in all received 3,000 votes, but not a single candidate was elected. In the November 1949 Syrian elections the trade-union federation entered candidates in Damascus, Homs, and Aleppo, but they were all defeated. In the 1953 general elections in Sudan the 'Atbara workers voted almost unanimously for the sectarian leader, while the secretary of the railway workers' union, an outstanding labour leader, received only a negligible number of votes.[1]

The reason for these defeats does not necessarily lie in the greater prestige or position of the non-labour leader. There are many ways by which election results can be influenced. At any rate, the total result has been that not a single representative of the workers was elected to any parliament of the Arab countries prior to the military revolutions. In the new Congress of the Popular Force, which met in May 1962, there were 250 representatives of workers out of a total of 1,500.[2]

None the less, the trade unions are sufficiently strong and consolidated to be used by political parties and movements as an avenue through which they can extend their influence among the workers, and the parties use the unions in order to organise the workers and win their support. The liaison between workers and political groups is maintained by the union leadership, which is made up of skilled workers and educated persons who subscribe to certain political ideologies, mostly leftist, or who have connections with the parties and national movements (such as the organisations recently established by the army-officer group). While it cannot be said that the rank and file has been deeply penetrated by these political movements, the labour organisations as such have assumed considerable importance in the national political arena.

[1] Egyptian Press of December 1944 and January 1945; *Hamizrah Hehadash*, I, p. 163; Fawzi, *Labour Movement*, p. 101.

[2] *OM*, 1962, pp. 244–6.

CONCLUSION

One common identifying trait is found to pervade Arab society of today, as it has been described in this volume: its transitional nature in a period of fundamental change.

Much of the traditional foundation is being undermined. The extended family and the tribe are breaking up; religion is no longer the only cause to which the settled populace is bound by ties of allegiance and membership; the city's traditional structure by family and district has undergone basic changes; and in some countries of the Arab East the power of the urban upper-class élite is foundering, while in earlier generations this group had dominated a largely rural populace. Finally, a fall in the death rate has upset the demographic equilibrium which had previously helped to maintain a balance between the growth of the population and the sources of livelihood.

With the disruption of the old forms, new groupings have interposed themselves between the smallest unit based on blood ties and the highly comprehensive religious framework. The most outstanding and important outcome is the appearance of national feelings, based on territorial or linguistic ties. Also, a certain degree of economic and social class consciousness has come into being.

It is natural that a transitional stage between two social orders should not be exactly a period of peace and quiet. Like other societies that passed through such stages, Arab society is undergoing profound upheavals. Moreover, there are special historical and internal social conditions in the Arab Middle East which lend its problems particular pungency. A fundamental point is that development has not generally been organic in nature. Changes are not chiefly due to forces which arose from within, but are generally the result of copying borrowed casts and a foreign civilisation. Hence these casts are not accepted equally by all sectors of the population. They do not conform organically to the old society, neither can they replace it in its entirety. The new forms encounter a society of outstanding polarity: the city is the exclusive centre of all economic, political, and cultural activity, while the village is peopled by an oppressed and ignorant populace, concerned only with agriculture; a small class of educated persons, bureaucrats, army officers, and the like, who are in contact with the outer world, are juxtaposed to the great majority of the population, poverty-stricken and ignorant. Infiltrating Western civilisation has, then, not found its natural medium—a broad middle class of some wealth, education, and initiative. As a result of all these conditions, it is clear that sometimes old and new patterns are to be found in combination, and sometimes there seems to be a vacuum where the old casts were destroyed, but nothing new has been formed in their place.

How do these matters appear in reality in the Arab East of today? Primarily, there is a gap between certain social developments and undeveloped economic resources, particularly in industry. In Egypt, for example, it has been seen that the population rose as a result of improved conditions of health, and a consequently lower mortality, but the population surplus could not be absorbed by Egyptian industry. The process of urbanisation in that country, due chiefly to over-population in the villages, is not accompanied by a parallel growth of sources of livelihood in the city. In Syria the dissolution of traditional craftsmanship (and its social organisation—the guilds) is not paralleled by a spread of modern industry. In nearly all the Arab states the educational system has been extended; but this, too, has external causes, and the educated class arising in its wake does not have sufficient sources of livelihood, because it strives towards the professions customarily prized in traditional society, generally officialdom.

Thus, most of the problems of modern Arab society are due to the fact that alongside social changes, part or even all the population retains the old social casts and the attitudes of generations past which were an organic part of traditional life. Egyptian population surpluses are growing more acute, not only because there are not enough sources of livelihood but also because the masses do not practise birth control; a large and prolific family has a strong position and commands respect. The prodigious changes in the education of girls have not yet found their complement in an improved economic status for women or in social and legal reform. Most of the efforts to plan a modern national state in the Arab East have been hampered by communities and tribes which are not so readily willing to make their exit.

This brings us to one of the basic problems of Arab society: allegiance—allegiance to sect, country, or Arab nation. The decline of religion as a way of life in the Arab East has not automatically curtailed the importance of the religious community as a social and political framework. With the rise of modern nationalism, loyalty to Islam or to the various Christian denominations has been maintained. There are even groups which remain loyal only to their religious community and have taken on no new allegiance of a national type. Furthermore, the new nationalism is still uncertain as to its basis—territorial or linguistic, pan-Arab or Egyptian, Iraqi, Syrian, and so on. The ties of blood and religion which formed the foundations of traditional society have, then, been joined by ties of territory and language trying to replace or to adapt themselves to the old scheme of allegiances.

But the upheavals passing over the Arab East today are due only in part to the preservation of old patterns by the side of the new ones. Also, in some regions and some strata of society a vacuum has been created where the old ways of life have disintegrated before new ones have made their appearance. The extended family, for example, is dissolving, but an individualistic society as the basis of a different family structure has not yet been formed. The religious orders have lost their function as social frameworks in the city (and to a certain extent in the village also), but no replacement has come into view. Many have thus lost that sense of security which was part of the traditional society with its well-defined patterns.

The new and the old side by side, and uneven social advancement in various spheres—these also characterise class structure in the Arab East. Even within the boundaries of a single country such as Syria, a modern working class has developed, while beduin tribes continue their traditional existence. Iraq, for example, has its army-officer group with nationalistic–leftist sympathies holding the reins of central government, while at the far reaches of that country shaikhs continue to impose semi-feudal rule. The origin of this situation is the absence of a broad midde class which might have formed the basis of a new political rule in place of the old domination of landowners. Even the agrarian reform of Egypt, which disrupted the economic status of estate-owners, did not result in the formation of an independent and solid peasantry. The old classes persist, and even in places where they are being abolished, no new group possesses the requisite power and economic backing to inherit their place. As a result, groups of army officers have periodically taken over the rule. A working class has emerged and grown to considerable dimensions, but for the past generation it, too, has been struggling with the heritage of the old order: ignorance and poverty, conditions unfavourable to strong organisation, workers' allegiances along lines other than class, and the influence of external social and political factors.

Finally, it is to be remembered that there are vast differences in the degree of social change, not only among the various communities, between village and city, and among different strata and classes but also among the various countries of the Arab Middle East. As a result of this and all the other factors mentioned above, we may understand the highly diversified opinions on the character of modern Arab society, quoted as being conservative and modern, 'feudal' and 'bourgeois', predominantly influenced by religion or by nationalistic feelings. Opinions of outsiders are no less sharply divided than those of members of that society and its spokesmen. Whether expressed by foreigners or Arabs, the opinions are often obscured by faulty vision; some tend to generalise from only a part of Arab society, and others give way to wishful thinking. The latter fault is particularly common among those who, for political reasons or in apologia and with exaggerated pride, intend to prove that modern Arab society is like any modern European society. Wishful thinkers are also found among those who want the Arabs to remain backward and are anxious to prove that they are indeed so. Both camps ignore the fact that their own misconceptions and wishful thinking cannot change the actual complex picture.

In all events, two facts are not to be denied: great changes are today engulfing Arab society, but it has not yet emerged as a new society. When will consolidation be completed and what form will the new society assume? This remains to be seen.

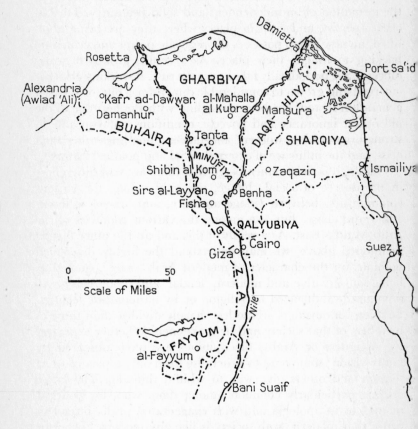

Lower and Middle Egypt

Scale of Miles

0   100

al-Fayyum

BANI SUAIF

Bani Suaif

MINYA

al-Minya

ASYUT

Asyut

GIRGA

Suhaj

Nag' Hamadi

Qena

QENA

Kiman

Silwa

Aswan

ASWAN

Red Sea

Nile

SUDAN

Upper Egypt

R

245

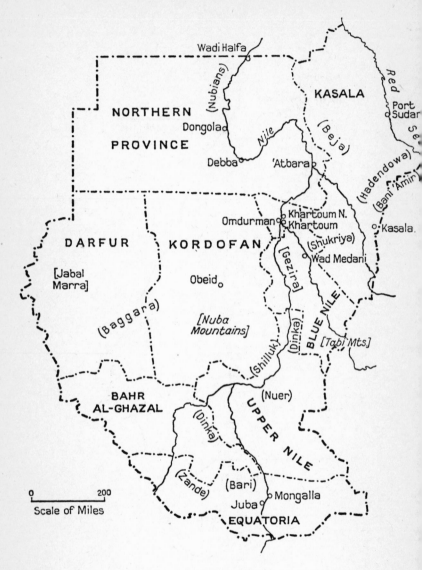

The Sudan

246

The Arabian Peninsula

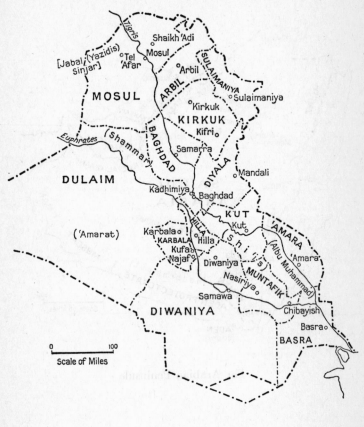

Iraq

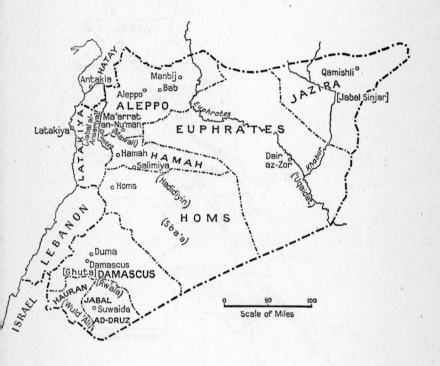

Syria

Lebanon

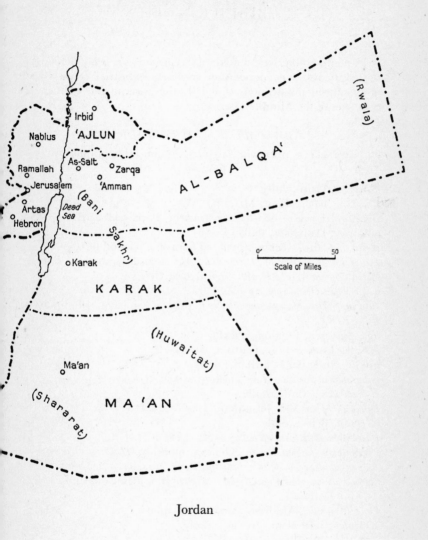

Nablus

Irbid

'AJLUN

As-Salt   Zarqa

Ramallah

Jerusalem   'Amman

Artas   *Dead*
Sea

Hebron

(Bani

S'akhr)

Karak

AL - BALQA'

(Rwala)

0'   50
Scale of Miles

KARAK

(Huwaitat)

Ma'an

MA 'AN

(Shararat)

Jordan

251

BIBLIOGRAPHY

Note. Unless otherwise stated, all figures have been taken from statistical abstracts, population censuses, industrial censuses, and other official publications issued by the governments of the Arab countries of the Middle East.

NEWSPAPERS AND PERIODICALS
(In brackets—abbreviations used in the bibliography and in footnotes.)

al-Ahram, Cairo, daily.
American Anthropologist, Menasha (Wisconsin), quarterly.
Annales Economies—Sociétés—Civilisations, Paris (*Annales*).
al-Ayyam, Damascus, daily.
al-Ba'th, Cairo, weekly (appeared for a short period in 1946).
Bulletin of the School of Oriental and African Studies, London (*BSOAS*).
Bulletin of the World Health Organisation, Geneva.
Cahiers de l'Orient contemporain, Paris.
Economic Development and Cultural Change, Chicago, Ill., quarterly (*EDCC*)
The Economist, London, weekly.
L'Égypte Contemporaine, Cairo, quarterly.
Filastin, Jerusalem (Jordan), daily.
Geographical Review, New York, quarterly (*GR*).
al-Gumhuriya, Cairo, daily.
Hamizrah Hehadash, Jerusalem (Israel), quarterly.
al-Hayat, Beirut, daily.
International Archives of Ethnography, Leiden (*IAE*).
International Labour Review, Geneva, monthly (*ILR*).
International Social Science Bulletin, Paris, quarterly (*ISSB*).
Journal of the Palestine Oriental Society, Jerusalem, quarterly (ceased publication).
Land Economics, Madison (Wisconsin), quarterly.
al-Manar, Jerusalem (Jordan), daily.
Mibifnim, 'Ayn Harod (Israel), quarterly.
Middle East Economic Papers, Beirut (*MEEP*).
Middle East Journal, Washington D.C., quarterly (*MEJ*).
Middle Eastern Affairs, New York, monthly (*ME Aff*).
Muslim World, Hartford, Conn., quarterly (*MW*).

New Outlook, Tel-Aviv, monthly.

Orient, Paris, quarterly.

Oriente Moderno, Rome, monthly (*OM*).

Palestine and Middle East, Tel-Aviv, monthly (ceased publication).

Population Studies, Cambridge, quarterly.

Revue du Monde musulman, Paris (ceased publication).

Southwestern Journal of Anthropology, Albuquerque (New Mexico), quarterly (*SWJA*).

Studia Islamica, Paris.

at-Tali'a, Cairo, monthly (appeared in 1945 and 1946).

The Times, London, daily.

al-Wahda, Damascus, daily.

Die Welt des Islams, Leiden (*WI*).

az-Zaman, Baghdad, daily.

YEARBOOKS, COLLECTIVE PUBLICATIONS, AND PUBLICATIONS OF INTERNATIONAL BODIES

Blattner, J. E. (ed.), *Who's Who in Egypt and the Near East*, Cairo, 1950.

Bullard, Sir Reader (ed.), *The Middle East, A Political and Economic Survey*, third ed., London, 1958.

Dangoor's Printing and Publishing House, *The Iraq Directory 1936*, Baghdad, n.d.

Darwish, M. F., and others, *Directory of the Republic of Iraq 1960* (in Arabic; Arabic title: *Dalil al-Jumhuriya al-Iraqiya*), Baghdad, 1961.

La Documentation française, Notes documentaires et études, *L'Évolution politique des états de la peninsule arabe*, Nos. 1041 and 1042, 21 and 22 December 1948.

La Documentation française, Notes et études documentaires, *Aperçu sur le problème du nomadisme au Moyen-Orient*, No. 2095, 3 November 1955.

La Documentation française, *Le Yemen, synthèse historique, sociale et politique*, No. 2141, Paris, 18 February 1956.

Europa Publications, *The Middle East 1958*, sixth edition, London 1958.

Food and Agricultural Organisation of the United Nations (FAO), *Agriculture in the Near East, Development and Outlook*, Rome, 1953.

Government of Palestine, General Monthly Bulletin of Statistics, *Survey of Social and Economic Conditions in Arab Villages, 1944*, Jerusalem, July and September 1945.

International Bank for Reconstruction and Development (IBRD), *The Economic Development of Iraq*, Baltimore, 1952.

Bibliography

IBRD, *The Economic Development of Syria*, Baltimore, 1955.

International Labour Organisation (ILO), Petroleum Committee, third session, *Social Conditions in the Petroleum Industry*, Geneva, 1950.

ILO, Regional Conference for the Near and Middle East, Teheran, April 1951, *Manpower Problems*, Geneva, 1951.

Jewish Agency for Palestine, Economic Research Institute, *Statistical Handbook of Middle Eastern Countries*, Jerusalem, 1944.

League of Nations, *Report submitted to the Council by the Commission instituted by the Council Resolution of September 30, 1924*, C 400, M. 147, 1925, VII.

Massignon, L. (ed.), *Annuaire du Monde musulman 1954*, Paris, 1955.

Oron, Y. (ed.), *Middle East Record 1960 (MER)*, Jerusalem, [1962].

Simmons, J. S., and others (ed.), *Global Epidemiology, III, The Near and Middle East*, Philadelphia–London–Montreal, 1954.

United Nations (UN), Department of Economic and Social Affairs, *Review of Economic Conditions in the Middle East 1951–2*, New York, 1953. *Economic Developments in the Middle East 1945–1954*, New York, 1955. *The Development of Manufacturing Industry in Egypt, Israel, and Turkey*, New York, 1958.

UNESCO, *Compulsory Education in the Arab States*, Paris, 1956.

United States, Department of Labor, *Directory of Labor Organizations, Asia and Australasia*, Washington, 1958 (quoted from *ME Aff*, March 1960, pp. 88–93).

BOOKS AND ARTICLES

Abbas, M., *The Sudan Question*, London, 1952.

Abbot, N., 'Woman', in R. N. Anshen (ed.), *Mid-East: World Center*, New York, 1956.

'Abd al-Qadir, M. Z., 'Ikhtiyar al-'umad', *al-Ahram*, 9 April 1942.

——, ' 'Ibrat al-kolira—khatt ad-difa' 'an al-aghniya fi buyut al-fuqara' *al-Ahram*, 30 October 1947.

Adams, C. C., *Islam and Modernism in Egypt*, Oxford, 1933.

Adams, D. G., *Iraq's People and Resources*, Berkeley and Los Angeles, 1958.

'Afifi, Hafiz, *'Ala hamish as-siyasa*, Cairo, 1938.

Allouni, A. A., 'The Labor Movement in Syria', *MEJ*, Winter 1959.

'Alluba, M. 'A., *Mabadi fi's-siyasa al-misriya*, Cairo, 1942.

Amin, Qasim, *Tahrir al-mar'a*, third ed., Cairo, n.d.

Ammar, H., *Growing Up in an Egyptian Village*, London, 1954.

Anderson, J. N. D., 'Recent Developments in Shari'a Law', *MW*, 1951, pp. 113–26, 271–88.

Bibliography

Anderson, J. N. D., 'The Jordanian Law of Family Rights 1951', *MW*, 1952, pp. 190–206.

——, 'The Personal Law of the Druse Community', *WI*, 1953, pp. 1–9, 83–94.

——, 'The Syrian Law of Personal Status', *BSOAS*, 1955, pp. 34–49.

——, *Islamic Law in the Modern World*, London, 1959.

Aouad, I., *Le Droit privé des Maronites 1697–1841*, Paris, 1933.

al-'Arabi, Dr. M. 'A., 'al-Qarya al-misriya fi'l-'ahd al-jadid', *al-Ahram*, 4 December 1952.

Awad, M., 'Settlement of Nomadic and Semi-Nomadic Tribal Groups in the Middle East', *ILR*, January 1959.

Ayrout, H. H., *Fellahs*, Cairo, 1942.

Badaoui, Z., *Les Problèmes du travail et les organisations ouvrières en Egypte*, Alexandria, 1948.

Badri, 'A., 'Khamsat awbi'a fi khamsat a'wam', *al-Ahram*, 30 October 1947.

Baer, G., 'Some Aspects of Beduin Sedentarization in 19th-Century Egypt', *WI* 1957, pp. 84–98.

——, 'Land Tenure in the Hashemite Kingdom of Jordan', *Land Economics*, August 1957.

——, 'Egyptian Attitudes towards Land Reform 1922–1955', in W. Z. Laqueur (ed.), *The Middle East in Transition*, London, 1958.

——, 'Waqf Reform in Egypt' in *St Antony's Papers, Middle Eastern Affairs*, Number One, London, 1958.

——, 'The Dissolution of the Egyptian Village Community', *WI*, 1959, pp. 56–70.

——, 'An Appraisal of Egyptian Land Reform', *New Outlook*, October 1959.

——, 'The Village Shaykh in Modern Egypt', in U. Heyd (ed.), *Studies in Islamic History and Civilisation, Scripta Hierosolymitana*, vol. IX, Jerusalem, 1961.

——, *A History of Landownership in Modern Egypt 1800–1950*, London, 1962.

Barth, F., 'Father's Brother's Daughter Marriage in Kurdistan', *SWJA*, Vol. 10, No. 2, pp. 164–71.

Beling, W. A., 'Recent Developments in Labor Relations in Bahrayn', *MEJ*, Spring 1959.

Berger, M., *Bureaucracy and Society in Modern Egypt*, Princeton, 1957.

——, 'The Middle Class in the Arab World', in W. Z. Laqueur (ed.), *The Middle East in Transition*, London, 1958.

Berque, J., 'Sur la structure sociale de quelques villages égyptiens', *Annales*, 1955, pp. 199–215.

Berque, J., *Histoire sociale d'un village égyptien au XXème siècle*, Paris, 1957.

——, *Les Arabes d'hier à demain*, Paris, 1960.

Besançon, J., *L'Homme et le Nil*, Paris, 1957.

Bint ash-Shati', 'Hudud Allah fi mirath al-untha', *al-Ahram*, 16 July 1960.

Blackman, W. S., *The Fellahin of Upper Egypt*, London, 1927.

Blanc, H., *Hadruzim*, Jerusalem, 1958.

Boktor, A., *School and Society in the Valley of the Nile*, Cairo, 1936.

Bonne, A., 'Land and Population in the Middle East', *MEJ*, Winter 1951.

Butt, A., *The Nilotes of the Anglo-Egyptian Sudan and Uganda*, London, 1952.

Canaan, I., 'Unwritten Laws affecting the Arab Woman of Palestine', *Journal of the Palestine Oriental Society*, Vol. XI, 1931.

Chamberet, R. de, *Enquête sur la condition du fellah égyptien*, Paris, 1909.

Chatila, Kh., *Le Mariage chez les musulmans en Syrie*, Paris, 1934.

Chehabe-ed-Dine, S., *Géographie humaine de Beyrouth*, Beirut, 1960.

Churchill, C. W., *The City of Beirut*, Beirut, 1954.

——, 'Village Life in the Central Beqa' Valley of Lebanon', *MEEP*, 1959.

Clergé, M., *Le Caire, Étude de géographie urbaine et d'histoire économique*, Cairo, 1934.

Cohen, A., *Tenu'ath hapo'alim ha'aravith*, Tel-Aviv, 1947.

——, *Ha'olam ha'aravi shel yameinu 1918–1958*, Merhavia, 1958.

Cromer, Earl of, *Modern Egypt*, London, 1908.

Daghestani, K. El, 'The Evolution of the Moslem Family in the Middle Eastern Countries', *ISSB*, Vol. V, 1953, No. 4.

Darling, Sir Malcolm, 'Land Reform in Italy and Egypt', *Yearbook of Agricultural Co-operation 1956*, Oxford, 1956.

Davis, H. M., *Constitutions, Electoral Laws, Treaties of States in the Near and Middle East*, Durham, N.C., 1953.

Davis, K., and Golden, H. H., 'Urbanisation and the Development of Pre-Industrial Areas', *EDCC*, October 1954.

Dowson, E., *An Inquiry into Land Tenure and Related Questions*, London and Baghdad, 1932.

Dupree, L., 'The Non-Arab Ethnic Groups of Libya,' *MEJ*, Winter 1958.

Edmonds, C. J., 'The Kurds of Iraq', *MEJ*, Winter 1957.

Epstein, E., 'The Nomad Problem in Transjordan', *Palestine and Middle East*, 2 February 1937.

Evans-Pritchard, E. E., *The Nuer*, London, 1940.

——, *The Sanusi of Cyrenaica*, London, 1949.

Fawzi, S., *Social Aspects of Low-Cost Housing in the Northern Sudan*, Khartoum, 1954.

——, *The Labour Movement in the Sudan 1946–1955*, London, 1957.

——, 'Manpower Distribution in the Sudan', *MEEP*, 1958.

Fayein, C., *Hakima, Eineinhalb Jahre Ärztin im Jemen*, Wiesbaden, 1956.

Finnie, D., 'Recruitment and Training of Labor—The Middle East Oil Industry', *MEJ*, Spring 1958.

Fuller, A. H., *Buarij, Portrait of a Lebanese Muslim Village*, Cambridge, Mass., 1961.

Gaitskell, A., *Gezira, A Story of Development in the Sudan*, London, 1959.

Ghali, B., *Siyasat al-ghad*, Cairo, 1944.

Gharzuzi, E., *Thawrat al-islah bi'l-arqam*, Cairo, 1959.

Gibb, H. A. R., and Bowen, H., *Islamic Society and the West*, Part I, London, 1950; Part II, London, 1957.

Goitein, S. D., and Ben-Shemesh, A., *Muslim Law in Israel* (in Hebrew), Jerusalem, 1957.

Granott, A., *The Land System in Palestine*, London, 1952.

Granqvist, H., *Marriage Conditions in a Palestinian Village*, Vol. I, Helsinki, 1931; Vol. II, Helsinki, 1935.

Greenberg, J. H., 'Studies in African Linguistic Classification', *SWJA*, Vols. 5 and 6.

Gritly, A. A. I., 'The Structure of Modern Industry in Egypt', *L'Égypte contemporaine*, November–December 1947.

Grunwald, K., 'Hati'us shel Surya ve-Halevanon', *Hamizrah Hehadash*, Vol. V, pp. 243–57.

Gulick, J., *Social Structure and Culture Change in a Lebanese Village*, New York, 1955.

Hadas, Y., 'Hapo'el hasuri', *Hamizrah Hehadash*, Vol. VII, pp. 99–109.

Halim, A., *Thamaniya ayyam fi's-Sa'id*, Cairo, 1944.

Hamdan, G., 'The Growth and Functional Structure of Khartoum', *GR*, January 1960.

Handley, W. J., 'The Labor Movement in Egypt', *MEJ*, July 1949.

Helaissi, A. S., 'The Bedouins and Tribal Life in Saudi Arabia', *ISSB*, Vol. XI, 1959, No. 4.

Hess, C. G., and Bodman, H. L., 'Confessionalism and Feudality in Lebanese Politics', *MEJ*, Winter 1954.

Heyworth-Dunne, J., 'The Yemen', *ME Aff.*, February 1958.

Himadeh, S., *an-Nizam al-iqtisadi fi'l-'Iraq*, Beirut, 1938.

Hourani, A., *Minorities in the Arab World*, London, 1946.

Ibnat ash-Shati', *Qadiyat al-fallah*, Cairo, [1938–9].

Bibliography

Ireland, P. W., *Iraq, A Study in Political Development*, London, 1937.

Issawi, C., *Egypt, An Economic and Social Analysis*, London, 1947.

——, *Egypt at Mid-Century*, London, 1954.

——, 'The Entrepreneur Class', in S. N. Fisher (ed.), *Social Forces in the Middle East*, Ithaca, N.Y., 1955.

Jamali, F., *The New Iraq—Its Problem of Bedouin Education*, New York, 1934.

Jaussen, J. A., *Coutumes des Arabes au pays de Moab*, Paris, 1908.

——, *Coutumes palestiniennes, I. Naplouse et son district*, Paris, 1927.

Khadduri, M., *Independent Iraq*, London, 1951.

Khalid, Kh. M., *Min huna nabda'*, Nazareth, 1959.

Khayyat, J., *al-Qarya al-'Iraqiya*, Beirut, 1950.

Konikoff, A., *Transjordan, An Economic Survey*, Jerusalem, 1946.

Lambardi, N., 'Divisioni amministrative del Yemen con notizie economiche e demografiche', *OM*, 1947, No. 7–9.

Lane, E. W., *The Manners and Customs of the Modern Egyptians* (1836), London, 1944.

Latron, A., *La Vie rurale en Syrie et au Liban*, Beirut, 1936.

Legrain, G., *Fellah de Karnak*, Paris, 1902.

Lenczowski, G., *Oil and State in the Middle East*, Ithaca, N.Y., 1960.

Lerner, D., and Pevsner, L., *The Passing of Traditional Society, Modernizing the Middle East*, Glencoe, Ill., 1958.

Levy, R., *The Social Structure of Islam*, Cambridge, 1957.

Lewis, B., *The Arabs in History*, London, 1950.

Lichtenstadter, I., 'An Arab Egyptian Family', *MEJ*, Autumn 1952.

Linant de Bellefonds, Y., 'Le Code du statut personnel irakien du 30 décembre 1959', *Studia Islamica*, XIII, 1960.

Lindberg, J., *A General Economic Appraisal of Libya*, New York, 1952.

Lipsky, G. A., and others, *Saudi Arabia, its People, its Society, its Culture*, New Haven, 1959.

Longrigg, S. H., *Four Centuries of Modern Iraq*, Oxford, 1925.

Macmichael, Sir Harold, *The Sudan*, London, 1954.

Makarius, R., *La Jeunesse intellectuelle d'Égypte au lendemain de la deuxième guerre mondiale*, Paris, 1960.

Mar'i, S., *al-Islah az-zira'i fi misr*, Cairo, 1957.

Marx, E., 'Bedouin Society in the Negev', *New Outlook*, Vol. II, 1958, No. 1 and 2.

Marzouk, G. A., 'Fertility of the Urban and Rural Population in Egypt', *L'Égypte contemporaine*, January 1957.

Massé, H., *Le Deuxième Congrès musulman général des femmes d'Orient*, Paris, 1933.

Matthews, R. D., and Akrawi, M., *Education in Arab Countries of the Near East*, Washington, D.C., 1949.

Meyer, A. J., *Middle East Capitalism*, Cambridge, Mass., 1959.

Montagne, R., *La Civilisation du désert*, Paris, 1947.

Moutran, N., *La Syrie de demain*, Paris, 1916.

Mubarak, 'Ali Pasha, *al-Khitat at-tawfiqiya al-jadida*, Cairo, 1887–9.

Muhsam, H. V., 'Fertility of Polygamous Marriages', *Population Studies*, Cambridge, July 1956.

——, 'Sedentarization of the Bedouin in Israel', *ISSB*, Vol. XI, 1959, No. 4.

Müller, V., *En Syrie avec les Bédouins*, Paris, 1931.

Munib, M. K., 'Lamha 'an hayat al-'ummal fi'l-Mahalla al-Kubra', *al-Ba'th*, 22 March 1946.

——, 'Ahwal al-'amilat fi'l-Mahalla al-Kubra', *at-Tali'a*, March 1946.

Murphy, R. F., and Kasdan, L., 'The Structure of Parallel Cousin Marriage', *American Anthropologist*, 1959.

Murray, G. W., *Sons of Ishmael*, London, 1935.

Musil, A., *Manners and Customs of the Rwala Bedouins*, New York, 1928.

Nahas, J., *Situation économique et sociale du fellah égyptien*, Paris, 1901.

Nahi, S., *Muqaddima fi'l-iqta' wanizam al-aradi fi'l-'Iraq*, Baghdad, 1955.

Nikitine, B., *Les Kurdes*, Paris, 1956.

Paret, R., *Zur Frauenfrage in der arabisch-islamischen Welt*, Stuttgart, 1934.

Patai, R. (ed.), *Jordan*, New Haven, 1957.

Phillips, D. G., 'Rural-to-Urban Migration in Iraq', *EDCC*, July 1959.

Piot Bey, *Causerie ethnographique sur le fellah*, Cairo, 1900.

Qubain, F. I., 'Social Classes and Tensions in Bahrain', *MEJ*, Summer 1955.

Robertson Smith, W., *Kinship and Marriage in Early Arabia*, London, 1907.

Rondot, P., *Les Tribus montagnards de l'Asie antérieur*, Cairo, 1937.

——, *Les Institutions politiques du Liban*, Paris, 1947.

——, *Les Chrétiens d'Orient*, Paris, 1955.

——, 'The Minorities in the Arab Orient Today', *ME Aff*, June–July 1959.

Rosenfeld, H., 'Temuroth bamivneh hahevrati shel hakfar ha'aravi Tayyiba', *Mibifnim*, April 1956.

——, 'An Analysis of Marriage and Marriage Statistics for a

Moslem and Christian Arab Village', *IAE*, Vol. XLVIII, 1957, No. 1.

Russell Pasha, Sir Thomas, *Egyptian Service 1902–1946*, London, 1949.

el-Saaty, H., 'The Middle Classes in Egypt', *L'Égypte contemporaine*, April 1957.

Sālim, 'A. M., 'Nizam al-qada wa't-tashri' fi'l-mamlaka al-'arabiya as-sa'udiya', *L'Égypte contemporaine*, October 1959.

Salim, Sh. M., *Ech-Chibayish, An Anthropological Study of a Marsh Village in Iraq* (in Arabic), Vol. I, Baghdad, 1956 (pp. 1–259); Vol. II, Baghdad, 1957 (pp. 260–482).

Sanger, R. H., *The Arabian Peninsula*, Ithaca, N.Y., 1954.

Sauvaget, J., and Weulersse, J., *Damas et la Syrie sud*, Damascus, 1936.

Sauvaget, J., *Alep*, Paris, 1941.

Schwally, F., *Beiträge zur Kenntnis des Lebens der mohammedanischen Städter, Fellachen und Beduinen im heutigen Ägypten*, Heidelberg, 1912.

Seligman, C. G., *Pagan Tribes of the Nilotic Sudan*, London, 1932.

Shafiq, D., and Abduh, I., *Tatawwur an-nahda an-nisa'iya fi misr*, Cairo, 1945.

Shafiq, D., *Al-mar'a al-misriya min al-fara'ina ila'l-yawm*, Cairo, 1955.

Shawqi, 'U., 'Bulaq—hayy al-'araq wa'd-dumu' wa'd-dam', *at-Tali'a*, 15 January 1946.

Shimoni, Y., '*Arvei Eretz Yisrael*, Tel-Aviv, 1947.

Stauffer, T. B., 'The Industrial Worker', in S. N. Fisher (ed.), *Social Forces in the Middle East*, Ithaca, N.Y., 1955.

Tannous, A. I., 'The Arab Village Community in the Middle East', *Annual Report of the Smithsonian Institution 1943*, Washington, 1944.

Thomas, F. C., 'The Libyan Oil Worker', *MEJ*, Summer 1961.

Thoumin, R., *Géographie humaine de la Syrie centrale*, Tours, 1936.

Tomiche, N., 'En Égypte: Le Gouvernement devant le problème démographique', *Orient*, July 1957.

Touma, T., *Un Village de montagne au Liban (Hadeth el-Jobbé)*, Paris, 1958.

Toynbee, A., *Survey of International Affairs*, 1925, I, London, 1927; 1930, London, 1931.

Trimingham, J. S., *Islam in the Sudan*, London, 1949.

Warriner, D., *Land and Poverty in the Middle East*, London, 1948.

——, *Land Reform and Development in the Middle East*, London, 1957.

Waschitz, J., *The Arabs in Palestine* (in Hebrew), Merhavia, 1947.

Weulersse, J., *Le Pays des Alaouites*, Tours, 1940.

Weulersse, J., *Paysans de Syrie et du Proche Orient*, Paris, 1946.

Wheelock, K., *Nasser's New Egypt*, London, 1960.

Winkler, H. A., *Bauern zwischen Wasser und Wüste*, Stuttgart, 1934.

——, *Ägyptische Volkskunde*, Stuttgart, 1936.

Al Witry, H., *Health Services in Iraq*, Jerusalem, 1944.

Woodsmall, R. F., *Der Aufsteig der mohammedanischen Frau*, Zürich, 1938.

Zarour, M., 'Ramallah: My Home Town', *MEJ*, Autumn 1953.

INDEX

Abadiya, 83, 103
Abbas, Makki, 29n
Abbot, N., 41n
'Abd al-Qadir, M. Z., 174n
'Abd an-Nasir, 30, 213
'Abduh, Ibrahim, 48n
'Abduh, Muhammad, 45, 47, 213
absenteeism, workers', 230
Adams, C. C., 45n, 107n
Adams, D. G., 20n, 52n, 175n, 188n
Aden (colony), 103, 225
  death rate, 25
  disease in, 21
  Jews, 90
  labour legislation, 238
  population, 3, 7, 179
  slavery, 223
  trade unions, 231, 236
Aden (protectorate),
  population, 3
  slavery, 223
'Afifi, Hafiz, 18, 23, 28n
Africa, Arabs in, 4
age,
  in city, 197
  groupings, population, 8–10
  at marriage, see marriage
    of working classes, 228
agha, 108, 111
Agrarian Reform, Institute of, 159f
ahl, see family, extended
Ahl al-Hilla, 126n
Ahmad, Muhammad, 79
'Ajlun, 122
'Akkar, 146
'Alawis, 81f, 111f
Aleppo, 6, 110, 180, 183, 191, 192, 213, 227
Alexandria, 52n, 96, 97, 98, 177, 178, 187, 195, 197, 198, 224, 227, 236
'Ali, Caliph, 79f, 82
'Ali Ilâhi, 91
allegiance, problem of, 242
Allouni, A. A., 230n
'Alluba, M. A., 28n
'Amaiza, 123, 124, 128
'Amara, 106, 147, 152, 179, 182f, 187
'Amarat, 125
America,
  Assyrians in, 86
  Druzes in, 83
  Maronites in, 88, 117

Amin, Qasim, 45, 47
'Amman, 147, 180, 182, 185, 191, 192
'Ammar, 'Abbas, 26n
Ammar, Hamed, 13, 24, 59n, 63n, 64, 78n, 123n, 138n, 165, 169n, 175
ancylostomiasis, 23
Anderson, J. N. D., 36n, 54n, 62n, 73n
Ansar, 79
Anuak, 93, 102
Aouad, I., 39n, 118n
Arab–Israel War, 221, 222, 235
al-'Arabi, M. 'A., 174n
'Arabi rebellion, 221, see 'Urabi
Arabian Peninsula,
  beduin, 119
  communal structure, 102–4
  map, 247
  population, 3; density, 7; urban, 179
  slavery, 223
  trade unions, 231
  wage-earners, 225
Arabic language, 91f, 100; dialects, 91
Aramco Petroleum Works, 103, 225, 229, 236
Arbil, 107, 179
'arifa, 126
aristocracy, absence of landed, 207
Armenians, 94
  Catholic, 89
  in Lebanon, 113, 116–17
  in Syria, 110
army officers,
  and politics, 220ff
  and Westernisation, 221
'ar-Rub 'al-Khali, 7
Artas, 37, 38, 65, 67
artisan class, 210, 213
'ashira, 124, 131
'al-'Asima', 118
'Asir, 7, 103
Assassins, 81
Association of Catholic Youth, 31
Assyrians/Assyrian Church, 84–6, 105
Aswan, 7, 147, 187, 188
Aswan High Dam, 27
Asyut, 7, 97, 146, 178, 187
'Ataiba, 125
'Atbara, 178, 184, 226, 239
autonomy,
  legal, of beduins, 135
  religious, 72

263

Index

Awad, M., 130n, 131n
Awlad 'Ali, 131n
Ayrout, H. H., 138, 152n, 165n, 173n

Bab, 146
Badaoui, Z., 233
al-Badiya, Bahithat, 43
Baer, G., 132n, 133n, 141n, 146n,
    148n, 149n, 152n, 153n, 155n,
    156n, 165n, 208m, 221n
Baggara, 100
Baghdad, 6, 38, 92, 106, 107, 179, 182,
    187, 188, 192, 194, 224, 227
Baha' Allah, 91
Baha'is, 91
Bahrain, 81, 95, 103, 179, 223
    Imamis, 103
    labour legislation, 238
    population, 3, 7
    strikes, 236
    trade unions, 231
    wage-workers, 225, 226f
Bahrain Petroleum Co., 225
bait at-ta'a, 35
Bani 'Amir, 100
Bani Suaif, 178
Banu Asad, 65, 67
Banu Khalid, 125
baqqara, 121f
al-Baquri, Hasan, 31
Barabra, 100
barber, village, 167
Bari, 93, 101
Barth, F., 65, 66n, 123n
Basra, 106, 179, 182, 187, 226, 227
baths, 196
beduins,
    and administration, 135–6
    and census, 2
    and class structure, 222
    distribution, 119
    law, 126f
    life of, 120ff
    migrations, 122
    and military service, 133f
    and modern State, 133ff
    and patriarchy, 61
    political representation, 136f
    relation to settled, 120
    religion, 126, 132
    settlement, 128ff
    social organisation, 122ff, 131
    transition to towns, 131
    see also nomads
Beir, language of, 93
Beirut, 6, 42, 53n, 60, 62n, 113, 116,
    180, 192, 194, 195, 227
Beja, 64, 100
Beling, W. A., 225n, 227n, 231n
Benghazi, 178, 183

Berbers, 4
    language, 93
Berger, M., 52n, 205n, 213n, 217, 218
Berque, J., 46n, 47n, 59n, 65, 77, 78n,
    138n, 158n, 165n, 169n, 172n,
    173, 175, 176, 192n, 200n, 203n,
    211n, 212n, 220
Besançon, J., 163n
bilharziasis, 23
Bint an-Nil, 47
al-Biqa', 15, 113, 116, 146
birkas, 20
birth control, 30f, 198
    in Lebanon, 32
    religion and, 30f
birth rates, 8, 10ff
    in cities, 198
    in Egypt, 12–13
    reasons for limitation, 11
    trends, 10–11
Black Saturday, 222
Blackman, W. S., 13n, 15n, 41n, 42n,
    98n, 165n, 169n, 175n
Blanc, H., 112n
Blattner, J. E., 69n
blind, in Egypt, 97f
blood feuds, 122, 123, 134, 135
Boktor, A., 15n, 42n, 98n, 150n
Bonne, A., 5n, 33n
brand, camel, 124
Brazil, marriage age, 14
bride price, 36, 37, 40f, 62
Britain,
    and Assyrians, 86
    and Druzes, 73
British, in Arab States, 96
British Guiana, marriage age, 14
Buarij, 174n
bubonic plague, 21, 22
Buhaira, 7, 147, 187
building materials, 16, 163
Bulaq quarter, 18
Bulgaria, marriage age, 14
Bullard, Sir Reader, 223n
bureaucracy, 205, 217f
    foreigners and, 218
Butt, A., 101n

café, 196
Cairo, 7, 38, 97, 98, 177, 178, 182, 187,
    191, 192, 193, 195, 196, 197, 198,
    224
    epidemics, 22
    housing, 18
camel raising, 120–2
Canaan, L., 39n, 41n
canals, irrigation, 19
capital, sources of, 210
caravans, decline of, 129
Carmathians, 81

264

Index

269